DRAMATISTS
AND
DRAMAS

DRAMATISTS AND DRAMAS

Harold Bloom
Sterling Professor of the Humanities
Yale University

Checkmark Books®
An imprint of Infobase Publishing

Dramatists and Dramas

Checkmark Books
An imprint of Infobase Publishing
132 West 31st Street
New York NY 10001

ISBN-10: 0-7910-9726-9
ISBN-13: 978-0-7910-9726-7

Library of Congress Cataloging-in-Publication Data
Bloom, Harold.
  Dramatists and dramas / Harold Bloom.
     p. cm. — (Bloom's 20th anniversary collection)
  ISBN 0-7910-8226-1 (hc: alk. paper)—ISBN 0-7910-9726-9 (pb: alk. paper)
  1. Drama—History and criticism. I. Title.
  PN1721.B66 2005
  809.2—dc22   2005003094

Checkmark Books are available at special discounts when purchased in
bulk quantities for businesses, associations, institutions, or sales promotions.
Please call our Special Sales Department in New York at (212) 967-8800 or
(800) 322-8755.

You can find Bloom's Literary Criticism on the World Wide Web
at http://www.chelseahouse.com

Cover design by Ben Peterson

Printed in the United States of America

Bang EJB 10 9 8 7 6 5 4 3 2 1

This book is printed on acid-free paper.

Table of Contents

Preface to the
20th Anniversary Edition

Harold Bloom

I BEGAN EDITING ANTHOLOGIES OF LITERARY CRITICISM FOR CHELSEA House in early 1984, but the first volume, *Edgar Allan Poe: Modern Critical Views*, was published in January, 1985, so this is the twentieth anniversary of a somewhat Quixotic venture. If asked how many separate books have been issued in this project, I no longer have a precise answer, since in so long a span many volumes go out of print, and even whole series have been discontinued. A rough guess would be more than a thousand individual anthologies, a perhaps insane panoply to have been collected and introduced by a single critic.

Some of these books have surfaced in unlikely places: hotel rooms in Bologna and Valencia, Coimbra and Oslo; used-book stalls in Frankfurt and Nice; on the shelves of writers wherever I have gone. A batch were sent by me in answer to a request from a university library in Macedonia, and I have donated some of them, also by request, to a number of prisoners serving life sentences in American jails. A thousand books across a score of years can touch many shores and many lives, and at seventy-four I am a little bewildered at the strangeness of the endeavor, particularly now that it has leaped between centuries.

It cannot be said that I have endorsed every critical essay reprinted, as my editor's notes have made clear. Yet the books have to be reasonably reflective of current critical modes and educational fashions, not all of them provoking my own enthusiasm. But then I am a dinosaur, cheerfully naming myself as "Bloom Brontosaurus Bardolator." I accept only three criteria for greatness in imaginative literature: aesthetic splendor, cognitive power, wisdom. What is now called "relevance" will be in the dustbins in less than a generation, as our society (somewhat tardily) reforms prejudices and inequities. The fashionable in literature and criticism always ebbs away into Period Pieces. Old, well-made furniture survives as valuable antiques, which is not the destiny of badly constructed imaginings and ideological exhortings.

Time, which decays and then destroys us, is even more merciless in obliterating weak novels, poems, dramas, and stories, however virtuous these may be. Wander into a library and regard the masterpieces of thirty years ago: a handful of forgotten books have value, but the iniquity of oblivion has rendered most bestsellers instances of time's revenges. The other day a friend and former student told me that the first of the Poets Laureate of twentieth-century America had been Joseph Auslander, concerning whom even my still retentive memory is vacant. These days, Mrs. Felecia Hemans is studied and taught by a number of feminist Romantic scholars. Of the poems of that courageous wisdom, who wrote to support her brood, I remember only the opening line of "Casabianca" but only because Mark Twain added one of his very own to form a couplet:

> The boy stood on the burning deck
> *Eating peanuts by the peck.*

Nevertheless, I do not seek to affirm the social inutility of literature, though I admire Oscar Wilde's grand declaration: "All art is perfectly useless." Shakespeare may well stand here for the largest benign effect of the highest literature: properly appreciated, it can heal part of the violence that is built into every society whatsoever. In my own judgment, Walt Whitman is the central writer yet brought forth by the Americas—North, Central, South, Caribbean—whether in English, Spanish, Portuguese, French, Yiddish or other tongues. And Walt Whitman is a healer, a poet-prophet who discovered his pragmatic vocation by serving as a volunteer, unpaid wound-dresser and nurse in the Civil War hospitals of Washington, D.C. To read and properly understand Whitman can be an education in self-reliance and in the cure of your own consciousness.

The function of literary criticism, as I conceive it in my gathering old age, is primarily appreciation, in Walter Pater's sense, which fuses analysis and evaluation. When Pater spoke of "art for art's sake' he included in the undersong of his declaration what D.H. Lawrence meant by "art for life's sake," Lawrence, the most provocative of post-Whitmanian vitalists, has now suffered a total eclipse in the higher education of the English-speaking nations. Feminists have outlawed him with their accusations of misogyny, and they describe him as desiring women to renounce sexual pleasure. On this supposed basis, students lose the experience of reading one of the major authors of the twentieth century, at once an unique novelist, story-teller, poet, critic, and prophet.

An enterprise as vast as Chelsea House Literary Criticism doubtless reflects both the flaws and the virtues of its editor. Comprehensiveness has been a goal throughout, and I have (for the most part) attempted to set aside many of my own literary opinions. I sorrow when the market keeps an important volume out of print, though I am solaced by the example of my idol, Dr. Samuel Johnson, in his *Lives of the Poets*. The booksellers (who were both publishers and retailers) chose the poets, and Johnson was able to say exactly what he thought of each. Who remembers such worthies as Yalden, Sprat, Roscommon, and Stepney? It would be invidious for me to name the contemporary equivalents, but their name is legion.

I have been more fully educated by this quest for comprehensivness, which taught me how to write for a larger audience. Literary criticism is both an individual and communal mode. It has its titans: Johnson, Coleridge, Lessing, Goethe, Hazlitt, Sainte-Beuve, Pater, Curtius, Valèry, Frye, Empson, Kenneth Burke are among them. But most of those I reprint cannot be of that eminence: one makes a heap of all that can be found. Over a lifetime in reading and teaching one learns so much from so many that no one can be certain of her or his intellectual debts. Hundreds of those I have reprinted I never will meet, but they have helped enlighten me, insofar as I have been capable of learning from a host of other minds.

Introduction

Harold Bloom

1

FROM ANY LITERARY PERSPECTIVE, THERE IS SOMETHING PROBLEMATIC about dramatic form, from at least the Renaissance to our twenty-first century situation. Drama both is and is not a literary genre, because it is contaminated (necessarily) by performance. Shakespeare survives bad direction and inadequate acting, on stage and on screen, because we always can go home and reread him. But Eugene O'Neill and Arthur Miller cannot survive travesties in the theater, because they do not reread with multiple reverberations. Except for his stage directions, O'Neill writes with only sporadic eloquence, and Miller scarcely writes well at all. Theater in some sense is an art of writing, but sometimes it performs better than it reads.

Benjamin Bennett argues that the novel is conservative as a form whereas theater is revolutionary, whatever the politics of the dramatist. "Revolutionary" to Bennett means the breaking-apart of genre, and not of society. The center cannot hold in dramatic performance: literature (in Western tradition) pervades drama, and yet theater can turn literature into mere anarchy. From the arrival of Shakespeare's own troupe of players in Act II, Scene 2 of *Hamlet* through the disruption of *The Mousetrap*'s performance in Act III, Scene 2, what is the literary form of the world's most notorious and influential play?

Commenting upon the ideas of the extraordinary Viennese dramatist Hoffmannsthal, Bennett remarks that the playwright:

> ... is always in the situation of speaking with two voices: a personal voice that arises ... and is never available for us to hear

directly; and a public voice whose whole sound and content is determined by circumstances.

As with Shakespeare, we hear only the second voice. Hence the dilemma of all performed drama: are we indeed listening to Shakespeare? Hamlet, who rebels against finding himself in the wrong play, one unworthy of his enormous consciousness, implicitly stands for Shakespeare's own uneasiness in regard to his needful reliance upon his players. Unlike his peers, from Cervantes to Joyce, Shakespeare wrote nothing during the final three years of his life. Why? We never will know, but one possibility is that, like Prospero, he wearied of the difficulties of directing his own art.

2

There are absences in this volume that I regret: Calderon, Racine, Congreve, Strindberg, among others. Yet the major Athenians are here, and Shakespeare occupies almost a third of this book, a proportion I do not judge excessive. His twenty-one most vital plays are here, accompanied by some of his major contemporaries: Marlowe, Jonson, Webster.

A sequence of Moliére, Ibsen, Wilde, Shaw and Chekhov carries us up to the twentieth century, whose major European dramatists are there: Pirandello, Synge, O'Casey, Brecht, Beckett, Ionesco, Pinter, and Stoppard. Lorca seems to me the largest omission. The principal American dramatists are here: O'Neill, Wilder, Williams, Miller and our contemporaries Albee, Shepard, August Wilson, Mamet, and Kushner.

There are some sports in this book: Gay's *The Beggar's Opera*, T.S. Eliot's Neo-Christian devotional, *Murder in the Cathedral*, and Neil Simon's popular theater. These multiply variety, though I would grant only Gay a dramatic eminence among the three. In so mixed a genre as theatrical literature, some outriders are inevitable.

3

Surveying my own economical appreciations, I find only Moliére and Ibsen able to achieve what Shakespeare surpasses all others in composing so vitally: characters who are "free artists of themselves" (Hegel). But Shakespeare remains an unquestionable miracle: how can he have happened? Falstaff, Hamlet, Iago, and Cleopatra are endless to our meditation, while Lear and Macbeth define the sublimity that makes us willing to surrender less difficult pleasures in order to experience a hurt that is itself the meaning. Reading and teaching Shakespeare, and only rarely seated in a theater, I am moved to that verge beyond which imagination cannot reach.

What is the right use of Shakespeare, whether in reading or in performance? The world's Scriptures, Bible and Koran included, and perhaps *Don Quixote* also, have something like Shakespeare's universal force, and they too seem out ahead of us, waiting for us to catch up. Yet religious writing, whatever its truth and wisdom may or may not be, rarely expands consciousness without a certain expense of deformation. Shakespeare, like Homer and the Athenian tragedians, stimulates consciousness without compelling it to exercise exclusions and self-curtailments. Drama may be the most mixed of literary genres, and yet Shakespeare so molded it as not to abandon us to even the richest of confusions. The Shakespearean exuberance peoples a heterocosm of men and women, abounding with a secular blessing of more life on into a time without boundaries.

Aeschylus

(c. 525–455 B.C.E)

The Oresteia

WHEN ODYSSEUS ENCOUNTERS THE GHOST OF AGAMEMNON IN THE underworld (*Odyssey*, Book XI) the embittered shade memorably recalls his slaughter by his extraordinary wife:

> As I lay dying the woman with the dog's eyes would not close my eyes for me as I descended into Hades.

One recalls that Faulkner took the title for his most original novel from those first four words, but Aeschylus created an Agamemnon who is less imposing than Homer's. Selective in his use of the story, Homer omits any mention of the sacrifice of Iphigeneia by Agamemnon, and does not tell us that the Furies harried Orestes for his matricide. The *Odyssey* intimates that Clytemnestra was hateful, but does not elaborate. Aeschylus, who somehow gives me the uncanny notion that he is more archaic than Homer, certainly more primordial, portrays a Clytemnestra far more vivid than any other role in the *Oresteia*.

Clytemnestra's hatred for her husband appears to transcend his ritual sacrifice of Iphigeneia, and pragmatically represents a desire to usurp the kingdom. Aeschylus could not have been unaware of the negative splendor with which he had endowed Clytemnestra. One hesitates to call her a heroine-villain, though the mixed metaphor of lioness-serpent, mother of the lion Orestes whom she calls a serpent, certainly applies to her.

Since Clytemnestra is dramatically and imaginatively stronger than Agamemnon, his slave-mistress Cassandra, and the avenging Electra and Orestes, she certainly is the most memorable figure not only in the trilogy, but in all of Aeschylus that has survived. She is superbly flamboyant, and fascinates us because she exults outrageously in her slaughter of Agamemnon, and also in her wholly gratuitous butchery of the innocent Cassandra. I employ here the translation of Richmond Lattimore (1947), to give Clytemnestra's speech as she stands over the bodies of Agamemnon and Cassandra:

Much have I said before to serve necessity,
but I will take no shame now to unsay it all.
How else could I, arming hate against hateful men
disguised in seeming tenderness, fence high the nets
of ruin beyond overleaping? Thus to me
the conflict born of ancient bitterness is not
a thing new thought upon, but pondered deep in time.
I stand now where I struck him down. The thing is done.
Thus have I wrought, and I will not deny it now.
That he might not escape nor beat aside his death,
as fishermen cast their huge circling nets, I spread
deadly abundance of rich robes, and caught him fast.
I struck him twice. In two great cries of agony
he buckled at the knees and fell. When he was down
I struck him the third blow, in thanks and reverence
to Zeus the lord of dead men underneath the ground.
Thus he went down, and the life struggled out of him;
and as he died he spattered me with the dark red
and violent driven rain of bitter savored blood
to make me glad, as gardens stand among the showers
of God in glory at the birthtime of the buds.

These being the facts, elders of Argos assembled here,
be glad, if it be your pleasure; but for me, I glory.
Were it religion to pour wine above the slain,
this man deserved, more than deserved, such sacrament.
He filled our cup with evil things unspeakable
and now himself come home has drunk it to the dregs.

Few utterances in drama before Shakespeare have so stunning a force. The third blow is a shocker, but less so than the image of the murderess as gardens gloried by the rain of her husband's blood. Even in Shakespeare's panoply of Lady Macbeth, Goneril, and Regan, there is no woman of similar violence. To go beyond this might seem unlikely, but

Aeschylus surpasses it in Clytemnestra's sadistic delight at having added Cassandra to the orgiastic slaughter:

> Now hear you this, the right behind my sacrament:
> By my child's Justice driven to fulfilment, by
> her Wrath and Fury, to whom I sacrificed this man,
> the hope that walks my chambers is not traced with fear
> while yet Aegisthus makes the fire shine on my hearth,
> my good friend, now as always, who shall be for us
> the shield of our defiance, no weak thing; while he,
> this other, is fallen, stained with this woman you behold,
> plaything of all the golden girls at Ilium;
> and here lies she, the captive of his spear, who saw
> wonders, who shared his bed, the wise in revelations
> and loving mistress, who yet knew the feel as well
> of the men's rowing benches. Their reward is not
> unworthy. He lies there; and she who swanlike cried
> aloud her lyric mortal lamentation out
> is laid against his fond heart, and to me has given
> a delicate excitement to my bed's delight.

It is wonderfully clear that Clytemnestra's hatred for Agamemnon is sexual, a woman's resentment of a male weaker than herself, who rules over her only because of gender. Her pride in her double-murder is exuberant, and her hatred extends both to Zeus and to Cassandra. Ironically extending reverence to Zeus as "lord of dead men underneath the ground," she implies a hatred towards him as well, presumably as supreme male. But why does she relish her murder of Cassandra, a captive? There is a sexual element in this hatred also: it is as though Clytemnestra has manned herself in unmanning Agamemnon.

Her final outcry is made to Orestes, just before he takes her inside the house to kill her:

> You are the snake I gave birth to, and gave the breast.

Her defiance and bitterness, her refusal of guilt or remorse, remains compellingly steadfast.

Sophocles

(c. 496–406 B.C.E)

Electra

SOPHOCLES WAS A CHILD OF THREE OR FOUR WHEN AESCHYLUS PRESENTED his first tragedy, in 499 B.C.E. At twenty-eight, Sophocles won the first prize competing against Aeschylus, and until 456, when Aeschylus died, there must have been many contests between the two. Sophocles's *Electra* has a complex relation to Aeschylus's *Libation-Bearers*, which was the second play of a trilogy; in Sophocles's case, *Electra* stood alone.

I intend to contrast *Electra* and the *Libation-Bearers*, employing Richmond Lattimore's version of the Aeschylus, and the new translation of the Sophocles by the Canadian poet Anne Carson. Carson, a major poet and a classical scholar, cites Virginia Woolf's essay, "On Not Knowing Greek," from *The Common Reader*. Woolf remarks that Electra's cries "give angle and outline to the play," and Carson (who shows a dark affinity for Electra) writes a remarkable foreword, emphasizing Electra's horror of the evil in her life, a horror virtually beyond measure: "she is someone off the scale." Strikingly comparing the Electra of Sophocles to Emily Dickinson's "equally private religion of pain," Carson observes that: "They touch a null point at the centre of the woman's soul."

Woolf, Dickinson, and Carson perhaps have only their literary greatness in common, and yet Carson's translation teaches us to uncover the Sophoclean Electra in the novelist and in both poets. Electra's grief is passionately personal in Sophocles, as John Jones noted in his *On Aristotle and Greek Tragedy*. "Personal" seems not strong enough, because we have debased the word, as when we speak of a "personal letter." That is too far from "Electra's private language of screams," as Carson phrases it, and too far also from Woolf's *Three Guineas*, Dickinson's Master poems, and Carson's tangos, *The Beauty of the Husband*.

4

In the *Libation-Bearers*, Electra is perhaps more angry than pained, a princess who fiercely resents her debasement, and who centers her love upon Orestes. The Electra of Sophocles has a death-absorbed imagination, as Carson says, and suffers the negation of her own sexuality. Here is Aeschylus's Electra, craving revenge, and unwilling to abandon life:

> Almighty herald of the world above, the world
> below: Hermes, lord of the dead, help me; announce
> my prayers to the charmed spirits underground, who watch
> over my father's house, that they may hear. Tell Earth
> herself, who brings all things to birth, who gives them strength,
> then gathers their big yield into herself at last.
> I myself pour these lustral waters to the dead,
> and speak, and call upon my father: Pity me;
> pity your own Orestes. How shall we be lords
> in our house? We have been sold, and go as wanderers
> because our mother bought herself, for us, a man,
> Aegisthus, he who helped her hand to cut you down.
> Now I am what a slave is, and Orestes lives
> outcast from his great properties, while they go proud
> in the high style and luxury of what you worked
> to win. By some good fortune let Orestes come
> back home. Such is my prayer, my father. Hear me; hear.
> And for myself, grant that I be more temperate
> of heart than my mother; that I act with purer hand.
>
> Such are my prayers for us; but for our enemies,
> father, I pray that your avenger come, that they
> who killed you shall be killed in turn, as they deserve.
> Between my prayer for good and prayer for good I set
> this prayer for evil; and I speak it against Them.
> For us, bring blessings up into the world. Let Earth
> and conquering Justice, and all gods beside, give aid.
>
> Such are my prayers; and over them I pour these drink
> offerings. Yours the strain now, yours to make them flower
> with mourning song, and incantation for the dead.

This woman contrasts sharply to the Sophoclean Electra:

Alright then, you tell me one thing—
at what point does the evil level off in my life?
you say ignore the deed—is that right?
Who could approve this?
It defies human instinct!
Such ethics make no sense to me.
And how could I nestle myself in a life of ease

while my father lies out in the cold,
outside honor?
My cries are wings:
they pierce the cage.
For if a dead man is earth and nothing,
if a dead man is void and dead space lying,
if a dead man's murderers
do not give
blood for blood
to pay for this,
then shame does not exist.
Human reverence
is gone.

Electra is believed to have come late in Sophocles's career, and the celebrated irony of *Oedipus Tyrannus* seems far away. The dramatic ironies of *Electra* turn upon freedom, rather than knowledge. Orestes frees Electra from her immediate torments, but he has arrived too late to save her from the negativity that has become her nature. Knowledge cannot liberate Oedipus: to know the truth causes the agony in which he blinds himself. It may even be that pity in Sophocles is only another irony. Electra, in Carson's version, cannot be said to have suffered and then broken free. Throwing the corpse of Aegisthus to the dogs will not cut the knot of evils inside Electra. Her irony is simply that there is no correcting the past, least of all for women.

Oedipus Rex

Whether there is a "tragic flaw", a *hamartia*, in King Oedipus is uncertain, though I doubt it, as he is hardly a figure who shoots wide of the mark. Accuracy is implicit in his nature. We can be certain that he is free of that masterpiece of ambivalence—Freud's Oedipal complex. In the Age of Freud, we are uncertain what to do with a guiltless Oedipus, but that does appear to be the condition of Sophocles' hero. We cannot read *Oedipus the*

King as we read the *Iliad* of Homer, where the gods matter enormously. And even more, we know it is absurd to read Oedipus as though it were written by Yahwist, or the authors of Jeremiah or Job, let alone of the Gospels. We can complete our obstacle course by warning ourselves not to compound Oedipus with *Hamlet* or *Lear*. Homer and the Bible, Shakespeare and Freud, teach us only how not to read Sophocles.

When I was younger, I was persuaded by Cedric Whitman's eloquent book on Sophocles to read Oedipus as a tragedy of "heroic humanism." I am not so persuaded now, not because I am less attracted by a humanistic heroism, but because I am uncertain how such a stance allows for tragedy. William Blake's humanism was more than heroic, being apocalyptic, but it too would not authorize tragedy. However the meaning of Oedipus is to be interpreted in our post–Nietzchean age, the play is surely tragedy, or the genre will lose coherence. E.R. Dodds, perhaps assimilating Sophocles to the Iliad, supposed that the tragedy of Oedipus honored the gods, without judging them to be benign or even just. Bernard Knox argues that the greatness of the gods and the greatness of Oedipus are irreconcilable, with tragedy the result of that schism. That reduces to the Hegelian view of tragedy as an agon between right and right, but Knox gives the preference to Oedipus, since the gods, being ever victorious, therefore cannot be heroic. A less Homeric reading than Dodds's, this seems to me too much our sense of heroism—Malraux perhaps, rather than Sophocles.

Freud charmingly attributed to Sophocles, as a precursor of psychoanalysis, the ability to have made possible a self–analysis for the playgoer. But then Freud called *Oedipus* an "immoral play," since the gods ordained incest and patricide. Oedipus therefore participates in our universal unconscious sense of guilt, but on this reading so do the gods. I sometimes wish that Freud had turned to Aeschylus instead, and given us the Prometheus complex rather than the Oedipus complex. Plato is Oedipal in regard to Homer, but Sophocles is not. I hardly think that Sophocles would have chastised Homer for impiety, but then, as I read it, the tragedy of Oedipus takes up no more skeptical stance than that of Plato, unless one interprets Plato as Montaigne wished to interpret him.

What does any discerning reader remember most vividly about *Oedipus the King*? Almost certainly, the answer must be the scene of the king's self–blinding, as narrated by the second messenger, here in David Grene's version:

> By her own hand. The worst of what was done
> you cannot know. You did not see the sight.
> Yet in so far as I remember it

you'll hear the end of our unlucky queen.
When she cam raging into the house she went
straight to her marriage bed, tearing her hair
with both her hands, and crying upon Laius
long dead—Do you remember, Laius,
that night long past which bred a child for us
to send you to your death and leave
a mother making children with her son?
And then she groaned and cursed the bed in which
she brought forth husband by her husband, children
by her own child, an infamous double bond.
How after that she died I do not know,—
for Oedipus distracted us from seeing.
He burst upon us shouting and we looked
to him as he paced frantically around,
begging us always: Give me a sword, I say,
to find this wife no wife, this mother's womb,
this field of double sowing whence I sprang
and where I sowed my children! As he raved
some god showed him the way—none of us there.
Bellowing terribly and led by some
invisible guide he rushed on the two doors,—
wrenching the hollow bolts out of their sockets,
he charges inside. There, there, we saw his wife
hanging, the twisted rope around her neck.
When he saw her, he cried out fearfully
and cut loose the dangling noose. Then, as she lay,
poor woman, on the ground, what happened after,
was terrible to see. He tore the brooches—
the gold chased brooches fastening her robe—
away from her and lifting them high
dashed them on his own eyeballs, shrieking out
such things as: they will never see the crime
I have committed or had done upon me!
Dark eyes, now on the days to come, look on
forbidden faces, do not recognize
those whom you long for—with such imprecations
he struck his eyes again and yet again
with the brooches. And the bleeding eyeballs gushed
and stained his beard—no sluggish oozing drops
but a black rain and bloody hail poured down.

So it has broken—and not on one head
but troubles mixed for husband and wife.
The fortune of the days gone by was true
good fortune—but today groans and destruction
and death and shame—of all ills can be named
not one is missing.
(1.1237–86)

The scene, too terrible for acting out, seems also too dreadful for representation in language. Oedipus, desiring to put a sword in the womb of Jocasta, is led by "some god" to where he can break through the two doors (I shudder as I remember Walt Whitman's beautiful trope for watching a woman in childbirth, "I recline by the sills of the exquisite flexible doors"). Fortunately finding Jocasta self–slain, lest he add the crime of matricide to patricide and incest, Oedipus, repeatedly stabbing his eyes with Jocasta's brooches, passes judgment not so much upon seeing as upon the seen, and so upon the light by which we see. I interpret this as his protest against Apollo, which brings both the light and the plague. The Freudian trope of blinding for castration seems to me less relevant here than the outcry against the god.

To protest Apollo is necessarily dialectical, since the pride and agility of the intellect of Oedipus, remorselessly searching out the truth, in some sense is also against the nature of truth. In this vision of reality, you shall know the truth, and the truth will make you mad. What would make Oedipus free? Nothing that happens in this play, must be the answer, nor does it seem that becoming an oracular god later on makes you free either. If you cannot be free of the gods, then you cannot be made free, and even acting as though your daemon is your destiny will not help you either.

The startling ignorance of Oedipus when the drama begins is the *given* of the play, and cannot be questioned or disallowed. Voltaire was scathing upon this, but the ignorance of the wise and the learned remains an ancient truth of psychology, and torments us every day. I surmise that this is the true force of Freud's Oedipus complex: not the unconscious sense of guilt, but the necessity of ignorance, lest the reality–principle destroy us. Nietzsche said it not in praise of art, but so as to indicate the essential limitation of art. Sophoclean irony is more eloquent yet:

CREON: Do not seek to be master in everything, for the
    things you mastered did not follow you throughout
    your life.
    (*As Creon and Oedipus go out.*)

CHORUS: You that live in my ancestral Thebes, behold
   this Oedipus,—him who knew the famous riddles
   and was a man most masterful; not a citizen who
   did not look with envy on his lot—see him now
   and see the breakers of misfortune swallow him!
   Look upon that last day always. Count no mortal
   happy till he has passed the final limit of his life secure from pain.

                              (1.1521–30)

The *Oedipus Plays*

Because of Freud's unfortunate formulation of "the Oedipus complex," we
find it difficult to interpret the Oedipus plays of Sophocles without
indulging in rather irrelevant Freudian considerations. Freud should have
named it "the Hamlet complex," since that is what he suffered from, an
accurate sense that "the poets" (meaning Shakespeare) had been there
before him. In this case, Sophocles had not been there before him, since
Oedipus in fact had no desire whatsoever, conscious or "unconscious," to
kill his father and marry his mother. Once we clear that confusion away, at
least we can confront the authentic difficulties presented by Sophocles'
three extraordinary dramas.

They are three very different plays, and do not always illuminate one
another. *Antigone* was first acted when Sophocles was around fifty-four
years old; it is a mature and powerful tragedy, and is very much Antigone's
own tragedy. *Oedipus the King* was first produced perhaps fifteen years later,
and was regarded by Aristotle as the exemplary tragedy. Sophocles lived
another twenty years, dying in 406 or 405 B.C.E., at the age of ninety or so.
It is generally assumed that *Oedipus at Colonus* was the work of his final
years, since its first staging was posthumous, about five years after the
poet's death. The play, highly original and difficult, has a subtle relationship to the initial drama of Oedipus, and makes us read *Oedipus the King*
differently, whether that is wholly valid or not. All three plays abound in
ambiguities, pragmatically in ironies, but the irony or ambiguous wordplay
of any one of them is not at all that of the other two.

Antigone, the Hegelian model of "a struggle between right and right,"
Antigone and Creon, turns upon the irony that Antigone's sense of "the
law" relates to the gods, and Creon's to the state. Creon's stance is not
intrinsically false, but it violates human dignity, and becomes something
ugly because it is not appropriate to the human moment, as Antigone's
position certainly is. *Hubris*, the arrogance of power, is now permanently

associated with Creon's name, even as the courageous stubbornness of principle is Antigone's legacy.

But there are no qualities or principles most of us are prepared to associate unambiguously with the name of Oedipus, in either of the Sophoclean plays that feature him in their titles. Once we have set aside the irrelevant Freudian reductions, *Oedipus the King* becomes a battlefield of conflicting Interpretations. Is Oedipus innocent, so that only the gods are culpable? Are we to prefer Oedipus or the Sophoclean gods? Is Oedipus to blame for being so intelligent that he destroys the illusions without which we cannot go on living? Or is fate alone guilty, however we judge the flaws of Oedipus and the gods? Are *all* notions of guilt or innocence of little interest to Sophocles, and does he care only for the strife between illusion and truth? Or are all these questions useless, because the language of Sophocles knows only ambiguity, at least in human terms? Shall we say finally that we can make no sense of Oedipus as long as he is alive, because his only authentic language is the language of the gods, who urge him to stop tarrying and to come join them as yet another oracular god, at the close of *Oedipus at Colonus*?

All of these interpretations have been subtly urged by distinguished, scholarly critics of Sophocles, and they cannot all be right, because they strongly contradict one another. *Hamartia*, Aristotle's tragic flaw, seems dubious when we apply it to Sophocles' Oedipus, who never aims inaccurately, and who seems to me absolutely guiltless, and horribly unlucky, that last phrase being quite ludicrous in the context of his terrible story. I do not think that Sophocles means to honor the gods, since clearly we are to prefer Oedipus to the gods. When Oedipus blinds himself, a Freudian tends to speak of symbolic castration, but I think that Oedipus is making a religious protest against Apollo, and so against the light that does not let us see. And yet the power and self-confidence of Oedipus, his proper faith in his own intellect—these are gifts of Apollo. Oedipus knows this, and so I interpret him as crying out against the nature of truth, since the truth can only drive you mad.

That is a very dark reading, and I would not assert that it applies also to *Oedipus at Colonus*, an uncanny work, resembling nothing else that I have read. Why are the gods not insane, since they know the truth? Oedipus, becoming a god, abandons his characteristic fur: Henceforth he will share in the anger of the gods, which evidently is very different from our own. Presumably the madness of the gods also has nothing in common with our own. Whatever it is that destroys us can have no effect upon them. A Bible-educated culture cannot fully understand *Oedipus at Colonus*. We begin to gain entrance into the play only when we apprehend that it is totally other from any idea of religion that we possess.

Euripides

(C. 484–406 B.C.E)

E.R. DODDS, IN HIS SPLENDID EDITION OF THE *BACCHAE* (1944, 1960), explains not only the nature of Dionysiac religion, but remarks also the particular place of the play in the work of Euripides. The poet, over seventy, left Athens for Macedonia in 408 B.C.E., and never returned, dying in the winter of 407–406. In abandoning Athens, Euripides may well have felt defeated by public taste and poetic satirists. At least he did not have to endure the *Frogs* of Aristophanes, presented at Athens in 408, the year after his death. In the *Frogs*, Dionysus goes down into Hades in order to bring back a tragic poet-playwright, severely lacking in Athens after the death of the three great figures: Aeschylus, Sophocles, Euripides. Poor Euripides is savaged by Aristophanes, though nowhere near so viciously as Socrates was debased in the *Clouds*.

Dodds, still the authority upon the Greeks and the irrational, reads the *Bacchae* as being beyond any single stance by Euripides upon the Dionysiac. Euripides presents Dionysus as soft and sinister, a fatal androgyne of a god. Pentheus, the god's destined victim, also receives an equivocal representation. Neither the god nor the tyrant moves our sympathy as audience or readers.

The *Bacchae* was not presented in Athens until after the death of Euripides. We do not have a complete text of the play, but what is missing is not necessarily central. In the Hellenistic period and in Rome, the *Bacchae* was very popular, and still seems the masterpiece of Euripides's nineteen extant tragedies. William Arrowsmith, whose turbulent, wonderful translation I will employ here, compares the *Bacchae* in eminence to Sophocles's *Oedipus Tyrannus* and Aeschylus's *Agamemnon*. Like those plays, the *Bacchae* makes us into what Shakespeare called "wonder-wounded hearers." Oedipus and Clytemnestra find their rival in Euripides's uncanny

Dionysus, who is a triumph of representation: disturbing, fascinating, ultimately terrifying.

Dionysiac worship came late to Hellas, and did not attempt to supplant the Olympian pantheon. In Hellenistic Alexandria and in Rome, Dionysus became Bacchus the wine-god, but in earlier Hellas he was a more comprehensive divinity, emblematic of natural abundance, of flowering life, the Power in the tree. The Maenads in the *Bacchae* have drunk no wine (Pentheus is wrong about this) but are ecstatic through mountain-dancing, a shamanistic practice, restricted in Hellas to women's societies, and still carried on by certain group of women in the United States today. Dodds is eloquent on Dionysiac dance:

> ... he is the cause of madness and the liberator from madness ... To resist Dionysus is to repress the elemental in one's own nature; the punishment is the sudden complete collapse ... when the elemental breaks through ...

This Dionysiac dance of enthusiastic women culminated in a *sparagmos*, in which an animal body was torn apart and devoured raw, thus repeating the Titanic act of rending and consuming the infant Dionysus. The women who destroy Pentheus think he is a lion; more usually the Bacchantes ripped asunder and ate a bull, whose innate strength of resistance testifies to the daemonic ferocity imparted by Dionysus to his Maenads. There is some evidence of human sacrifice and ritual murder associated with Dionysiac celebration in the classical world. The Bacchantes achieved both the vitality of animal life and the group ecstasy in which individual consciousness vanished, for a time.

The origins of this shamanism may have been in Thrace, but in any rate it was tamed in Hellas, until the dark times of the Peloponnesian War, when it returned under the name of various mystery gods: Attis, Adonis, and Sabazius, to be deprecated and attacked by Plato, among others.

Dodds categorizes the *Bacchae* as the most severely formalized of Euripides's plays, and warns us against seeing it either as an exaltation of Dionysus or as an enlightened protest against orgiastic religions, since Penthues is very hard to like, and Dionysus is absolutely beyond human moral categories. There is a renewed force in the aged, self-exiled Euripides of the *Bacchae*, but it is neither Dionysiac nor counter-Dionysiac. Euripides, at the end, perfected his own art as poet-dramatist. It is as though he answered his enemy Aristophanes in advance, by demonstrating that, in his own way, he could raise himself to the Sublime measure of Sophocles and of Aeschylus.

William Arroswmith was a great humanist, who died in 1992, fighting heroically against the tides of Resentment that since have totally drowned humanism in the universities of the English-speaking world. I mourn him still, as we were close friends, and he restored my spirits, each time we met. A lover of both Euripides and Aristophanes, he refrained from translating the *Frogs*, while giving us superb version of the *Birds* and the *Clouds*, and of the *Bacchae* and four other tragedies by Euripides. Arrowsmith saw in the *Bacchae*, as in *Hippolytus* and in *Heracles*, an unique Euripidean compassion: "the pity that is born from shared suffering." To Arrowsmith, this was Euripidean humanism: "that faith and that fate which, in Euripides, makes man human, not mere god." Whether Arrowsmith, in his moral generosity and genial humaneness, imparted his own qualities to Euripides seems to me something of a question. Here is the close of the play, in Arrowsmith's version:

AGAVE
> I pity you, Father.

CADMUS
>   And I pity you, my child,
> and I grieve for your poor sisters. I pity them.

AGAVE
> Terribly has Dionysus brought
> disaster down upon this house.

DIONYSUS
> I was terribly blasphemed,
> my name dishonored in Thebes.

AGAVE
> Farewell, Father.

CADMUS
> Farewell to you, unhappy child.
> Fare well. But you shall find your faring hard.

(*Exit Cadmus*)

AGAVE
> Lead me, guides, where my sisters wait,
> poor sisters of my exile. Let me go
> where I shall never see Cithaeron more,
> where that accursed hill may not see me,
> where I shall find no trace of thyrsus!
> That I leave to other Bacchae.

(*Exit Agave with attendants.*)

CHORUS

    The gods have many shapes.
    The gods bring many things
    to their accomplishment.
    And what was most expected
    has not been accomplished.
    But god has found his way
    for what no man expected.
               So ends the play.

I hear ironies that are far stronger than the traumatized pity exchanged by Cadmus and his daughter Agave, who has led the Bacchantes in slaying her own son, Pentheus. Were I a director, I would be at a loss to tell the actor playing Dionysus how to speak his frightening lines: perhaps tonelessly, or at least matter-of-fact? An actress can do virtually anything with the blinding irony of: "That I leave to other Bacchae." Since the chorus are Asian Maenads, they are no problem: their tone is triumphant, if no longer ecstatic. Tragic irony is stronger in Euripides than is any humanism. If Aristophanes attended the *Bacchae*, he would have had his view of Euripidean nihilism confirmed. But that is what I find most Shakespearean about Euripides, whose own uncanniness somehow gets into the Shakespeare of *Troilus and Cressida*.

Aristophanes

(450–388 B.C.E)

> "There is a God, and his name is Aristophanes"
> —Heinrich Heine

OF THE ELEVEN EXTANT COMEDIES OF ARISTOPHANES, THE *BIRDS* SEEMS BEST of all to me, perhaps because it is even more outrageous than the *Clouds* and the *Frogs*. Aristophanes, outraged by his Athens and his Hellas, turned outrageousness into all but the highest art, to be surpassed only by the greatest of the Shakespearean comedies. Fortunately, we have a superb version of the *Birds* by the late William Arrowsmith, which is the text I will rely upon here.

Arrowsmith avoids the deep pit into which so any of the translators of Aristophanes have tumbled, which is to make the *Birds* or the *Clouds* ring forth like Gilbert and Sullivan. Though imperial Athens in 414 B.C.E. had its parallels with Victorian Britain, W.S. Gilbert's England was not treading near disaster. In 415–414, Athens was, when Alcibiades and his Athenian fleet sailed off to the Sicilian catastrophe. Athens was a place of hysteria, political frenzy, McCarthyite witch-hunting, and balked aggressivity. Aristophanes therefore sends forth his two confidence men, the daemonic Pisthetairos (let us call him "Plausible," which his name means) and his accomplice Euelpides ("Hopeful") to the wilderness of the Birds. There they suborn Hoopoe, who helps persuade all the other Birds to join in the Plausible-Hopeful project of building a New City, Cloudcuckooland. This City of the Birds will usurp the air-space between Olympus and Athens and so will come to dominate both. At the play's end, Plausible (who should have been played by the late Zero Mostel) is crowned King of the cosmos, displacing Zeus, and marries Miss Universe. The wedding feast is a delicious stew of jailbirds, victims of the Athenian-style "democracy" of King Plausible.

Any summary of outrageousness necessarily fails, particularly because

Aristophanes, in an antithetical reaction to Athenian disaster, is in hilarious high spirits throughout the *Birds*. Moses Hadas usefully remarks that Aristophanes "erases the world that is and constructs another," which is in part what Heine meant when he proclaimed: "There is a God and his name is Aristophanes." As befits God, Aristophanes in the *Birds* avoids bitterness, happy to escape with us to Cloudcuckooland.

Prometheus, being a Titan and so anti-Olympian, arrives to offer pragmatic counsel to Plausible:

> PROMETHEUS:
>> But give me your attention. At present these Triballoi gods
>> have joined with Zeus to send an official embassy
>> to sue for peace. Now here's the policy you must follow:
>> flatly reject any offers of peace they make you
>> until Zeus agrees to restore his sceptre to the Birds
>> and consents to give you Miss Universe as your wife.
>
> PISTHETAIROS:
>> But who's Miss Universe?
>
> PROMETHEUS:
>>   A sort of Beauty Queen,
>> the sign of Empire and the symbol of divine supremacy.
>> It's she who keeps the keys to Zeus' thunderbolts
>> and all his other treasures—Divine Wisdom,
>> Good Government, Common Sense, Naval Bases,
>> Slander, Libel, Political Graft, Sops to the Voters—
>
> PISTHETAIROS:
>> And *she* keeps the keys?
>
> PROMETHEUS:
>> Take it from me, friend.
>> Marry Miss Universe and the world is yours.
>> —You understand
>> why I had to tell you this? As Prometheus, after all,
>> my philanthropy is proverbial.
>
> PISTHETAIROS:
>> Yes, we worship you
>> as the inventor of the barbecue.
>
> PROMETHEUS:
>>   Besides, I loathe the gods.
>
> PISTHETAIROS:
>> The loathing's mutual, I know.

PROMETHEUS:

Just call me

TIMON:

I'm a misanthrope of gods.

—But I must be running along.
Give me my parasol. If Zeus spots me now,
he'll think I'm an ordinary one-god procession. I'll pretend
to be the girl behind the boy behind the basket.

PISTHETAIROS:

Here—take this stool and watch yourself march by.

*Exit Prometheus in solemn procession, draped in his
blanket, the umbrella in one hand, the stool in the
other. Pisthetairos and the Attendants retire.*

This is the *Birds* in miniature, wonderfully relevant to the United
States of 2001, where Plausible II rules as our court-selected President.
The sop to the Voters is of course the six-hundred-dollar-tax-rebate, even
though the equivalents of Miss Universe tempted our previous ruler.
Aristophanes is at his most amiable when he ends with the apotheosis of
Plausible. We live in Cloudcuckooland, and why should we not?

Christopher Marlowe

(c. 1564–1593)

LIKE SHAKESPEARE, BORN ONLY A FEW MONTHS AFTER HIM, MARLOWE began as an Ovidian poet. Killed at twenty-nine, in what may have been a mere tavern brawl, or possibly a political intrigue (fitter end for a double agent), Marlowe had the unhappy poetic fate of being swallowed up by Shakespeare's unprecedented powers of dramatic representation. We read Marlowe now as Shakespeare's precursor, remembering that Shakespeare also began as a poet of Ovidian eros. Read against Shakespeare, Marlowe all but vanishes. Nor can anyone prophesy usefully how Marlowe might have developed if he had lived another quarter century. There seems little enough development between *Tamburlaine* (1587) and *Doctor Faustus* (1593), and perhaps Marlowe was incapable of that process we name by the critical trope of "poetic development," which seems to imply a kind of turning about or even a wrapping up.

There has been a fashion, in modern scholarly criticism, to baptize Marlowe's imagination, so that a writer of tragic caricatures has been converted into an orthodox moralist. The vanity of scholarship has few more curious monuments than this Christianized Marlowe. What the common reader finds in Marlowe is precisely what his contemporaries found: impiety, audacity, worship of power, ambiguous sexuality, occult aspirations, defiance of moral order, and above all else a sheer exaltation of the possibilities of rhetoric, of the persuasive force of heroic poetry. The subtlest statement of the scholar's case is made by Frank Kermode:

> Thus Marlowe displays his heroes reacting to most of the temptations that Satan can contrive; and the culminating temptation ... is the scholar's temptation, forbidden knowledge ... [Marlowe's] heroes do not resist the temptations, and he provides us, not with

a negative proof of virtue and obedience to divine law, but with positive examples of what happens in their absence. Thus, whatever his intentions may have been, and however much he flouted conventions, Marlowe's themes are finally reducible to the powerful formulae of contemporary religion and morality.

"Finally reducible" is the crucial phrase here; is final reduction the aim of reading or of play-going? As for "Marlowe's themes," they count surely rather less than Marlowe's rhetoric does, and, like most themes or topics, indubitably do ensue ultimately from religion and morality. But Marlowe is not Spenser or Milton, and there is one originality he possesses that is not subsumed by Shakespeare. Call that originality by the name of Barabas, Marlowe's grandest character, who dominates what is certainly Marlowe's most vital and original play, *The Jew of Malta*. Barabas defies reduction, and his gusto represents Marlowe's severest defiance of all moral and religious convention.

II

Barabas (or Barabbas, as in the Gospels) means "son of the Father" and so "son of God," and may have begun as an alternate name for Jesus. As the anti-Jewish tenor of the Gospels intensified from Mark to John, Barabbas declined from a patriotic insurrectionist to a thief, and as either was preferred by "the Jews" to Jesus. This is a quite Marlovian irony that the scholar Hyam Maccoby puts forward, and Marlowe might have rejoiced at the notion that Jesus and Barabbas were historically the same person. One Richard Baines, a police informer, insisted that Marlowe said of Jesus: "If the Jews among whom he was born did crucify him they best knew him and whence he came." The playwright Thomas Kyd, arrested after his friend Marlowe's death, testified that the author of *The Jew of Malta* tended to "jest at the divine Scriptures, gibe at prayers, and strive in argument to frustrate and confute what hath been spoke or writ by prophets and such holy men." Are we to credit Baines and Kyd, or Kermode and a bevy of less subtle scholars?

Marlowe, who was as sublimely disreputable as Rimbaud or Hart Crane, is more of their visionary company than he is at home with T.S. Eliot or with academic moralists. *The Jew of Malta* contrasts sharply with *The Merchant of Venice*, which may have been composed so as to overgo it on the stage. It cannot be too much emphasized that Marlowe's Barabas is a savage original, while Shakespeare's Shylock, despite his supposed humanization, is essentially the timeless anti-Semitic stock figure, devil and usurer, of Christian tradition. Stating it more plainly, Shakespeare indeed is as anti-Semitic as the Gospels or T.S. Eliot, whereas Marlowe employs his Barabas as a truer surrogate for himself than are Tamburlaine, Edward II, and Dr. Faustus. Barabas is Marlowe the satirist:

> It's no sin to deceive a Christian;
> For they themselves hold it a principle,
> Faith is not to be held with heretics.
> But all are heretics that are not Jews;
> This follows well ...

And so indeed it does. The art of Barabas is to better Christian instruction, unlike Shylock, who has persistence but who lacks art. Shylock is obsessive-compulsive; Barabas delights because he is a free man, or if you would prefer, a free fiend, at once a monstrous caricature and a superb image of Marlowe's sly revenge upon society. What Hazlitt gave us as a marvelous critical concept, gusto, is superbly manifested by Barabas, but not by poor Shylock. "Gusto in art is power or passion defining any object." Hazlitt accurately placed Shakespeare first among writers in this quality:

> The infinite quantity of dramatic invention in Shakespeare takes from his gusto. The power he delights to show is not intense, but discursive. He never insists on anything he might, except a quibble.

But Shylock is the one great exception in Shakespeare, and surprisingly lacks invention. Marlowe's superior gusto, in just this one instance, emerges as we contrast two crucial speeches. Barabas is outrageous, a parody of the stage-Jew, and Shylock speaks with something like Shakespeare's full resources, so that the power of language is overwhelmingly Shakespeare's, and yet Barabas becomes an original representation, while Shylock becomes even more the nightmare bogey of Christian superstition and hatred:

> SALERIO: Why, I am sure if he forfeit thou wilt not take his flesh. What's that good for?
> SHYLOCK: To bait fish withal. If it will feed nothing else, it will feed my revenge. He hath disgraced me, and hind'red me half a million, laughed at my losses, mocked at my gains, scorned my nation, thwarted my bargains, cooled my friends, heated mine enemies-and what's his reason? I am a Jew. Hath not a

Jew eyes? Hath not a Jew hands, organs, dimensions, senses, affections, passions?—fed with the same food, hurt with the same weapons, subject to the same diseases, healed by the same means, warmed and cooled by the same winter and summer as a Christian is? If you prick us, do we not bleed? If you tickle us, do we not laugh? If you poison us, do we not die? And if you wrong us, shall we not revenge? If we are like you in the rest, we will resemble you in that. If a Jew wrong a Christian, what is his humility? Revenge! If a Christian wrong a Jew, what should his sufferance be by Christian example? Why revenge! The villainy you teach me I will execute, and it shall go hard but I will better the instruction.

"If you prick us, do we not bleed? If you tickle us, do we not laugh?" Shylock himself is not changed by listening to these, his own words, and neither are the audience's prejudices changed one jot. No one in that audience had seen a Jew, nor had Shakespeare, unless they or he had watched the execution of the unfortunate Dr. Lopez, the Queen's physician, condemned on a false charge of poisoning, or had glimpsed one of the handful of other converts resident in London. Shylock is rendered more frightening by the startling reminders that this dangerous usurer is flesh and blood, a man as well as a devil. Jews after all, Shakespeare's language forcefully teaches his audience, are not merely mythological murderers of Christ and of his beloved children, but literal seekers after the flesh of the good and gentle Antonio.

Can we imagine Barabas saying: "If you prick us, do we not bleed? If you tickle us, do we not laugh?" Or can we imagine Shylock intoning this wonderful and parodistic outburst of the exuberant Barabas?

As for myself, I walk abroad a-nights,
And kill sick people groaning under walls.
Sometimes I go about and poison wells;
And now and then, to cherish Christian thieves,
I am content to lose some of my crowns,
That I may, walking in my gallery,
See 'em go pinion'd along by my door.
Being young, I studied physic, and began
To practise first upon the Italian;
There I enrich'd the priests with burials,
And always kept the sexton's arms in ure
With digging graves and ringing dead men's knells.

And, after that, was I an engineer,
And in the wars 'twixt France and Germany,
Under the pretence of helping Charles the Fifth,
Slew friend and enemy with my stratagems:
Then after that was I an usurer,
And with extorting, cozening, forfeiting,
And tricks belonging unto brokery,
I fill'd the gaols with bankrupts in a year,
And with young orphans planted hospitals;
And every moon made some or other mad,
And now and then one hang himself for grief,
Pinning upon his breast a long great scroll
How I with interest tormented him.
But mark how I am blest for plaguing them:
I have as much coin as will buy the town.
But tell me now, how has thou spent thy time?

This would do admirably in a Gilbert and Sullivan opera, had the anti-Semitic Gilbert (see *The Bab Ballads*) been willing to mock his own prejudices. We do not know how the more sophisticated among Marlowe's audience received this, but properly delivered it has the tang and bite of great satire. A more fascinating surmise is: How did Shakespeare receive this? And how did he react to Barabas in what we can call the mode of Hemingway, sparring with his holy friars?

FRIAR BARNARDINE: Barabas, thou hast—
FRIAR JACOMO: Ay, not what thou hast—
BARABAS: True, I have money; what though I have?
FRIAR BARNARDINE: Thou art a—
FRIAR JACOMO: Ay, that thou art, a—
BARABAS: What needs all this? I know I am a Jew.
FRIAR BARNARDINE: Thy daughter—
FRIAR JACOMO: Ay, thy daughter—
BARABAS: O, speak not of her! Then I die with grief.
FRIAR BARNARDINE: Remember that—
FRIAR JACOMO: Ay, remember that—
BARABAS: I must needs say that I have been a great usurer.
FRIAR BARNARDINE: Thou hast committed—
BARABAS: Fornication: but that was in another country,
    And besides the wench is dead.

We can say that Shakespeare refused the hint. Shylock's grim repetitions ("I will have my bond") come out of a different universe, the crimes of Christendom that Shakespeare had no thought of rejecting. This is hardly to say that Marlowe was in any sense humane. *The Jew of Malta* is bloody farce, more than worthy of Jarry or Artaud. Barabas emerges from the world of Thomas Nashe and Thomas Kyd, Marlowe's half-world of espionage and betrayal, of extravagant wit and antithetical lusts, which was the experiential scene that must have taught Shakespeare to go and live otherwise, and write otherwise as well.

III

The Australian poet Alec Hope, in a remarkable essay upon Marlowe, ascribes to *Tamburlaine* "a thoroughgoing morality of power, aesthetics of power and logic of power." Hope is clearly right about *Tamburlaine*. I would go further and suggest that there is no other morality, aesthetics or logic anywhere in Marlowe's writings. Where Hope usefully quotes Hazlitt on the congruence between the language of power and the language of poetry, I would cite also the great American theoretician of power and poetry, the Emerson of *The Conduct of Life*:

> A belief in causality, or strict connection between every trifle and the principle of being, and, in consequence, belief in compensation, or, that nothing is got for nothing,—characterizes all valuable minds, and must control every effort that is made by an industrious one. The most valiant men are the best believers in the tension of the laws ...
>
> All power is of one kind, a sharing of the nature of the world. The mind that is parallel with the laws of nature will be in the current of events, and strong with their strength.

Like Marlowe, Hazlitt and Emerson are agonists who understand that there are no accidents. In Marlowe, the implicit metaphysics of this understanding are Epicurean-Lucretian. Barabas and Tamburlaine seek their own freedom, and ultimately fail, but only because they touch the ultimate limits at the flaming ramparts of the world. Edward II and Dr. Faustus fail, but they are weak, and their fate does not grieve Marlowe. Indeed, the aesthetic satisfaction Marlowe hints at is not free from a sadistic pleasure the poet and his audience share at observing the dreadful ends of Edward and Faustus. Marlowe's heroes, Tamburlaine and Barabas, die defiantly, with Tamburlaine still naming himself "the scourge of God," and Barabas, boiling in a cauldron, nevertheless cursing his enemies with his customary vehemence:

> And, villains, know you cannot help me now.
> Then, Barabas, breathe forth thy latest fate,
> And in the fury of thy torments strive
> To end thy life with resolution.
> Know, Governor, 'twas I that slew thy son,
> I fram'd the challenge that did make them meet.
> Know, Calymath, I aim'd thy overthrow:
> And, had I escap'd this stratagem,
> I would have brought confusion on you all,
> Damn'd Christians, dogs, and Turkish infidels!
> But now begins the extremity of heat
> To pinch me with intolerable pangs.
> Die, life! fly, soul! tongue, curse thy fill, and die!

Shylock, alas, ends wholly broken, "content" to become a Christian, a resolution that is surely the most unsatisfactory in all of Shakespeare. I cannot envision the late Groucho Marx playing Shylock, but I sometimes read through *The Jew of Malta*, mentally casting Groucho as Barabas. T.S. Eliot, whose admiration for *The Jew of Malta* was strong, was also a fan of the sublime Groucho. I rejoice, for once, to share two of Eliot's enthusiasms, and enjoy the thought that he too might have wished to see Groucho play Barabas.

Doctor Faustus

Though it seems to me less impressive than *The Jew of Malta* and the first part of *Tamburlaine*, *Doctor Faustus* is now regarded by most critics as Marlowe's greatest play. I have seen several performances of *Doctor Faustus* and of *Edward II*, but only one of *Tamburlaine* (a superb enactment by Anthony Quayle) and regret deeply that I have not yet seen *The Jew of Malta* on stage. Marlowe had a collaborator (perhaps two) in *Doctor Faustus*, and we do not seem to have an authentic text of the play. Many of the comic scenes are scarcely readable, and no other Elizabethan play mixes superb and dreadful writing to the extent that this one does.

Marlowe, whose learning was curious and extensive, presumably knew that Faustus (Latin for "the favored one") was the cognomen taken by Simon Magus, founder of the Gnostic heresy, when he went to Rome. *Doctor Faustus* is a Hermetic drama in its range and implications, but it has few

Gnostic overtones. It scarcely matters whether its overt theology is Catholic, Lutheran, or Calvinist, since the theology is there as a good, boisterous mythology that the hyperbolist Marlowe is happy to exploit. As many critics have recognized, Marlowe maintains his distance from Faustus and expresses himself fairly directly through the splendidly bitter Mephostophilis, who walks about in the likeness of a friar and who suffers a profound nostalgia for the loss of heaven. Marlowe is not representing himself in or as Mephostophilis and yet clearly Mephostophilis, not Faustus, is the play's intellectual, its advanced, or modern, thinker. He cannot exactly be called disinterested and yet he is remarkably detached, while carefully always knowing both his limits and his allegiances. Though a loyal follower of Lucifer, his rhetoric indicates a personal and poignant distance from his own camp and conveys a more formidable pathos than Faustus himself will evoke until his final speech. The opening dialogue between Faustus and his personal devil (as it were) provides a remarkable dramatic contrast between the two, a contrast in which we find we prefer Mephostophilis to the human magus who thinks he has summoned this spirit:

> MEPHOSTOPHILIS: I am a servant to great Lucifer,
>   And may not follow thee without his leave:
>   No more than he commands must we perform.
> FAUSTUS: Did not he charge thee to appear to me?
> MEPHOSTOPHILIS: No. I came now hither of mine own accord.
> FAUSTUS: Did not my conjuring speeches raise thee? Speak.
> MEPHOSTOPHILIS: That was the cause, but yet per accidens;
>   For when we hear one rack the name of God.
>   Abjure the scriptures and his saviour Christ.
>   We fly in hope to get his glorious soul;
>   Nor will we come unless he use such means
>   Whereby he is in danger to be damned.
>   Therefore the shortest cut for conjuring
>   Is stoutly to abjure the Trinity
>   And pray devoutly to the prince of hell.
> FAUSTUS: So Faustus hath already done, and holds this principle:
>   There is no chief but only Belzebub,
>   To whom Faustus doth dedicate himself.
>   This word "damnation" terrifies not him,
>   For he confounds hell in Elysium.
>   His ghost be with the old philosophers.
>   But leaving these vain trifles of men's souls,
>   Tell me, what is that Lucifer, thy lord?

MEPHOSTOPHILIS: Arch-regent and commander of all spirits.

FAUSTUS: Was not that Lucifer an angel once?

MEPHOSTOPHILIS: Yes Faustus, and most dearly loved of God.

FAUSTUS: How come it then that he is prince of devils?

MEPHOSTOPHILIS: O, by aspiring pride and insolence,
    For which God threw him from the face of heaven.

FAUSTUS: And what are you that live with Lucifer?

MEPHOSTOPHILIS: Unhappy spirits that fell with Lucifer,
    Conspired against our God with Lucifer,
    And are for ever damned with Lucifer.

FAUSTUS: Where are you damned?

MEPHOSTOPHILIS: In hell.

FAUSTUS: How 'comes it then that thou art out of hell?

MEPHOSTOPHILIS: Why, this is hell, nor am I out of it.
    Think'st thou that I who saw the face of God
    And tasted the eternal joys of heaven,
    Am not tormented with ten thousand hells
    In being deprived of everlasting bliss?
    O Faustus, leave these frivolous demands,
    Which strikes a terror to my fainting soul.
    (3.40–82)

Lucifer would not be pleased by the language of his loyal but elaborately wistful follower, we must suspect. The hints that Milton took from Marlowe are plain enough, but even the sublimity of the Miltonic Satan of the early books of *Paradise Lost* does not allow for anything quite like the epigrammatic snap of the justly famous "Why, this is hell, nor am I out of it," the most Gnostic Statement in the drama. Harry Levin rather strangely compared Mephostophilis to Dostoevsky's Porfiry, the examining magistrate in *Crime and Punishment*. But Porfiry is a good man; Mephostophilis, I venture, is Marlowe's version of the Accuser, the Satan who appears at the opening of the Book of Job. Blake, in a Gnostic insight, called the Accuser the God of this world. Mephostophilis has no such pretensions and is closer to the biblical Book of Job's Accuser because he functions as what Saul Bellow rather nastily calls a Reality Instructor. Mephostophilis has uncanny insight into Faustus, indeed he seems to be the Daemon or Genius of Faustus, perhaps the spiritual form that Faustus will take on in Hell.

Mephostophilis has a horror of marriage, not merely because it is a sacrament but because this "ceremonial toy" might threaten his curious intimacy with Faustus. This aversion to connubial bliss is mild compared

to the exalted view of man held by this surprising spirit, who seems both
more of a Hermeticist and more of a Humanist than either Marlowe or
Faustus:

> FAUSTUS: When I behold the heavens then I repent,
>   And curse thee, wicked Mephostophilis,
>   Because thou hast deprived me of those joys.
> MEPHOSTOPHILIS: 'Twas thine own seeking, Faustus, thank thyself.
>   But think'st thou heaven is such a glorious thing?
>   I tell thee, Faustus, it is not half so fair
>   As thou or any man that breathes on earth.
> FAUSTUS: How prov'st thou that?
> MEPHOSTOPHILIS: 'Twas made for man; then he's more excellent.
> FAUSTUS: If heaven was made for man, 'twas made for me.
>   I will renounce this magic and repent.
> (6.1–11)

Mephostophilis evidently desires Faustus, at least aesthetically, and we
remember his initial insistence that he first came to Faustus not because he
was conjured, but of his own accord. Forbidden by Lucifer to love the creator, Mephostophilis loves the creature and refuses to discuss origins:

> FAUSTUS: Well, I am answered. Now tell me, who made the
>   world?
> MEPHOSTOPHILIS: I will not.
> FAUSTUS: Sweet Mephostophilis, tell me.
> MEPHOSTOPHILIS: Move me not, Faustus.
> FAUSTUS: Villain, have not I bound thee to tell me anything?
> MEPHOSTOPHILIS: Ay, that is not against our kingdom:
>   This is. Thou art damned, think thou of hell.
> FAUSTUS: Think, Faustus, upon God, that made the world.
> MEPHOSTOPHILIS: remember this—
> FAUSTUS: ay, go, accursed spirit to ugly hell.
>   'Tis thou hast damned distressed Faustus' soul.
>   Is't not too late?
> (6.67–78)

It is definitely too late, and I wonder at the exegetes who debate the
supposedly relevant theologies—Catholic, Calvinist, Lutheran—and their
presumed effect upon whether Faustus either will not or cannot repent.
Marlowe is no more interested in letting Faustus escape than in giving the

wretched Edward II a good death. The play's glory is in the last speech of Faustus, an extraordinary rhapsody whose sixty lines form one of the great dramatic poems in the language. All of it is magnificent and subtle, but the final line almost transcends Faustus and his situation:

I'll burn my books!—Ah, Mephostophilis!

To burn his books of magic or Hermetic knowledge would be to burn himself, for he has become what he desired to become, his daemonic books. That "Ah, Mephostophilis!" spoken to the spirit who leads him off the stage is a sigh of surrender, a realization that, like Mephostophilis, he goes, after all, of his own accord and not just because he is summoned. We are not much moved by this damnation, any more than Marlowe could be much moved. Barabas has an extraordinary personality, and so in very different ways do Tamburlaine and Edward II. Doctor Faustus is scarcely a person and so hardly a personality at all. He is Marlowe's victim or scapegoat, sacrificed in Marlowe's own Black Mass, so as to utter a gorgeous, broken music in his demise. Simon Magus, the original Faustus, was a sublime charlatan; the nihilistic genius of Marlowe was content at the end with a merely eloquent charlatan.

William Shakespeare

(1564-1616)

THE COMEDIES

THE GREATNESS OF SHAKESPEARE'S HIGH COMEDIES—*A MIDSUMMER Night's Dream, As You Like It, The Merchant of Venice*, and *Twelfth Night, or What You Will*—fully matches the magnificence of his four High Tragedies: *Hamlet, Othello, King Lear*, and *Macbeth*. Shakespeare's natural gift was for comedy; he is already fully himself in the early farces, *The Comedy of Errors* and *The Taming of the Shrew*. The shadow of Christopher Marlowe darkens *Titus Andronicus* and *Richard III*, but Marlowe had no interest and little talent for comedy. *The Tempest* is still essentially comedy, little as we tend to apprehend this.

II

A Midsummer Night's Dream is unique in Shakespeare, because it is the most visionary of his dramas, beyond even *The Tempest* as a transcendental enterprise. Ariel and the spirits are of another order of representation than are Puck, Titania, Oberon and Bottom's good friends: Cobweb, Mustardseed, Peaseblossom, and Moth, all elves of the greatest charm and amiability, worthy of the sublime Bottom himself. Of Bottom, no praise can be excessive. Ancestor of Joyce's Poldy Bloom, Bottom radiates good will and good sense; he is sound at the core, and is the skein upon which the play's elaborate designs is wound. One of Shakespeare's great originals, Bottom is not always well served by modern criticism, which tends to underestimate his innate dignity. Natural man, so much maligned by moralists, whether Christian or Marxist, achieves an apotheosis in Bottom.

And yet there is much more to Bottom than even that grand dignity.

He alone, of the play's humans, is open to the realm of the fairies, and he
alone enjoys the bottomless dream that in some sense is the ethos of
Shakespeare's visionary play. Weavers are in touch with uncanny forces,
and Bottom is the prince of weavers. He holds God's secrets, even if he is
unaware of them. There is a link between Bottom's sweet good nature and
the high, good spirits of Shakespeare's true genius Sir John Falstaff.

III

If Falstaff (and Hamlet) have a rival for audacious intelligence, and
slyly agile wit in all Shakespeare, then she must be the superb Rosalind,
heroine of *As You Like It*, the most joyous of the comedies. The Forest of
Arden may not be an earthly paradise, but in Shakespeare it is the best
place to be, and Rosalind is the best person to be with in all of literature.
William Hazlitt wonderfully said of Rosalind: "She talks herself out of
breath, only to get deeper in love." I myself tend to emphasize her originality, in which she fully rivals Falstaff and Hamlet. In one crucial way, she
transcends even them. As the audience, we can achieve perspectives upon
Falstaff and Hamlet that are not available to them, but we enjoy no such
privilege in regard to Rosalind. Dramatic irony can and does victimize
Falstaff and Hamlet, but never Rosalind. She sees herself and her play all
around, as it were; she arranges her own surprises. You cannot close the
doors upon Rosalind's wit; it will out at the casement. Neither passive nor
aggressive, Rosalind's wit is the subtlest I have encountered in literature.

IV

The Merchant of Venice, insofar as it is Portia's play, is high comedy, but
history has made it Shylock's play also, which has rendered this great work
highly problematic. Shylock's play can be done as farce, as tragicomedy, or
as something for which we lack a name. One doesn't have to be Jewish to
be horrified by forced conversion, on threat of death, to Christianity, but
of course there is a particular shudder involved for Jewish playgoers and
readers, like myself. What are we to do with *The Merchant of Venice*? Portia,
though she squanders herself, is almost of Rosalind's splendor. Shylock's
energy of being, the heroism of his malevolent will, and most of all his
shattering eloquence: these combine to render him as memorable as he is
frightening, a permanent slander against the Jewish people and its traditions of trusting to Yahwistic righteousness. I yield to no one in Bardolatry,
but still must affirm that the role of Shylock has done grievous harm.

Yet *The Merchant of Venice* remains a masterwork of Shakespearean comedy, even if we do not laugh with it as Shakespeare's own audiences did. The ravishing Act V, set in Portia's Belmont, is a lyrical triumph, juxtaposing fulfilled Romantic love with ironic overtones of love's betrayal. Shylock's absence in the final act is both a tribute to the sophisticated power of Portia's world, and a critique of its limitations.

V

Of Shakespeare's early farces, *The Taming of the Shrew* maintains a perpetual popularity. The loving struggle for supremacy between Kate and Petruchio is an epitome of a crucial element in nearly every marriage, and the war between men and women is of universal relevance. It is too easy to get this play quite wrong; there are feminist visions of the "brutal" Petruchio pursuing Kate with a whip! In mere fact, she slaps him, and he confines his assaults to language. What Shakespeare actually gives us is the subtle self-education of Kate, who achieves dominion over the swaggering Petruchio through a parody of submission. What is profoundly moving is the representation of two ferocious beings who fall in love at first sight (though Kate conceals it) and who eventually make a strong alliance against the rest of the world. Beneath the surface of this knockabout farce, Shakespeare pursues one of his most illuminating contentions: the natural superiority of women over men.

VI

Twelfth Night is Shakespeare's farewell to high comedy, and may be his greatest achievement in that mode. Whose play is it; does it center upon Viola, Olivia, Malvolio, or Feste? That is rather like asking whether *King Lear* centers upon Edmund, the Fool, Edgar, or Lear himself? A beautifully complex comedy, *Twelfth Night* refuses the perspective that would make it poor, victimized Malvolio's tragicomedy. Like Shylock, Malvolio is one of Shakespeare's displaced spirits; he is not at home in the comic world of the play. And yet the play *needs* Malvolio; his undeserved downfall is essential to Shakespeare's vision. There is no poetic justice (or Christian consolation) in Shakespeare: the whirligig of time accomplishes its revenges. A delight and a madness, *Twelfth Night*'s only sane character is the remarkable Feste, the most admirable of Shakespeare's clowns. Viola is benign and lovable, yet she is as much a zany as Orsino, whom she will marry or Olivia, who rarely gets anything straight. *Twelfth Night*, a sublime Feast of Fools, is a crowning an achievement as are *King Lear* and *The Tempest*, all summits of their mode.

The Taming of the Shrew

The Taming of the Shrew, when acted, seems almost the simplest of performance pieces, a fine farce in an immemorial tradition of male supremacy. Well before the advent of feminist criticism of Shakespeare, Harold Goddard declined to accept such an interpretation:

> *Richard III* proves that *double-entendre* was a passion of the youthful Shakespeare, and both *The Two Gentlemen of Verona* and *Love's Labor's Lost* illustrate the fact that he was fond of under- and over-meanings he could not have expected his audience as a whole to get. But it is *The Taming of the Shrew* that is possibly the most striking example among his early works of his love of so contriving a play that it should mean, to those who might choose to take it so, the precise opposite of what he knew it would mean to the multitude. For surely the most psychologically sound as well as the most delightful way of taking *The Taming of the Shrew* is the topsy-turvy one. Kate, in that case, is no shrew at all except in the most superficial sense. Bianca, on the other hand, is just what her sister is supposed to be. And the play ends with the prospect that Kate is going to be more nearly the tamer than the tamed, Petruchio more nearly the tamed than the tamer, though his wife naturally will keep the true situation under cover. So taken, the play is an early version of *What Every Woman Knows*—what every woman knows being, of course, that the woman can lord it over the man so long as she allows him to think he is lording it over her. This interpretation has the advantage of bringing the play into line with all the other Comedies in which Shakespeare gives a distinct edge to his heroine. Otherwise it is an unaccountable exception and regresses to the wholly un-Shakespearean doctrine of male superiority, a view which there is not the slightest evidence elsewhere Shakespeare ever held.

In Goddard's reading, the Christopher Sly induction is an intentional analogue to the subtle gulling of Petruchio by Kate:

> In the Induction to *The Taming of the Shrew*, Christopher Sly the tinker, drunk with ale, is persuaded that he is a great lord who has been the victim of an unfortunate lunacy. Petruchio, in the play which Sly witnesses (when he is not asleep), is likewise persuaded that he is a great lord—over his wife. Sly is obviously in for a rude

awakening when he discovers that he is nothing but a tinker after all. Now Petruchio is a bit intoxicated himself—who can deny it?—whether with pride, love, or avarice, or some mixture of the three. Is it possible that he too is in for an awakening? Or, if Kate does not let it come to that, that *we* at least are supposed to see that he is not as great a lord over his wife as he imagined? The Induction and the play, taken together, do not allow us to evade these questions. Can anyone be so naive as to fancy that Shakespeare did not contrive his Induction for the express purpose of forcing them on us? Either the cases of Sly and Petruchio are alike or they are diametrically opposite. Can there be much doubt which was intended by a poet who is so given to pointing out analogies between lovers and drunkards, between lovers and lunatics? Here surely is reason enough for Shakespeare not to show us Sly at the end when he no longer thinks himself a lord. It would be altogether too much like explaining the joke, like solving the equation and labeling the result ANSWER. Shakespeare wants us to find things for ourselves. And in this case in particular: why explain what is as clear, when you see it, as was Poe's Purloined Letter, which was skilfully concealed precisely because it was in such plain sight all the time?

This is consonant with Northrop Frye's observation that Kate in act 5 is engaged in much the same occupation as in act 1, getting back at Bianca for being the favorite (and spoiled) daughter, except that Kate, schooled by her husband, now has social convention on her side against Bianca. And yet the most celebrated of Kate's speeches remains a permanent scandal:

> KATHERINA: Fie, fie, unknit that threat'ning unkind brow,
>   And dart not scornful glances from those eyes,
>   To wound thy lord, thy king, thy governor.
>   It blots thy beauty, as frosts do bite the meads,
>   Confounds thy fame, as whirlwinds shake fair buds,
>   And in no sense is meet or amiable.
>   A woman mov'd is like a fountain troubled,
>   Muddy, ill-seeming, thick, bereft of beauty,
>   And while it is so, none so dry or thirsty
>   Will deign to sip, or touch one drop of it.
>   Thy husband is thy lord, thy life, thy keeper,
>   Thy head, thy sovereign; one that cares for thee,
>   And for thy maintenance; commits his body

To painful labor, both by sea and land;
To watch the night in storms, the day in cold,
Whilst thou li'st warm at home, secure and safe;
And craves no other tribute at thy hands
But love, fair looks, and true obedience
Too little payment for so great a debt.
Such duty as the subject owes the prince,
Even such a woman oweth to her husband;
And when she is froward, peevish, sullen, sour,
And not obedient to his honest will,
What is she but a foul contending rebel,
And graceless traitor to her loving lord?
I am asham'd that women are so simple
To offer war where they should kneel for peace,
Or seek for rule, supremacy, and sway,
When they are bound to serve, love, and obey.
Why are our bodies soft, and weak, and smooth,
Unapt to toil and trouble in the world,
But that our soft conditions, and our hearts,
Should well agree with our external parts?
Come, come, you froward and unable worms!
My mind hath been as big as one of yours,
My heart as great, my reason haply more,
To bandy word for word and frown for frown;
But now I see our lances are but straws,
Our strength as weak, our weakness past compare,
That seeming to be most which we indeed least are.
Then vail your stomachs, for it is no boot,
And place your hands below your husband's foot;
In token of which duty, if he please,
My hand is ready, may it do him ease.

Unlike John Milton's "He for God only, she for God in him," I rather doubt that any audience ever could have taken this to heart. A good actress can do marvelous things with: "I am asham'd that women are so simple." The clearest representational truth of *The Taming of the Shrew* is that Kate and Petruchio, both violent expressionists, were made for one another, and doubtless are likelier to live happily ever after than any other married couple in Shakespeare. If you had the Bianca-doting Baptista for a father, and you were Kate, then the amiable ruffian Petruchio would become an ideal, indeed an over-determined match.

That still leaves the puzzle of the induction, with the curious status it assigns to the Kate–Petruchio agon as a play-within-a-play or rather farce-within-a-farce. Brilliant as the induction is, it performs strangely in our mobile society, where class distinctions hardly are as they are in England now, or were in England then. Goddard may have been imaginatively correct in analogizing Sly's delusion and Petruchio's (if he is deluded), but socially the analogy cannot hold. Petruchio and Kate are in the same social class, but the drunken Sly is indeed lunatic when he accepts the deceit practiced upon him. Shakespeare's meanings are necessarily ours, but his social judgments remain those of another nation, at another time.

A Midsummer Night's Dream

On the loftiest of the world's thrones we still are sitting only on our own Bottom.
                    —MONTAIGNE, "Of Experience"

I will get Peter Quince to write a ballet of this dream. It shall be call'd "Bottom's Dream," because it hath no bottom.

I wish Shakespeare had given us Peter Quince's ballet (ballad), but he may have been too wise to attempt the poem. *A Midsummer Night's Dream*, for me, is Puck and Bottom, and I prefer Bottom. Perhaps we reduce to Puckish individuals or Bottoms. Pucks are more charming, but Bottoms are rather more amiable. Shakespeare's Bottom is surpassingly amiable, and I agree with Northrop Frye that Bottom is the only mortal with experience of the visionary center of the play. As the possible lover (however briefly) of the Fairy Queen, Bottom remains a lasting reproach to our contemporary fashion of importing sacred violence, bestiality, and all manner of sexual antics into Shakespeare's most fragile of visionary dramas. For who could be more mild mannered, better natured, or sweetly humorous than the unfailingly gentle Bottom? Titania ends up despising him, but he is simply too good for her!

Bottom, when we first encounter him, is already a Malaprop, inaccurate at the circumference, as it were, but sound at the core, which is what his name means, the center of the skein upon which a weaver's wool is wound. And surely that is his function in the play; he is its core, and also he is the most original figure in *A Midsummer Night's Dream*. Self-assertive, silly, ignorant, he remains a personage of absolute good will, a kind of remote ancestor to Joyce's amiable Poldy. Transformed into an outward monstrosity by Puck, he yet retains his courage, kindness, and humor, and goes through his uncanny experience totally unchanged within. His initial dialogue with Titania is deliciously ironic, and he himself is in full control of the irony:

> TITANIA: I pray thee, gentle mortal, sing again.
>   Mine ear is much enamored of thy note;
>   So is mine eye enthralled to thy shape;
>   And thy fair virtue's force (perforce) doth move me
>   On the first view to say, to swear, I love thee.
> BOTTOM: Methinks, mistress, you "should have little reason
>   for that. And yet, to say the truth, reason and love keep
>   little company together now-a-days. The more the pity
>   that some honest neighbors will not make them friends.
>   Nay, I can gleek upon occasion.
> TITANIA: Thou art as wise as thou art beautiful.
> BOTTOM: Not so, neither; but if I had wit enough to get out of this
>   wood, I have enough to serve mine own turn.

Knowing that he lacks both beauty and wisdom, Bottom is realistic enough to see that the faery queen is beautiful but not wise. Charmed by (and charming to) the elve foursome of Peaseblossom, Cobweb, Moth, and Mustardseed, Bottom makes us aware that they mean no more and no less to him than Titania does. Whether or not he has made love to Titania, a subject of some nasty debate among our critical contemporaries, seems to me quite irrelevant. What does matter is that he is sublimely unchanged, for worse or for better, when he wakes up from his bottomless dream:

> BOTTOM: [*Awaking.*] When my cue comes, call me, and I will
>   answer. My next is, "Most fair Pyramus." Heigh-ho! Peter
>   Quince! Flute the bellowsmender! Snout the tinker!
>   Starveling! God's my life, stol'n hence, and left me asleep! I
>   have had a most rare vision. I have had a dream, past the wit
>   of man to say what dream it was. Man is but an ass, if he go
>   about [t'] expound this dream. Methought I was—there is no
>   man can tell what. Methought I was, and methought I had—
>   but man is but [a patch'd] fool, if he will offer to say what
>   methought I had. The eye of man hath not heard, the ear of
>   man hath not seen, man's hand is not able to taste, his tongue
>   to conceive, nor his heart to report, what my dream was. I will
>   get Peter Quince to write a ballet of this dream. It shall be
>   ca-l'd "Bottom's Dream," because it hath no bottom; and I

will sing it in the latter end of a play, before the Duke.
Peradventure, to make it the more gracious, I shall sing it at
her death.

Bottom's revision of 1 Corinthians 2:9–10 is the heart of the matter:

Eye hath not seen, nor ear heard, neither have entered into the
heart of man, the things which God hath prepared for them that
love him.
    But God hath revealed them unto us by his Spirit.
(ST. PAUL)

The eye of man hath not heard, the ear of man hath not seen,
man's hand is not able to taste, his tongue to conceive, nor his
heart to report, what my dream was.
(BOTTOM)

Bottom's scrambling of the senses refuses St. Paul's easy supernatural-
ism, with its dualistic split between flesh and spirit. Our prophet Bottom is
a monist, and so his dream urges upon us a synesthetic reality, fusing flesh
and spirit. That Bottom is one for whom God has prepared the things
revealed by his Spirit is made wonderfully clear in the closing dialogue
between the benign weaver and Theseus:

BOTTOM: [*Starting up.*] No, I assure you, the wall is down that
        parted their fathers. Will it please you to see the epilogue, or
        to hear a Bergomask dance between two of our company?
THESEUS: No epilogue, I pray you; for your play needs no excuse.

Only Bottom could assure us that the wall is down that parted all our
fathers. The weaver's common sense and natural goodness bestow upon
him an aesthetic dignity, homely and humane, that is the necessary coun-
terpoise to the world of Puck that otherwise would ravish reality away in
Shakespeare's visionary drama.

II

Puck, being the spirit of mischief, is both a hobgoblin and "sweet
Puck," not so much by turns but all at once. *A Midsummer Night's Dream*
is more Puck's play than Bottom's, I would reluctantly agree, even as *The
Tempest* is more Ariel's drama than it is poor Caliban's. If Puck, rather than

Oberon, were in charge, then Bottom never would resume human shape and the four young lovers would continue their misadventures forever. Most of what fascinates our contemporaries about *A Midsummer Night's Dream* belongs to Puck's vision rather than to Bottom's. Amidst so much of the Sublime, it is difficult to prefer any single passage, but I find most unforgettable Puck's penultimate chant:

> Now the hungry [lion] roars,
> And the wolf [behowls] the moon;
> Whilst the heavy ploughman snores,
> All with weary task foredone.
> Now the wasted brands do glow,
> Whilst the screech-owl, screeching loud,
> Puts the wretch that lies in woe
> In remembrance of a shroud.
> Now it is the time of night
> That the graves, all gaping wide,
> Every one lets forth his sprite,
> In the church-way paths to glide.
> And we fairies, that do run
> By the triple Hecat's team
> From the presence of the sun,
> Following darkness like a dream,
> Now are frolic. Not a mouse
> Shall disturb this hallowed house.
> I am sent with broom before,
> To sweep the dust behind the door.

Everything problematic about Puck is summed up there; a domestic, work-a-day spirit, yet always uncannily *between*, between men and women, faeries and humans, nobles and mechanicals, nature and art, space and time. Puck is a spirit cheerfully amoral, free because never in love, and always more amused even than amusing. The triple Hecate—heavenly moon maiden, earthly Artemis, and ruler of Hades—is more especially Puck's deity than she is the goddess worshipped by the other faeries. Hazlitt wisely contrasted Puck to Ariel by reminding us that "Ariel is a minister of retribution, who is touched with the sense of pity at the woes he inflicts," while Puck "laughs at those whom he misleads." Puck just does not care; he has nothing to gain and little to lose. Only Oberon could call him "gentle," but then Oberon could see Cupid flying between moon and earth, and Puck constitutionally could not. Puck says that things please him best "that befall preposterously," where I think the last word takes on the force of the later coming earlier and the earlier later. As a kind of flying metalepsis or trope of transumption, Puck is indeed what the rhetorician Puttenham called a far-fetcher.

The midsummer night's dream, Puck tells us in his final chant, is ours, since we "but slumb'red here, / While these visions did appear." What are we dreaming when we dream Puck? "Shadows" would be his reply, in a familiar Shakespearean trope, yet Puck is no more a shadow than Bottom is. Free of love, Puck becomes an agent of the irrational element in love, its tendency to over-value the object, as Freud grimly phrased it. A man or woman who incarnates Puck is sexually very dangerous, because he or she is endlessly mobile, invariably capable of transforming object-libido back into ego-libido again. Puckish freedom is overwhelmingly attractive, but the blow it strikes you will cause it no pain. Falling in love with a Puck is rather like turning life into the game of hockey.

Theseus, in the play's most famous speech, associates the lover with the poet and the lunatic in a perfectly Freudian conglomerate, since all forsake the reality principle, all assert the omnipotence of thought, and all thus yield themselves up to an ultimate narcissism. If Theseus is a Freudian, Bottom is not, but represents an older wisdom, the amiable sapience, mixed with silliness, of the all-too-natural man. Puck, quicksilver and uncaring, defines the limits of the human by being so far apart from the human.

How can one play contain both Bottom and Puck? Ariel and Caliban both care, though they care on different sides and in different modes. Puck has no human feelings, and so no human meaning; Bottom is one of the prime Shakespearean instances of how human meaning gets started, by a kind of immanent overflow, an ontological excess of being in excess of language. Only a dream, we might think, could contain both Bottom and Puck, but the play, however fantastic, is no fantasy, but an imitation that startles the reality principle and makes it tremble, rather like a guilty thing surprised.

The Merchant of Venice

Shylock is to the world of the comedies and romances what Hamlet is to the tragedies, and Falstaff to the histories: a representation so original as to be perpetually bewildering to us. What is beyond us in Hamlet and Falstaff is a mode of vast consciousness crossed by wit, so that we know authentic disinterestedness only by knowing the Hamlet of act 5, and know the wit that enlarges existence best by knowing Falstaff before his rejection by King Henry V, who has replaced Hal. Shylock is not beyond us in any way, and yet he resembles Hamlet and Falstaff in one crucial regard: he is a much more problematical representation than even Shakespeare's art could have intended. Like Hamlet and Falstaff, he dwarfs his fellow characters. Portia, despite her aura, fades before him just as Claudius recedes in the clash of mighty opposites with Hamlet, and as Hotspur is dimmed by Falstaff.

I know of no legitimate way in which *The Merchant of Venice* ought to be regarded as other than an anti-Semitic text, agreeing in this with E.E. Stoll as against Harold Goddard, my favorite critic of Shakespeare. Goddard sees Antonio and Portia as self-betrayers, who should have done better. They seem to me perfectly adequate Christians, with Antonio's anti-Semitism being rather less judicious than Portia's, whose attitude approximates that of the T.S. Eliot of *After Strange Gods*, *The Idea of a Christian Society*, and the earlier poems. If you accept the attitude towards the Jews of the Gospel of John, then you will behave towards Shylock as Portia does, or as Eliot doubtless would have behaved towards British Jewry, had the Nazis defeated and occupied Eliot's adopted country. To Portia, and to Eliot, the Jews were what they are called in the Gospel of John: descendants of Satan, rather than of Abraham.

There is no real reason to doubt that the historical Shakespeare would have agreed with his Portia. Shakespeare after all wrote what might as well be called *The Jew of Venice*, in clear rivalry with his precursor Marlowe's *The Jew of Malta*. Were I an actor, I would take great pleasure in the part of Barabas, and little or none in that of Shylock, but then I am a Jewish critic, and prefer the exuberance of Barabas to the wounded intensity of Shylock. There is nothing problematic about Barabas. We cannot imagine him asking: "If you prick us, do we not bleed?," anymore than we can imagine Shylock proclaiming: "As for myself, I walk abroad a-nights ... and poison wells." Marlowe, subtly blasphemous and cunningly outrageous, gives us Christians and Muslims who are as reprehensible as Barabas, but who lack the Jew of Malta's superb delight in his own sublime villainy. Despite his moralizing scholars, Marlowe the poet is Barabas, or rhetorically so akin to his creation as to render the difference uninteresting. Shakespeare possibly intended to give us a pathetic monster in Shylock, but being Shakespeare, he gave us Shylock, concerning whom little can be said that will not be at least oxymoronic, if not indeed self-contradictory.

That Shylock got away from Shakespeare seems clear enough, but that is the scandal of Shakespearean representation; so strong is it that nearly all his creatures break out of the temporal trap of Elizabethan and Jacobean mimesis, and establish standards of imitation that do seem to be, not of an age, but for all time. Shylock also—like Hamlet, Falstaff, Cleopatra—compels us to see differences in reality we otherwise could not have seen. Marlowe is a great caricaturist; Barabas is grotesquely magnificent, and his extravagance mocks the Christian cartoon of the Jew as usurer and fiend. It hardly matters whether the mockery is involuntary, since inevitably the hyperbolic force of the Marlovian rhetoric raises word-consciousness to a level where everything joins in an overreaching. In a cosmos where all is excessive, Barabas is no more a Jew than Tamburlaine is a Scythian or Faustus a Christian. It is much more troublesome to ask: Is Shylock a Jew? Does he not now represent something our culture regards as being essentially Jewish? So immense is the power of Shakespearean mimesis that its capacity for harm necessarily might be as substantial as its enabling force has been for augmenting cognition and for fostering psychoanalysis, despite all Freud's anxious assertions of his own originality.

II

Harold Goddard, nobly creating a Shakespeare in his own highly humane image, tried to persuade himself "that Shakespeare planned his play from the outset to enforce the irony of Portia's failure to be true to her inner self in the trial scene." E.E. Stoll, sensibly declaring that Shakespeare's contemporary audience set societal limits that Shakespeare himself would not have thought to transcend, reminds us that Jew-baiting was in effect little different from bear-baiting for that audience. I do not hope for a better critic of Shakespeare than Goddard. Like Freud, Goddard always looked for what Shakespeare shared with Dostoevsky, which seems to me rather more useful than searching for what Shakespeare shared with Kyd or even with Marlowe or Webster. Despite his authentic insistence that Shakespeare always was poet as well as playwright, Goddard's attempt to see *The Merchant of Venice* as other than anti-Semitic was misguided.

At his very best, Goddard antithetically demonstrates that the play's "spiritual argument" is quite simply unacceptable to us now:

> Shylock's conviction that Christianity and revenge are synonyms is confirmed. "If a Christian wrong a Jew, what should his suffer-ance be by Christian example? Why, revenge." The unforgettable speech from which that comes, together with Portia's on mercy, and Lorenzo's on the harmony of heaven, make up the spiritual argument of the play. Shylock asserts that a Jew is a man. Portia

declares that man's duty to man is mercy—which comes from heaven. Lorenzo points to heaven but laments that the materialism of life insulates man from its harmonies. A celestial syllogism that puts to shame the logic of the courtroom.

Alas, the celestial syllogism is Goddard's, and Portia's logic is Shakespeare's. Goddard wanted to associate *The Merchant of Venice* with Chekhov's bittersweet "Rothschild's Fiddle," but Dostoevsky again would have been the right comparison. Shakespeare's indubitable anti-Semitism is no lovelier than Dostoevsky's, being compounded similarly out of xenophobia and The Gospel of John. Shylock's demand for justice, as contrasted to Portia's supposed mercy, is part of the endless consequence of the New Testament's slander against the Pharisees. But the authors of the New Testament, even Paul and John, were no match for the authors of the Hebrew Bible. Shakespeare, more even than Dostoevsky, is of another order, the order of the Yahwist, Homer, Dante, Chaucer, Cervantes, Tolstoy—the great masters of Western literary representation. Shylock is essentially a comic representation rendered something other than comic because of Shakespeare's preternatural ability to accomplish a super-mimesis of essential nature. Shakespeare's intellectual, Hamlet, is necessarily the paradigm of *the* intellectual, even as Falstaff is the model of wit, and Cleopatra the sublime of eros. Is Shakespeare's Jew fated to go on being the representation of *the* Jew?

"Yes and no," would be my answer, because of Shakespeare's own partial failure when he allows Shylock to invoke an even stronger representation of *the* Jew, the Yahwist's vision of the superbly tenacious Jacob tending the flocks of Laban and not directly taking interest. Something very odd is at work when Antonio denies Jacob's own efficacy:

> This was a venture, sir, that Jacob serv'd for;
> A thing not in his power to bring to pass,
> But sway'd and fashion'd by the hand of heaven.

That is certainly a Christian reading, though I do not assert necessarily it was Shakespeare's own. Good Christian merchant that he is, Antonio distinguishes his own profits from Shylock's Jewish usury, but Shylock, or rather the Yahwist, surely wins the point over Antonio, and perhaps over Shakespeare. If the Jewish "devil can cite Scripture for his purpose," so can the Christian devils, from John through Shakespeare, and the polemical point turns upon who wins the agon, the Yahwist or Shakespeare? Shakespeare certainly intended to show the Jew as caught in the repetition of a revenge morality masking itself as a demand for justice. That is the rhetorical force of Shylock's obsessive "I will have my bond," with all its dreadfully compulsive ironic plays upon "bond." But if Shylock, like the Yahwist's Jacob, is a strong representation of the Jew, then "bond" has a tenacity that Shakespeare himself may have underestimated. Shakespeare's most dubious irony, as little persuasive as the resolution of *Measure for Measure*, is that Portia triumphantly out-literalizes Shylock's literalism, since flesh cannot be separated from blood. But Shylock, however monstrously, has a true bond or covenant to assert, whether between himself and Antonio, or between Jacob and Laban, or ultimately between Israel and Yahweh. Portia invokes an unequal law, not a covenant or mutual obligation, but only another variant upon the age-old Christian insistence that Christians may shed Jewish blood, but never the reverse. Can it be said that we do not go on hearing Shylock's "I will have my bond," despite his forced conversion?

III

Shakespearean representation presents us with many perplexities throughout the comedies and romances: Angelo and Malvolio, among others, are perhaps as baffling as Shylock. What makes Shylock different may be a strength in the language he speaks that works against what elsewhere is Shakespeare's most original power. Shylock does not change by listening to himself speaking; he becomes only more what he always was. It is as though the Jew alone, in Shakespeare, lacks originality. Marlowe's Barabas sounds less original than Shylock does, and yet Marlowe employs Barabas to satirize Christian moral pretensions. The curious result is that Marlowe, just this once, seems "modern" in contrast to Shakespeare. What are we to do with Shylock's great outbursts of pathos when the play itself seems to give them no dignity or value in context? I do not find it possible to contravene E.E. Stoll's judgment in this regard:

> Shylock's disappointment is tragic to him, but good care is taken that it shall not be to us ... The running fire assails him to the very moment—and beyond it—that Shylock says he is not well, and staggers out, amid Gratiano's jeers touching his baptism, to provoke in the audience the laughter of triumph and vengeance in his own day and bring tears to their eyes in ours. How can we here for a moment sympathize with Shylock unless at the same time we indignantly turn, not only against Gratiano, but against Portia, the Duke, and all Venice as well?

We cannot, unless we desire to read or see some other play. *The Merchant of Venice* demands what we cannot accept: Antonio's superior goodness, from the start, is to be demonstrated by his righteous scorn for Shylock, which is to say, Antonio most certainly represents what now is called a Jew-baiter. An honest production of the play, sensitive to its values, would now be intolerable in a Western country. The unhappy paradox is that *The Jew of Malta*, a ferocious farce, exposes the madness and hypocrisy of Jew-baiting, even though its Machiavel, Barabas, is the Jewish monster or Devil incarnate, while *The Merchant of Venice* is at once a comedy of delightful sophistication and a vicious Christian slander against the Jews.

In that one respect, Shakespeare was of an age, and not for all time. Bardolatry is not always an innocent disease, and produces odd judgments, as when J. Middleton Murry insisted: "*The Merchant of Venice* is not a problem play; it is a fairy story." For us, contemporary Jews and Gentiles alike, it had better be a problem play, and not a fairy story. Shylock, Murry admitted, was not "coherent," because a Shakespearean character had no need to be coherent. Yet Shylock is anything but incoherent. His palpable mimetic force enhances his rapacity and viciousness, and works to make an ancient bogeyman come dreadfully alive. For the reader or playgoer (though hardly the latter, in our time), Shylock is at once comic and frightening, a walking embodiment of the death drive.

We must not underestimate the power and influence of Shakespearean mimesis, even when it is *deliberately* unoriginal, as it is in Shylock. Hamlet and Falstaff contain us to our enrichment. Shylock has the strength to contain us to our destruction. Something of the same could be said for Angelo, in *Measure for Measure*, or of Malvolio, in *Twelfth Night*, or of nearly everyone in *Troilus*. History renders Shylock's strength as representation socially destructive, whereas Angelo and Malvolio inhabit the shadows of the individual consciousness. I conclude by noting that Shakespeare's comedies and romances share in the paradox that Gershom Scholem said the writings of Kafka possessed. They have for us "something of the strong light of the canonical, of the perfection that destroys."

Much Ado About Nothing

A.P. Rossiter found the essence of the Beatrice–Benedick relationship in misprision or mutual misreading by those two fierce wits:

Benedick and Beatrice misapprehend both each other *and* themselves: each misprizes the other sex, and misapprehends the possibility of a complete agreement between them, as individuals, on what causes that misprision: love of freedom and a superior conceit of themselves as "wise" where others are fools; as "free" and untied; and as having a right to enjoy kicking over other people's traces.

That is an interestingly dark view of Beatrice and Benedick, and is akin to Harold Goddard's judgment when he wrote of "antiromantic and intellectual egotism in Beatrice and Benedick" as being an aspect of the "egotism of youth." Both Rossiter and Goddard were among the double handful of critics who stood out among earlier modern Shakespearean expositors, but I have never been easy with the stance either adopted towards Beatrice and Benedick. Why moralize in regard to this couple, of all couples? Do they not represent, in *Much Ado about Nothing*, a freedom that misinterprets precisely because it is the freedom to misinterpret? And is such freedom, as represented by them, merely a youthful egotism?

If these questions are answerable, then it may be that the answers turn upon change, and the representation of change, in Beatrice and Benedick. Comedy is, of course, a much more difficult genre in which to depict change than is tragedy or history, but one of Shakespeare's uncanniest gifts was to abolish genre, and not just in what we have agreed to call his "problem plays." Here are Beatrice and Benedick in their full splendor:

BENEDICK: Thou and I are too wise to woo peaceably.
BEATRICE: It appears not in this confession; there's not one wise man among twenty that will praise himself.
BENEDICK: An old, an old instance, Beatrice, that liv'd in the time of good neighbors. If a man do not erect in this age his own tomb ere he dies, he shall live no longer in monument than the bell rings and the widow weeps.
BEATRICE: And how long is that, think you?
BENEDICK: Question: why, an hour in clamor and a quarter in rheum; therefore is it most expedient for the wise, if Don Worm (his conscience) find no impediment to the contrary, to be the trumpet of his own virtues, as I am to myself.

Do they misinterpret one another or themselves? We must acknowledge that, like all great wits, they are self-conscious and self-congratulatory, failings (if those are failings) present also in Falstaff, Rosalind, and Hamlet. I think that *Much Ado about Nothing* generates its highest humor, properly performed, precisely because Beatrice and Benedick understand their rituals all too well. Nor will age wither their youthful egotism; mutually supportive, it will last out their lives together. Shakespeare represents them as changing, but only into stronger versions of their initial selves. Anne Barton usefully compares them to Katherina and Petruchio in *The Taming of the Shrew*, another "unconventional couple who arrive at love and understanding by way of insult and aggression." Her characterization is closer to those earlier lovers than to Beatrice and Benedick, who understand (and probably love) one another from the start or even before the start.

Rossiter thought that *Much Ado about Nothing* was "a fantasy of equivocal appearances in a glittering world of amiable fools of all sorts." It is certainly the most amiably nihilistic play ever written, and is most appositely titled. Beatrice and Benedick are Nietzscheans before Nietzsche, just as they are Congreveans before Congreve. The abyss glitters in every exchange between the fencing lovers, whose mutual wit does not so much defend against other selves as it defends against meaninglessness. You make much ado about nothing because nothing will come of nothing. Emersonians also before Emerson, Beatrice and Benedick confront and pass the pragmatic test, the experiential law of Compensation, that nothing is got for nothing. When they totally accept that, the play can end, because by then they have changed altogether into the strongest version of their own selves:

BENEDICK: Do not you love me?
BEATRICE: Why, no, no more than reason.
BENEDICK: Why then your uncle and the Prince and Claudio
　　Have been deceived. They swore you did.
BEATRICE: Do not you love me?
BENEDICK: Troth, no, no more than reason.
BEATRICE: Why then my cousin, Margaret, and Ursula
　　Are much deceiv'd, for they did swear you did.
BENEDICK: They swore that you were almost sick for me.
BEATRICE: They swore that you were well-nigh dead for me.
BENEDICK: 'Tis no such matter. Then you do not love me?
BEATRICE: No, truly, but in friendly recompense.
LEONATO: Come, cousin, I am sure you love this gentleman.
CLAUDIO: And I'll be sworn upon't that he loves her,
　　For here's a paper written in his hand,
　　A halting sonnet of his own pure brain,
　　Fashion'd to Beatrice.
HERO: And here's another

Writ in my cousin's hand, stol'n from her pocket,
Containing her affection unto Benedick.
BENEDICK: A miracle! here's our own hands against our hearts.
Come, I will have thee, but by this light, I take thee for pity.
BEATRICE: I would not deny you, but by this good day, I yield upon
great persuasion, and partly to save your life, for I was told
you were in a consumption.
[BENEDICK]: Peace, I will stop your mouth.
[*Kissing her.*]

As You Like It

As You Like It is Rosalind's play as *Hamlet* is Hamlet's. That so many critics have linked her to Hamlet's more benign aspects is the highest of com-
pliments, as though they sensed that in wit, intellect, and vision of herself
she truly is Hamlet's equal. Orlando is a pleasant young man, but audiences
never quite can be persuaded that he merits Rosalind's love, and their
resistance has its wisdom. Among Shakespearean representations of
women, we can place Rosalind in the company only of the Portia of act 5
of *The Merchant of Venice*, while reserving the tragic Sublime for Cleopatra.
All of us, men and women, like Rosalind best. She alone joins Hamlet and
Falstaff as absolute in wit, and of the three she alone knows balance and
proportion in living and is capable of achieving harmony.

That harmony extends even to her presence in *As You Like It*, since she
is too strong for the play. Touchstone and Jaques are poor wits compared
to her, and Touchstone truly is more rancid even than Jaques. Neither is
capable of this wise splendor, typical of Rosalind's glory:

ROSALIND: No, faith, die by attorney. The poor world is almost six
thousand years old, and in all this time there was not any man
died in his own person, *videlicet*, in a love-cause. Troilus had
his brains dash'd out with a Grecian club, yet he did what he
could to die before, and he is one of the patterns of love.
Leander, he would have liv'd many a fair year though Hero
had turn'd nun, if it had not been for a hot midsummer night;
for, good youth, he went but forth to wash him in the
Hellespont, and being taken with the cramp was drown'd; and
the foolish chroniclers of that age found it was—Hero of
Sestos. But these are all lies: men have died from time to time,
and worms have eaten them, but not for love.

It seems a miracle that so much wit should be fused with such benignity. Rosalind's good humor extends even to this poor world, so aged, and to the amorous heroes she charmingly deromanticizes: the wretched Troilus who is deprived even of his honorable end at the point of the great Achilles's lance, and Marlowe's Leander, done in by a cramp on a hot midsummer night. Cressida and Hero are absolved: "men have died from time to time, and worms have eaten them, but not for love." Heroic passion is dismissed, not because Rosalind does not love romance, but because she knows it must be a sentimental rather than a naive mode. In the background to *As You Like It* is the uneasy presence of Christopher Marlowe, stabbed to death six years before in a supposed dispute over "a great reckoning in a little room," and oddly commemorated in a famous exchange between Touchstone and Audrey:

> TOUCHSTONE: When a man's verses cannot be understood, nor a man's good wit seconded with the forward child, understanding, it strikes a man more dead than a great reckoning in a little room. Truly, I would the gods had made thee poetical.
> AUDREY: I do not know what "poetical" is. Is it honest in deed and word? Is it a true thing?
> TOUCHSTONE: No, truly; for the truest poetry is the most feigning, and lovers are given to poetry; and what they swear in poetry may be said as lovers they do feign.

Touchstone is sardonic enough to fit into Marlowe's cosmos, even as Jaques at moments seems a parody of Ben Jonson's moralizings, yet Rosalind is surely the least Marlovian being in Elizabethan drama. That may be why Marlowe hovers in *As You Like It*, not only in the allusions to his death but in an actual quotation from *Hero and Leander*, when the deluded shepherdess Phebe declares her passion for the disguised Rosalind:

> Dead shepherd, now I find thy saw of might,
> Who ever lov'd that lov'd not at first sight?

Marlowe, the dead shepherd, defines *As You Like It* by negation. Rosalind's spirit cleanses us of false melancholies, rancid reductions, corrupting idealisms, and universalized resentments. An actress capable of the role of Rosalind will expose both Jaques and Touchstone as sensibilities inadequate to the play's vision. Jaques is an eloquent rhetorician, in Ben Jonson's scalding vein, but Arden is not Jonson's realm; while

Touchstone must be the least likeable of Shakespeare's clowns. I suspect that the dramatic point of both Jaques and Touchstone is how unoriginal they are in contrast to Rosalind's verve and splendor, or simply her extraordinary originality. She is the preamble to Hamlet's newness, to the Shakespearean inauguration of an unprecedented kind of representation of personality.

Richard III, Iago, and Edmund win their dark if finally self-destructive triumphs because they have quicker minds and more power over language than anyone else in their worlds. Rosalind and Hamlet more audaciously manifest the power of mind over the universe of sense than anyone they could ever encounter, but their quickness of thought and language is dedicated to a different kind of contest, akin to Falstaff's grosser agon with time and the state. It is not her will but her joy and energy that Rosalind seeks to express, and Hamlet's tragedy is that he cannot seek the same. Richard III, Iago, and Edmund superbly deceive, but Rosalind and Hamlet expose pretensions and deceptions merely by being as and what they are, superior of windows, more numerous of doors. We could save Othello and Lear from catastrophe by envisioning Iago and Edmund trying to function if Rosalind or Hamlet were introduced into their plays. Shakespeare, for reasons I cannot fathom, chose not to give us such true clashes of mighty opposites. His most intelligent villains are never brought together on one stage with his most intelligent heroes and heroines. The possible exception is in the confrontation between Shylock and Portia in *The Merchant of Venice*, but the manipulated clash of Jew against Christian there gives Shylock no chance. Even Shakespeare's capacities would have been extended if he had tried to show Richard III attempting to gull Falstaff, Iago vainly practising upon Hamlet, or Edmund exercising his subtle rhetoric upon the formidably subtle Rosalind. Poor Jaques is hopeless against her; when he avers "why, 'tis good to be sad and say nothing," she replies: "why, then, 'tis good to be a post," and she sweeps away his boasts of melancholy experience. And what we remember best of Touchstone is Rosalind's judgment that, like a medlar, he will be rotten ere he is ripe.

Perhaps Rosalind's finest remark, amid so much splendor, is her reply when Celia chides her for interrupting. There are many ways to interpret: "Do you not know I am a woman? When I think, I must speak. Sweet, say on." We can praise Rosalind for spontaneity, for sincerity, for wisdom, and those can be our interpretations; or we can be charmed by her slyness, which turns a male complaint against women into another sign of their superiority in expressionistic intensity. Rosalind is simply superior in everything whatsoever.

Twelfth Night

Clearly a kind of farewell to unmixed comedy, *Twelfth Night* nevertheless seems to me much the funniest of Shakespeare's plays, though I have yet to see it staged in a way consonant with its full humor. As some critics have noted, only Feste the clown among all its characters is essentially sane, and even he allows himself to be dragged into the tormenting of the wretched Malvolio, whose only culpability is that he finds himself in the wrong play, as little at home there as Shylock is in Venice.

Everything about *Twelfth Night* is unsettling, except for Feste again, and even he might be happier in a different play. Perhaps *Twelfth Night* was Shakespeare's practical joke upon his audience, turning all of them into Malvolios. Like *Measure for Measure*, the play would be perfectly rancid if it took itself seriously, which it wisely refuses to do. *Twelfth Night*, I would suggest, is a highly deliberate outrage, and should be played as such. Except for Feste, yet once more, none of its characters ought to be portrayed wholly sympathetically, not even Viola, who is herself a kind of passive zany, since who else would fall in love with the self-intoxicated Orsino?

What is most outrageous about *Twelfth Night* is Shakespeare's deliberate self-parody, which mocks his own originality at representation and thus savages representation or aesthetic imitation itself. Nothing happens in *Twelfth Night*, so there is no action to imitate anyway; *The Tempest* at least represents its opening storm, but *Twelfth Night* shrugs off its own, as if to say perfunctorily: let's get started. The shrug is palpable enough when we first meet Viola, at the start of scene 2:

VIOLA. What country, friends, is this?
CAPTAIN. This is Illyria, lady.
VIOLA. And what should I do in Illyria?
　　My brother he is in Elysium.
　　Perchance he is not drown'd—what think you, sailors?

Illyria is a kind of madcap elysium, as we have discovered already, if we have listened intently to the superbly eloquent and quite crazy opening speech of its duke:

If music be the food of love, play on,
Give me excess of it; that surfeiting,
The appetite may sicken, and so die.
That strain again, it had a dying fall;

O, it came o'er my ear like the sweet sound
That breathes upon a bank of violets,
Stealing and giving odor. Enough, no more,
'Tis not so sweet now as it was before.
O spirit of love, how quick and fresh art thou,
That notwithstanding thy capacity
Receiveth as the sea, nought enters there,
Of what validity and pitch soe'er,
But falls into abatement and low price
Even in a minute. So full of shapes is fancy
That it alone is high fantastical.

Shakespeare himself so liked Orsino's opening conceit that he returned to it five years later in *Antony and Cleopatra* where Cleopatra, missing Antony, commands: "Give me some music; music, moody food / Of us that trade in love." Orsino, not a trader in love but a glutton for the idea of it, is rather more like John Keats than he is like Cleopatra, and his beautiful opening speech is inevitably echoed in Keats's "Ode on Melancholy." We can call Orsino a Keats gone bad, or even a little mad, returning us again to the mad behavior of nearly everyone in *Twelfth Night*. Dr. Samuel Johnson, who feared madness, liked to attribute rational design even where it seems unlikely:

Viola seems to have formed a very deep design with very little pre-meditation: she is thrown by shipwreck on an unknown coast, hears that the prince is a batchelor, and resolves to supplant the lady whom he courts.

Anne Barton more accurately gives us a very different Viola, whose "boy's disguise operates not as a liberation but merely as a way of going underground in a difficult situation." Even that seems to me rather more rational than the play's Viola, who never does come up from underground, but, then, except for Feste, who does? Feste surely speaks the play's only wisdom: "And thus the whirligig of time brings in his revenges." "Time is a child playing draughts; the lordship is to the child" is the dark wisdom of Heracleitus. Nietzsche, with some desperation, had his Zarathustra proclaim the will's revenge against time, and in particular against time's assertion, "It was." Shakespeare's time plays with a spinning top, so that time's revenges presumably have a circular aspect. Yet Feste sings that when he was a young fool, he was taken as a toy, certainly not the way we take him now. He knows what most critics of Shakespeare will not learn, which is that *Twelfth Night* does not come to any true resolution, in which anyone has learned anything. Malvolio might be an exemplary figure if we could smuggle him into a play by Ben Jonson, but *Twelfth Night*, as John Hollander long ago noted, appears to be a deliberately anti Jonsonian drama. No one could or should be made better by viewing or reading it.

If it has no moral coherence, where then shall its coherence be found? Orsino, baffled by the first joint appearance of the twins Viola and Sebastian, is driven to a famous outburst:

> One face, one voice, one habit, and two persons,
> A natural perspective, that is and is not!

Anne Barton glosses this as an optical illusion naturally produced, rather than given by a distorting perspective glass. Dr. Johnson gives the same reading rather more severely: "that nature has here exhibited such a show, where shadows seem realities; where that which 'is not' appears like that which 'is.'" A natural perspective is in this sense oxymoronic, unless time and nature are taken as identical, so that time's whirligig then would become the same toy as the distorting glass. If we could imagine a distorting mirror whirling in circles like a top, we would have the compound toy that *Twelfth Night* constituted for Shakespeare. Reflections in that mirror are the representations in *Twelfth Night*: Viola, Olivia, Sir Toby and Sir Andrew, Orsino, Sebastian, and all the rest except for Malvolio and Feste.

It is difficult for me to see Malvolio as an anti-Puritan satire, because Sir Toby, Sir Andrew, and Maria are figures even more unattractive, by any imaginative standards. Sir Toby is not a Falstaffian personage, no matter what critics have said. Falstaff without preternatural wit is not Falstaff, and Belch is just that: belch, rather than cakes and ale. Malvolio is an instance of a character who gets away even from Shakespeare, another hobgoblin run off with the garland of Apollo, like Shylock or like both Angelo and Barnardine in *Measure for Measure*. The relations between Ben Jonson and Shakespeare must have been lively, complex, and mutually ambivalent, and Malvolio seems to me Shakespeare's slyest thrust at Jonsonian dramatic morality. But even as we laugh at Malvolio's fall, a laughter akin to the savage merriment doubtless provoked in the Elizabethan audience by the fall of Shylock, so we are made uneasy at the fate of Malvolio and Shylock alike. Something in us rightly shudders when we are confronted by the vision of poor Malvolio bound in the dark room. An uncanny cognitive music emerges in the dialogue between Feste, playing Sir Topas the curate, and "Malvolio the lunatic":

MALVOLIO. Sir Topas, Sir Topas, good Sir Topas, go to my lady.

CLOWN. Out, hyperbolical fiend! how vexest thou this man! Talkest thou nothing but of ladies?

SIR TOBY. Well said, Master Parson.

MALVOLIO. Sir Topas, never was man thus wrong'd. Good Sir Topas, do not think I am mad; they have laid me here in hideous darkness.

CLOWN. Fie, thou dishonest Sathan! I call thee by the most modest terms, for I am one of those gentle ones that will use the devil himself with courtesy. Say'st thou that house is dark?

MALVOLIO. As hell, Sir Topas.

CLOWN. Why, it hath bay windows transparent as barricadoes, and the [clerestories] toward the south north are as lustrous as ebony; and yet complainest thou of obstruction?

MALVOLIO. I am not mad, Sir Topas, I say to you this house is dark.

CLOWN. Madman, thou errest. I say there is no darkness but ignorance, in which thou art more puzzled than the Egyptians in their fog.

MALVOLIO. I say this house is as dark as ignorance, though ignorance were as dark as hell; and I say there was never man thus abus'd. I am no more mad than you are; make the trial of it in any constant question.

CLOWN. What is the opinion of Pythagoras concerning wild-fowl?

MALVOLIO. That the soul of our grandam might happily inhabit a bird.

CLOWN. What think'st thou of his opinion?

MALVOLIO. I think nobly of the soul, and no way approve his opinion.

CLOWN. Fare thee well. Remain thou still in darkness. Thou shalt hold th' opinion of Pythagoras ere I will allow of thy wits, and fear to kill a woodcock lest thou dispossess the soul of thy grandam. Fare thee well.

MALVOLIO. Sir Topas, Sir Topas!

We are almost in the cosmos of *King Lear*, in Lear's wild dialogues with Edgar and Gloucester. Feste is sublimely wise, warning Malvolio against the ignorance of his Jonsonian moral pugnacity, which can make one as stupid as a woodcock. But there is a weirder cognitive warning in Feste's Pythagorean wisdom. Metempsychosis or the instability of identity is the essence of *Twelfth Night*, the lesson that none of its characters are capable of learning, except for Feste, who learns it better all the time, even as the whirligig of time brings in his revenges:

A great while ago the world begun,
　　With hey ho, the wind and the rain,
But that's all one, our play is done,
　　And we'll strive to please you every day.

Measure for Measure

Northrop Frye observes that among all the principal characters of *Measure for Measure*, only Lucio seems sane. I would add the spectacular Barnardine, who sensibly judges that in the mad world of this drama, the only way to avoid execution is to stay safely asleep. If you fall into the error of applying moral realism to *Measure for Measure*, then you will conclude that the Duke, Angelo, Claudio, Isabella, and Mariana all are crazy, with the Duke the craziest of all. Clearly, the play is a fantastic story, a deliberate wildness, as outrageous as *Twelfth Night* or *The Winter's Tale*.

Measure for Measure seems to cohere only as a kind of erotic romance, a very original kind. Though it achieves plausibility only within the parameters of its curious assumptions, those assumptions are not so much Elizabethan conventions as they are purely Shakespearean. If they seem not so curious to us, that is because we live on them still, because as mimetic conventions they have become our assumptions and help govern our expectations as to what it is that makes verbal representation convincing to us.

The Duke's manipulations, though ultimately (and rather mechanically) benign in their effects, are as theatrical and amoral as Iago's or Edmund's, and his motivations always must remain inscrutable. He interests us only in relation to his views on death, which is Claudio's only claim upon our interest also. Since Angelo, on close scrutiny, is what we might now call a case history, that leaves only Isabella, who indeed is interesting, all too interesting. Her militant chastity is the play's center, the origin of its mode of producing meaning.

To remark of Isabella that she is unsympathetic is obvious, all too obvious, but then the Duke, Angelo, Claudio, and even poor Mariana are in their ways unsympathetic also. That only the obsessive slanderer Lucio and the dissolute Barnardine attract us makes clear the deliberate estrangement of Shakespearean representation in this play. The gap between natural being and role-playing in the Duke and Angelo is absolute, while in Isabella it is almost frightening. Lucio and Barnardine win us because they are precisely what they present themselves as being.

When I think of *Measure for Measure* I first remember Barnardine and then Lucio among the characters, but the speeches that come first to mind are all from act 3, scene 1, in which the Duke, Claudio, and Isabella all manifest preternatural eloquence and simultaneously descend even lower in our esteem. I sometimes believe that the most sublime passage of all in Shakespeare is the Duke's astonishing speech in reply to Claudio's: "I have hope to live, and am prepar'd to die." Yet what could be more problematic than this surpassing rhetorical persuasiveness spoken in a supposed comedy by a ruling figure to someone absurdly condemned to death? And this is rendered yet more dubious by the speaker's duplicity, since he is peculiarly disguised as a friar and yet clearly does not offer anything like Christian comfort:

> DUKE: Be absolute for death: either death or life
> Shall thereby be the sweeter. Reason thus with life:
> If I do lose thee, I do lose a thing
> That none but fools would keep. A breath thou art,
> Servile to all the skyey influences,
> That dost this habitation where thou keep'st
> Hourly afflict. Merely, thou art death's fool,
> For him thou labor'st by thy flight to shun,
> And yet run'st toward him still. Thou art not noble,
> For all th' accommodations that thou bear'st
> Are nurs'd by baseness. Thou'rt by no means valiant,
> For thou dost fear the soft and tender fork
> Of a poor worm. Thy best of rest is sleep,
> And that thou oft provok'st, yet grossly fear'st
> Thy death, which is no more. Thou art not thyself,
> For thou exists on many a thousand grains
> That issue out of dust. Happy thou art not,
> For what thou hast not, still thou striv'st to get,
> And what thou hast, forget'st. Thou art not certain,
> For thy complexion shifts to strange effects,
> After the moon. If thou art rich, thou'rt poor,
> For like an ass, whose back with ingots bows,
> Thou bear'st thy heavy riches but a journey,
> And death unloads thee. Friends hast thou none,
> For thine own bowels, which do call thee [sire],
> The mere effusion of thy proper loins,
> Do curse the gout, sapego, and the rheum
> For ending thee no sooner. Thou hast nor youth nor age,
> But as it were an after-dinner's sleep,
> Dreaming on both, for all thy blessed youth

> Becomes as aged, and doth beg the alms
> Of palsied eld; and when thou art old and rich,
> Thou hast neither heat, affection, limb, nor beauty,
> To make thy riches pleasant. What's yet in this
> That bears the name of life? Yet in this life
> Lie hid moe thousand deaths; yet death we fear
> That makes these odds all even.

Most of the great speeches in Shakespeare gain, as they should, by being read or delivered in context, but this is enormously more powerful and dignified when we rip it away from the play and forget both situation and speaker. What does that tell us about the dialectical interplay of Shakespearean representation and Shakespearean rhetoric? Here the strength of representation is at best equivocal in its force, since we cannot accept the reality of this speech as comfort, intended or actual, and even wonder if Claudio is not being ironical when he begins his reply with "I humbly thank you." Northrop Frye dryly remarks that the speech urges Claudio to "welcome death because if he lives he may get a lot of uncomfortable diseases." As addressed to a young man that is silly, but out of context I suggest the speech naturally falls into the mode in which each of us addresses him- or herself. As a meditation of the self directed to the self, the lines become at once bracing and elegiac, until they achieve an extraordinary triumph in a passage that haunted T.S. Eliot, who made them the epigraph to his "Gerontion," and that deeply engaged Dr. Samuel Johnson:

> Thou has nor youth nor age,
> But as it were an after-dinner's sleep,
> Dreaming on both.

Johnson memorably commented:

> This is exquisitely imagined. When we are young we busy ourselves in forming schemes for succeeding time, and miss the gratifications that are before us; when we are old we amuse the languour of age with the recollection of youthful pleasures or performances; so that our life, of which no part is filled with the business of the present time, resembles our dreams after dinner, when the events of the morning are mingled with the designs of the evening.

"Dinner," to Shakespeare and to Johnson, was the midday meal we now call lunch. Johnson, with his keen sense that human life was everywhere a condition in which much was to be endured and little to be enjoyed, reads in Shakespeare's lines the profound representation of our perpetual inability to live in the present moment. Caught as we are between wistfulness and nostalgia, never-to-come future and illusory past, the afternoon and morning of our existence, we confound midday with evening. Johnson has uncovered one of *Measure for Measure*'s uncanniest ranges of meaning: its protagonists' joys are either completed or deferred, and only the disreputable Lucio and Barnardine are alive in the present. If the immediacy of the moment is available only to the dissolute, then we see the malady that has crazed the Duke's Vienna, a mad city indeed.

Lucio, though sane, has nothing about him that is not rank, while the outrageous Barnardine is not only the sane foil to nearly the entire *personae* but is admirably vital, somewhat in the mode of that greatest of vitalists, Sir John Falstaff, though Barnardine is no wit. His fundamental recourse is sleep: "He will not wake," and when they insist upon waking him, he sublimely remarks: "I swear I will not die to-day for any man's persuasion." We like the Duke best, at the end, when he pardons Barnardine, thus giving the triumph to the most humane sentiment in the play, Barnardine's: "I will not consent to die this day, that's certain."

What is least humane in *Measure for Measure* is not even Angelo, let alone the enigmatic Duke, but Isabella. I cannot agree with Anne Barton's observation that "like Angelo, she has arrived at a new and juster knowledge of herself" by the drama's end. She seems not so much changed as distracted, while Angelo's new and just knowledge is just that he has been found out! Shakespeare in *Measure for Measure* cares not a jot for our moral outrage, or else he delights in provoking it. Consider the shock of juxtaposition he gives us between Claudio's eloquent fear and Isabella's sadistic display of enraged virtue:

CLAUDIO: Death is a fearful thing.
ISABELLA: And shamed life a hateful.
CLAUDIO: Ay, but to die, and go we know not where;
  To he in cold obstruction, and to rot;
  This sensible warm motion to become
  A kneaded clod; and the delighted spirit
  To bathe in fiery floods, or to reside
  In thrilling region of thick-ribbed ice;
  To be imprison'd in the viewless winds
  And blown with restless violence round about

> The pendant world; or to be worse than worst
> Of those that lawless and incertain thought
> Imagine howling—'tis too horrible!
> The weariest and most loathed worldly life
> That age, ache, [penury], and imprisonment
> Can lay on nature is a paradise
> To what we fear of death.
> ISABELLA: Alas, alas!
> CLAUDIO: Sweet sister, let me live.
>   What sin you do to save a brother's life,
>   Nature dispenses with the deed so far,
>   That it becomes a virtue.
> ISABELLA: O you beast!
>   O faithless coward! O dishonest wretch!
>   Wilt thou be made a man out of my vice?
>   Is't not a kind of incest, to take life
>   From thine own sister's shame? What should I think?
>   Heaven shield my mother play'd my father fair!
>   For such a warped slip of wilderness
>   Ne'er issu'd from his blood. Take my defiance!
>   Die, perish! Might but my bending down
>   Reprieve thee from thy fate, it should proceed.
>   I'll pray a thousand prayers for thy death,
>   No word to save thee.
> CLAUDIO: Nay, hear me, Isabel.   (ll. 115–147)

Whether or not there is a Dantesque overtone in Claudio's extraordinary speech on the fear of death, we now hear Milton in it, since it prefigures much that is Satanic in *Paradise Lost*, and something that is Belial's there as well. Johnson, whose imagination was so stirred by the prospect of death, did not comment on this speech, perhaps because it moved him too strongly. Of Isabella's harsh reaction, Johnson noted that we ought to "consider her not only as a virgin but a nun," to which one must rejoin that nuns do not marry dukes. Frye points to an obsession with the figure of the father in Isabella's rhetoric, which is certainly there, but the horror of incest is even more direct:

> Wilt thou be made a man out of my vice?
> Is't not a kind of incest, to take life
> From thine own sister's shame?

Evidently Isabella can envision coitus only as incest, but that is the dark, central insight of the play, if it can be called insight. Vienna in *Measure for Measure* is Isabella's vision; she defines its mode and its ambiance. Her passional life is a deferred torment, and the entire drama can be regarded as her version of the return of the repressed. She does not speak at all during the last eighty-five lines of the long scene in the act that ends the play and we do not even know that she definitely will accept the Duke's offer of marriage. Nor do we know how to interpret the final speech she makes, when she joins Mariana in pleading for Angelo's life: "Thoughts are no subjects, / Intents but merely thoughts." If a murderous intention, like Angelo's, is not answerable to justice, then presumably incestuous desires also need not be subject to a moral or spiritual authority. When I think of *Measure for Measure*, my final thought is always of Isabella, who is neither likeable nor endless to meditation, but who is finally more problematical even than the Duke, in this most problematic of all of Shakespeare's plays.

THE TRAGEDIES

Shakespeare's five major tragedies are widely recognized as among the supreme achievements of Western literature. One can think of the J-Writer's strand of Genesis-Exodus-Numbers, of the *Iliad*, of Dante's *Comedy*, as comparable eminences, together with the principal surviving dramas of Aeschylus, Sophocles, and Euripides. Though it is customary to group Shakespeare's major tragedies, *Hamlet* clearly is in a class of one, since its inwardness is unique, and enigmatic, while *Antony and Cleopatra*, at the other chronological extreme of these masterworks, also stands apart. *Othello*, *King Lear*, and *Macbeth* have more affinities with one another than with *Hamlet* or *Antony and Cleopatra*.

Hamlet is a radical theatrical experiment, perhaps the most radical we have known. Shakespeare cuts a gap into the play, from Act II, scene two, through Act III, scene two, that ought to destroy any audience's belief in the reality of what is being represented. Since the play co-opts us as accomplices, we accept every bewilderment we are shown. Hamlet himself is displayed as an authorial consciousness, and also as a great hero-villain, loved but unloving, and perfectly capable of acting as a casual slaughterer. Yet, despite the well-founded cavils of a few critics, audiences tend to love Hamlet the more intensely even as he demonstrates that he neither wants nor needs such love. William Hazlitt, speaking for the audience, said that we were Hamlet, a fusion that has been endemic for two centuries, and that may never depart. The drama is a "poem unlimited," of no genre really, and its protagonist, who has inspired so many imitators, continues to be an unique figure, the most isolated character in Shakespeare, perhaps indeed in all of Western literature.

Is Hamlet a tragic hero? So various are both the prince and his play that the answer may tell us more about you than about Hamlet. Something deeply personal, perhaps familial, enters into this play, whose lost original very likely was by the young Shakespeare himself (though some scholars, on dubious evidence, vote for Thomas Kyd, author of the celebrated *Spanish Tragedy*). Perhaps the deaths of Shakespeare's father and of Hamnet, his only son, are more relevant to *Hamlet* than we know, or perhaps Shakespeare is atoning for an earlier dramatic defeat, though that again is much more than we know.

Hamlet is all that is central to his play; even Claudius and Gertrude seem more peripheral than not. No other consciousness can assert much for itself in Hamlet's charismatic and overwhelming presence. Yet *Othello*, while the Moor's tragedy, is Iago's play, his triumphal march to the psychic and moral annihilation of his superb captain. Iago's malignity is anything but motiveless. He has been passed over for promotion by his war-god, Othello, and this partial rejection has been a vastation for the ensign or flag-officer, loyally pledged to perish rather than permit Othello's colors to be taken in battle. John Milton, involuntarily Shakespeare's closest student, made his Satan into a disciple of Iago. Satan's Sense of Injured Merit is precisely Iago's, but Othello is considerably more vulnerable than Milton's God. Othello falls, and only Emilia, at the price of her life, prevents Iago's absolute triumph.

Shakespeare wrote *King Lear*, *Macbeth*, and *Antony and Cleoptra* in a continuous burst of creativity for fourteen consecutive months. I cannot think of anything comparable in the history of literature. *King Lear*, though very oddly handled by recent politicized critics, is the most awesome poetic drama that I know. It is a great dance of contraries, a quarrel between sublimity and human clay. Whether the character of King Lear is too grand for the stage, as Charles Lamb argued, is hardly a popular question these days, but remains pragmatically quite real to me, as I have never seen an actor wholly adequate to the role. Shakespeare risked a tragedy beyond limits, and yet we have no choice but to share in the play's extravagance. No other drama seems to me to make such large demands upon an audience.

Macbeth emanates out of cosmological emptiness akin to *King Lear's*. In both plays, we have been thrown into realms that touch the limits of nature. Macbeth himself, more even than Lear, becomes a theater open to the night-sky, and to the forces that ride the air. What is most surprising and most sublime about *Macbeth* is that we cannot separate ourselves from the hero-villain, no matter how deeply he recedes into his heart of darkness. Shakespeare lavished intellect upon Hamlet and spirit upon Lear, but no one else receives so vast an imaginative endowment as does Macbeth. The paradox, tragically ironic, is that this man of blood is Shakespeare's greatest poet.

After the enormities of *King Lear* and *Macbeth*, Shakespeare breaks out into the world that destroys Antony and Cleopatra, whose heroic era dies with them. Though a double tragedy, *Antony and Cleopatra* is also a joyous display of Shakespeare's art at its most comprehensive. The largeness of personality in both Cleopatra and Antony is answered by the psychic and representational largeness of the play. Shakespeare's superb panoply of gifts, as comprehensive and generous as ever has been offered to us, come together in *Antony and Cleopatra* with a splendor that Shakespeare never sought again.

Romeo and Juliet

Except for *Hamlet* and *Macbeth*, *Romeo and Juliet* seems the most popular of Shakespeare's tragedies, though it is necessarily dwarfed by the heroic sequence of *Hamlet*, *Othello*, *King Lear*, *Macbeth*, and *Antony and Cleopatra*. Some critics prefer *Coriolanus* to the High Romanticism of *Romeo and Juliet*, and I myself would rather reread *Julius Caesar* than turn again to *Romeo and Juliet*. Yet the massive, permanent popularity of *Romeo and Juliet* is well-deserved. Its appeal is universal and world-wide, and its effect upon world literature is matched among the tragedies only by *Hamlet*. Stendhal, who with Victor Hugo is the great partisan of Shakespeare in equivocal France, wrote his own sublime tribute to *Romeo and Juliet* in his last completed novel, *The Charterhouse of Parma*.

I desire here to make some brief reflections upon the relative aesthetic eminence of the play in the full context of Shakespeare's achievement. So prodigal was Shakespeare's inventiveness, particularly in the creation of personalities, that I myself, in earlier years, tended to undervalue *Romeo and Juliet* in the full panoply of Shakespeare. There are perhaps twenty plays by him that I rated higher, even if some of them lacked the enormous popularity of *Romeo and Juliet*. I do not know whether I merely have aged, or have matured, but Juliet herself moves me now in many of the same ways that I find Desdemona and Cordelia to be almost unbearably poignant. What Robert Penn Warren called her "pure poetry" remains astonishingly vital and powerful, as when she wishes her lover's vow to Romeo could be inaugurated again:

> But to be frank and give it thee again;
> And yet I wish but for the thing I have.
> My bounty is as boundless as the sea,
> My love as deep: The more I give to thee
> The more I have, for both are infinite.

That is a transcendently persuasive utterance of love's reality, as rich as literature affords, so distant from vainglory or self-deception that Romeo is transfigured by receiving it. Shakespeare is reputed to have said that he had to kill off Mercutio lest Mercutio kill the play. I think it likelier that the full revelation of Juliet's greatness made it necessary to dispose of the prurient Mercutio, whose lively blasphemies against the splendors of Juliet's love might well have wearied us.

Juliet's is a difficult role to play, for the curse of our theaters are "high-concept" directors, and some of them do not seem to know clearly the difference between Juliet and the Cressida of *Troilus and Cressida*! Properly performed, or adequately interpreted by a sensitive reader, Juliet is an essential part of Shakespeare's unmatched invention of the human.

Hamlet ✓

Hamlet is the most persuasive representative we have of intellectual skepticism, with the single exception of Montaigne's self-portrayal, which would appear to have had considerable effect upon Shakespeare the dramatist. Montaigne's skepticism was so beautifully sustained that he very nearly could persuade us to share his conviction that Plato essentially was a skeptic. Hamlet's skepticism, though powerful and protracted, dominates the prince rather less than Montaigne's preoccupies the greatest of all essayists. In the mimesis of a consciousness, Hamlet exceeds Montaigne's image of himself as man thinking. Even Plato's Socrates does not provide us with so powerful and influential an instance of cognition in all its processes as does Hamlet.

Yet Hamlet is as much a man of action as he is an intellectual. His intellectuality indeed is an anomaly; by rights he should resemble Fortinbras more than he does those equally formidable wits, Rosalind and Falstaff, or those brilliant skeptics gone rancid, Iago and Edmund. We tend not to situate Hamlet between Rosalind and Edmund, since good and evil hardly seem fit antinomies to enfold the Western hero of consciousness, the role that Hamlet has fulfilled since he first was enacted. Harry Levin eloquently warns against sentimentalizing Hamlet's tragedy, against "the obscurantist conclusion that thought is Hamlet's tragedy; Hamlet is the man who thinks too much; ineffectual because he is intellectual; his nemesis is failure of nerve, a nervous prostration." Surely Levin is accurate; Hamlet thinks not too much but too well, and so is a more-than-Nietzsche, well in advance of Nietzsche. Hamlet abandons art, and perishes of the truth, even becomes the truth in the act of perishing. His tragedy is not the tragedy of thought, but the Nietzschean tragedy of truth.

The character of Hamlet is the largest literary instance of what Max Weber meant by charisma, the power of a single individual over nature, and so at last over death. What matters most about Hamlet is the universality of his appeal; the only rival representation of a secular personality would appear to be that of King David in 2 Samuel, and David is both of vast historical consequence, and perhaps not wholly secular, so that Hamlet's uniqueness is not much diminished. David, after all, has the eternal blessing of Yahweh, while Hamlet's aura is self-generated, and therefore more mysterious. No other figure in secular literature induces love in so universal an audience, and no one else seems to need or want that love so little. It may be that negative elements in Hamlet's charisma are the largest single component in our general psychological sense that it is easier to love than to accept love. Hamlet is the subject and object of his own quest, an intolerable truth that helps render him into so destructive an angel, so dangerous an aesthetic pleasure that he can survive only as a story able to be told by Horatio, who loves Hamlet precisely as the audience does, because we are Horatio. Remove Horatio from the play, and we would have no way into the play, whether now or later.

What are we to make of Horatio as a literary character? He is the character as playgoer and reader, passive yet passionately receptive, and necessarily the most important figure in the tragedy except for Hamlet himself. Why? Because, without Horatio, Hamlet is forbiddingly beyond us. The prince is an agonist who engages supernal powers, even while he attempts to see his uncle Claudius as his almighty opposite. Hamlet's contention is with forces within his own labyrinthine nature, and so with the spirit of evil in heavenly places. Like wrestling Jacob, Hamlet confronts a nameless one among the Elohim, a stranger god who is his own Angel of Death. Does Hamlet win a new name? Without Horatio, the question would be unanswerable, but the presence of Horatio at the close allows us to see that the new name is the old one, but cleansed from the image of the dead father. Horatio is the witness who testifies to the apotheosis of the dead son, whose transfiguration has moved him, and us, from the aesthetics of being outraged to the purified aesthetic dignity of a final disinterestedness, beyond ritual sacrifice, and beyond the romances of the family and of society.

Why does Horatio attempt suicide, when he realizes that Hamlet is dying? I blink at this moment, which strikes me as the most negative of all the many negative moments in the play:

HAMLET: Horatio, I am dead,
    Thou livest. Report me and my cause aright
    To the unsatisfied.
HORATIO: Never believe it,
    I am more an antique Roman than a Dane.
    Here's yet some liquor left.

Are we to associate Horatio with Eros, Antony's follower who kills himself to "escape the sorrow / Of Anthony's death," or with other heroic sacrificers to a shame culture? The court and kingdom of the wretched Claudius constitute something much closer to a guilt culture, and Horatio, despite his assertion of identity, hardly has wandered in from one of Shakespeare's Roman tragedies. Horatio's desire to die with Hamlet is a contamination from the audience that Shakespeare creates as a crucial element in *The Tragedy of Hamlet, Prince of Denmark*. Even as Iago writes a play with Othello and Desdemona as characters, or as Edmund writes with Gloucester and Edgar, so Shakespeare writes with Horatio and ourselves. Freud's Death Drive beyond the Pleasure Principle is a hyperbolical trope that we barely recognize as a trope, and similarly, we have difficulty seeing that Horatio's suicidal impulse is a metaphor for the little death that we die in conjunction with the apocalyptic end of a charismatic leader. Horatio truly resembles not the self-slain Eros of *Antony and Cleopatra* but the self-castrating Walt Whitman who gives up his tally of the sprig of lilac in his extraordinary elegy for Lincoln, the best of all American poems ever. The most extraordinary of Hamlet's universal aspects is his relationship to death. Whitman's Lincoln dies the exemplary death of the martyred father, the death of God, but Hamlet dies the death of the hero, by which I do not mean the death so much of the hero of tragedy but of the hero of Scripture, the death of Jonathan slain upon the high places. The death of Hamlet is upon the highest of all high places, the place of a final disinterestedness, which is otherwise inaccessible to us.

Can we not name that highest of high places as Hamlet's place, a new kind of stance, one that he himself does not assume until he returns in Act V from his abortive voyage to England? Strangely purged of mourning and melancholia for the dead father, Hamlet seems also beyond incestuous jealousy and a revenger's fury. In his heart there is a kind of fighting, and a sense of foreboding, not of death but of the inadequacies of life: "Thou wouldst not think how ill all's here about my heart." Speaking to Horatio, and so to us, Hamlet announces a new sense that there are no accidents, or need not be:

> If it be now, 'tis not to come; if it be not to come, it will be now;
> if it be not now, yet it will come. The readiness is all. Since no
> man, of aught he leaves, knows aught, what is't to leave betimes?
> Let be.

"It" has to be the moment of dying, and "the readiness is all" might be regarded as Hamlet's motto throughout Act V. "To be or not to be" is answered now by "let be," which is a sort of heroic quietism, and clearly is the prince's final advice to the audience. There is an ultimate skepticism in Hamlet's assurance that none of us knows anything of what we will leave behind us when we die, and yet this skepticism does not dominate the prince as he dies:

> You that look pale and tremble at this chance,
> That are but mutes or audience to this act,
> Had I but time—as this fell sergeant, Death,
> Is strict in his arrest—O, I could tell you—
> But let it be.

What he could tell us might concern a knowledge that indeed he has achieved, which I think is a knowledge of his relationship to us, and necessarily to our surrogate, Horatio. Hamlet's extraordinary earlier praise of Horatio (Act III, Scene 2, lines 54–74) may seem excessive or even hyperbolical, but not when we consider it as being in what Emerson called the optative mood, particularly in regard to the audience, or to the ideal of an audience:

>   ... for thou hast been
> As one in suff'ring all that suffers nothing,
> A man that Fortune's buffets and rewards
> Hast ta'en with equal thanks; and blest are those
> Whose blood and judgment are so well co-meddled,
> That they are not a pipe for Fortune's finger
> To sound what stop she please. Give me that man
> That is not passions' slave, and I will wear him
> In my heart's core, ay, in my heart of heart,
> As I do thee.

Hamlet himself is hardly one who, in suffering all, suffers nothing, but then Hamlet is the hero, beyond Horatio and ourselves, and perhaps, at the close, so far beyond that he transcends the limits of the human. Horatio is the man that the wily Claudius would not be able to use, partly because Horatio, like the audience, loves Hamlet, but partly also because Horatio stands apart from passion, from self-interest, from life. We are Horatio because he too is a spectator at Elsinore, yet a spectator who has taken sides, once and for all. Hamlet does not need Horatio's love, or ours, though he has it anyway. He needs Horatio to survive to tell his story, and us to receive his story, but he does not need our passion.

To discuss Hamlet as a literary character is to enter a labyrinth of speculation, past and present, that is bewildering in its diversity and in its self-contradictions. The personalities of Hamlet are a manifold, a veritable picnic of selves. Excess is the mark of Hamlet as it is of Falstaff, but the Falstaffian gusto, despite all its complexities, does not compare either to Hamlet's vitalism or to Hamlet's negative exuberance. To be the foremost single representation in all of Western literature, you ought to be the hero of an epic or at least a chronicle, but not the protagonist of a revenge tragedy. A consciousness as vast as Hamlet's ought to have been assigned a Faustian quest, or a journey to God, or a national project of renewal. All Hamlet has to do (if indeed he ought to do it) is chop down Claudius. Avenging the father does not require a Hamlet; a Fortinbras would be more than sufficient. What it was that could have inspired Shakespeare to this amazing disproportion between personage and enterprise seems to me fit subject for wonder.

The wonder is not that Hamlet should be too large for Elsinore, but that he may be too comprehensive for tragedy, just as Nietzsche may be too aesthetic for philosophy. We can envision Hamlet debating Freud, or Nietzsche; hardly a role for Lear or Othello, Yet we do not think of Hamlet as running away from the play, the way that Falstaff takes on a mimetic force that dwarfs the action of *Henry the Fourth, Part One*. Rather, Hamlet transforms his drama from within, so that as its center he becomes also a circumference that will not cease expanding. Long as the play is, we sense that Shakespeare legitimately could have made it much longer, by allowing Hamlet even more meditations upon the perplexities of being human. Indeed it is hardly possible to exclude any matter whatsoever as being irrelevant to a literary work centering upon Hamlet. We welcome Hamlet's opinions upon everything, just as we search the writings of Nietzsche or of Freud to see what they say upon jealousy or mourning or art or authority or whatsoever. Hamlet, a mere literary character, seems the only literary character who has and is an authorial presence, who could as well be a Montaigne, or a Proust, or a Freud. How Shakespeare renders such an illusion persuasive has been illuminated by a rich tradition of criticism. Why he should have ventured so drastic and original an illusion remains a burden for critics to come.

Doubtless it is wrong to see Hamlet as a Shakespearean self-portrait, but though wrong it seems inevitable, and has a sanction in Joyce's witty interpretation, when Stephen expounds his theory of *Hamlet* in *Ulysses*. What is clear is that Shakespeare has lavished intelligence upon Hamlet, who is not so much the most intelligent personage ever to be represented in language, as he is a new kind of intelligence, one without faith either in itself or in language. Hamlet is the precursor of Schopenhauer and Wittgenstein, as well as of Nietzsche and Freud. The prince understands that each of us is her own worst enemy, unable to distinguish desire from playacting, and liable to create disaster out of her equivocal doom-eagerness, a drive against death that courts death. The diseases of consciousness, one by one, seem invented by Hamlet as defenses that contaminate and are contaminated by the drive. Hamlet invents Freud in the sense that Freud is always in Hamlet's wake, condemned to map Hamlet's mind as the only route to a general map of the mind.

The consequence is that *Hamlet* is a Shakespearean reading of Freud that makes redundant any Freudian reading of Shakespeare. Hamlet is the theologian of the unconscious, anticipating Wordsworth as well as Freud. In the same way, Hamlet precedes Kafka and Beckett, by systematically evading every interpretation that might confine him to some reductive scheme that too easily transcends the realities of suffering. Hamlet, as an intelligence, is perpetually ahead of all later literature, which cannot deconstruct his dilemmas any more forcefully or overtly than he himself has done. Shakespeare makes all theorists of interpretation into so many instances of poor Rosencrantz and Guildenstern, who would pluck out the heart of the mystery yet cannot play upon Hamlet, call him what instrument they will. Historicizing Hamlet, whether in old modes or new, ends in reducing the exegete to an antiquarian, unable to separate past values from impending immediacies. There is a politics to Hamlet's spirit, but it is not our politics, though it remains our spirit.

The sickness of the spirit, in Hamlet as in our lives, is perhaps the most perplexing issue of the tragedy. Feigning derangement, Hamlet also becomes deranged, and then returns, apparently self-purged of his alienations from reality. We never do learn the precise nature of his illness, except that it ensued from the trauma brought on by the murder of the father and the mother's fast remarriage. But for a moral intelligence that extraordinary, the squalors of the family romance, or even the king's murder, do not seem the necessary origins of the falling away from self-hood. Imaginative revulsion seems the source of madness in Shakespeare, whether in *Hamlet*, *Timon of Athens*, or *Macbeth* Hamlet was as much a new kind of man as the King David of 2 Samuel had been: a figure who seemed to realize all of human possibility, an ultimate charismatic whose aura promised almost a triumph over nature. The biblical David has a superb pragmatic intelligence, but his changes are natural, or else presided over by the favor of God's blessing. Hamlet changes in the Shakespearean way, by overhearing himself, whether he speaks to himself or to others. His study of himself is absolute, and founded upon a pondering of his own words. Divinity lies principally within himself, and manifests itself in his fate, as in the fates of all connected with him. His character is his *daimon*, and overdetermines every event.

Literary character, like authorial presence, always returns, whatever the tides of critical fashion. Hamlet's particular union of representational force and linguistic authority has much to do with his universal appeal, and makes it likely also that a return to the study of personality in literature must find one of its centers in this most radiant of all fictional consciousnesses.

Julius Caesar ✓

The Tragedy of Julius Caesar is a very satisfying play, as a play, and is universally regarded as a work of considerable aesthetic dignity. We tend to read it first when we are in school, because it is so clear and simple a drama that our teachers find it suitable for us there. I have seen it only once on stage, once on television, and once as a film, and found none of these three presentations quite adequate, the problem in each case being with the actor who misplayed Brutus. Directors and actors seem to place more of Hamlet in Brutus than Shakespeare himself set there, and Brutus just cannot sustain Hamlet's aura. Hamlet scarcely can speak without extending our consciousness into the farthest ranges, but there is a narcissistic, rather spoiled quality to the perhaps excessively noble Brutus, and he does not achieve ghostlier demarcations, keener sounds, until his fortunes begin to fail.

Modern critics find somewhat problematical Shakespeare's supposed political stance in *Julius Caesar*. Presumably Shakespeare, as an Elizabethan royalist, is unhappy about the assassination of Caesar, and yet Brutus is the tragic hero. Caesar is in decay, a touch vainglorious, the conqueror dwindled into a ruler who accepts flattery. But however the politics of *Julius Caesar* are to be resolved, the play seems problematical in no other

respect. Its characters, including even Brutus, are not endless to meditation, and its rhetoric does not reverberate so as to suggest a beyond. There
is no Marlovian element in *Julius Caesar*, no hero-villains of Hermetic
ambition or Machiavellian intensity, no surpassingly eloquent and outrageous overreachers. Whether from North's Plutarch or from Seneca, or
more likely from a strain in his own nature, Shakespeare brings forth a
Stoic music with its own dying falls, but without a grudge or bias against
our given condition. Brutus essentially is a Stoic, acutely self-conscious and
self-regarding, with a touch of Virgil's Aeneas in him. But he has been too
much admired in Rome, and he greatly admires himself. A.D. Nuttall is
useful in contrasting Brutus and his Stoicism to Antony's affective oppor-
tunism:

> Brutus, the aristocrat, his theoretic Stoicism borne on a founda-
> tion of shame-culture, on ancient heroic dignity, belongs to the
> Roman past. He can do the Stoic trick (rather like "isolating" a
> muscle) of separating his reason from his passions but he cannot
> exploit his own motivating passions with the coolness of an
> Antony. With all his fondness for statuesque postures Brutus
> remains morally more spontaneous than Antony.

Where is Cassius on this scale of moral spontaneity? He plays upon
Brutus in order to bring him into the conspiracy, but then yields to Brutus
both as to Antony's survival and on granting Antony permission to speak at
Caesar's funeral. When he yields a third time and consents, against his will,
to stake everything upon battle at Philippi, he completes the irony of his
own undoing and Caesar's ghost is avenged. The irony could be interpreted as a dialectic of conscience and affection, since Cassius politically
seduced Brutus by exploiting the Stoic hero's moral spontaneity. Cassius is
destroyed by Brutus's incompetent political and military decisions, to
which Cassius yields out of affection, but also because he must accept the
moral consequences of having seduced Brutus into leadership, the only
role possible for Brutus in any enterprise.

Cassius is the one figure in the play who might have benefited by a
touch of Marlovian force or antithetical intensity, but Shakespeare preferred to maintain his own Stoic control in representing a Stoic tragedy.
We ought to marvel that Shakespeare, a year or so later, could venture
upon the infinite by writing *Hamlet*, where every current is antithetical and
far beyond merely rational controls. *Julius Caesar* has more in common
with *Henry V* than with *Hamlet*, just as the two parts of *Henry IV* reach out
to *As You Like It* and *Hamlet*. What is excluded from *Julius Caesar* is the

madness of great wit, the exuberance of Falstaff, of Rosalind, and of one of the endless aspects of Hamlet. As we miss Falstaff in *Henry V* so we miss someone, anyone, who could cause *Julius Caesar* to flare up for us. Shakespeare, with a curiously Stoic forbearance, subdued himself to his subject, though we do not know why.

The results of this uncharacteristic *ascesis* are surely mixed. We receive clarity and nobility, and lose nearly everything that makes Shakespeare unique. Dr. Samuel Johnson's summary speaks to this better than I can:

> Of this tragedy many particular passages deserve regard, and the contention and reconcilement of Brutus and Cassius is universally celebrated; but I have never been strongly agitated in perusing it, and think it somewhat cold and unaffecting, comparing with some other of Shakespeare's plays; his adherence to the real story, and to Roman manners, seems to have impeded the natural vigour of his genius.

Whatever the impediments, *Julius Caesar* is an anomaly among Shakespeare's mature plays in that it possesses his originality in language, to a fair degree, yet is almost wholly devoid of his principal originality in representation. Not even Brutus changes by listening to himself ruminate. How much difference can we hear between Brutus at the beginning of act 2 and Brutus near to the end of act 5? Brooding upon the probable change in a crowned Caesar, Brutus takes the responsibility of prophesying the change:

> It is the bright day that brings forth the adder,
> And that craves wary walking.

Poor Brutus, once embarked upon his venture, never encounters his own bright day. Shakespeare subtly allows the Stoic hero a continuous nobility down to the end, while also allowing Brutus to be deaf to the irony of his final self-praise:

> Countrymen,
> My heart doth joy that yet in all my life
> I found no man but he was true to me.

We wince, however sympathetic we find Brutus, since he seems to have forgotten Caesar's last words, with their shock that Brutus, of all men, should have been untrue to his friend Caesar. Brutus's "As Caesar lov'd me,

I weep for him" does not linger in us, but we do remember Antony's bitter eloquence:

> For Brutus, as you know, was Caesar's angel.

Perhaps Shakespeare's politics did inhibit his profoundest powers in *Julius Caesar*. The tragedy of Brutus and the crime against the monarch could not be reconciled with one another, and Shakespeare, divided against himself, found he could not be wholly true to Brutus.

Othello

Dr. Samuel Johnson found in the representation of Othello, Iago, and Desdemona "such proofs of Shakespeare's skill in human nature, as, I suppose, it is vain to seek in any modern writer." The High Romantic Victor Hugo gave us the contrary formula: "Next to God, Shakespeare created most," which does not seem to me a remystification of Shakespeare's characters, but rather a shrewd hint in what might be called the pragmatics of aesthetics. Shakespeare was a mortal god (as Hugo aspired to be) because his art was not a mimesis at all. A mode of representation that is always out ahead of any historically unfolding reality necessarily contains us more than we can contain it. A.D. Nuttall wonderfully remarks of Iago that he "chooses which emotions he will experience. He is not just motivated, like other people. Instead he *decides* to be motivated." Though Nuttall says that makes of Iago a Camus-like existentialist, I would think Iago is closer to a god, or a devil, and so perhaps resembles his creator, who evidently chose emotions to be experienced, and decided whether or not to be motivated. We do not feel Othello to be a critique of Shakespeare, but in some sense Iago is just that, being a playwright, like Edmund in *King Lear*, like Hamlet, and like William Shakespeare. Hamlet's "the rest is silence" has a curious parallel in Iago's "from this time forth I never will speak word," even though Hamlet dies immediately and Iago survives to die mutely under torture.

It is not that Iago is in Hamlet's class as an intellectual consciousness. No, Iago is comparable to Edmund, who in *King Lear* out-plots everyone else in the royal world of the play. Othello is a glorious soldier and a sadly simple man, who could have been ruined by a villain far less gifted than Iago. A.C. Bradley's charming notion is still true: exchange Othello and Hamlet in one another's plays, and there would be no plays. Othello would chop Claudius down as soon as the ghost had convinced him, and Hamlet would have needed only a few moments to see through Iago, and to begin destroying him by overt parody. But there are no Hamlets, Falstaffs, or inspired clowns in *Othello, The Moor of Venice*, and poor Desdemona is no Portia.

The Moor of Venice is sometimes the neglected part of the tragedy's title. To be the Moor of Venice, its hired general, is an uneasy honor, Venice being, then and now, the uneasiest of cities. Othello's pigmentation is notoriously essential to the plot. He is hardly a natural man in relation to the subtle Venetians, but the sexual obsessiveness he catches from Iago develops into a dualism that renders him insane. A marvelous monism has yielded to the discontents of Venetian civilization, and we remain haunted by intimations of a different Othello, as though Desdemona, even before Iago's intervention, has been loss as well as gain for the previously integral soldier. Many critics have noted Othello's ruefulness when he speaks in act 1 of having exchanged his "unhoused free condition" for his love of "the gentle Desdemona." When we think of him in his glory we remember his ending a street battle with one line of marvelous authority:

Keep up your bright swords, for the dew will rust them.

"Sheathe or die" would be the reductive reading, but Othello in his zenith defies reduction, and a fuller interpretation would emphasize the easiness and largeness of this superbly military temperament. How does so spacious and majestic an authority degenerate so rapidly into an equivalent of Spenser's Malbecco? Like Malbecco, Othello forgets he is a man and his name in effect becomes jealousy. Jealousy in Hawthorne becomes Satan, after having been Chillingworth, while in Proust, first Swann and then Marcel become art historians of jealousy, as it were, obsessive scholars desperately searching for every visual detail of betrayal. Freud's *delusional* jealousy involves repressed homosexuality, and seems inapplicable to Othello, though not wholly so to Iago. Jealousy in Shakespeare—parent to its presence in Hawthorne, Proust, and Freud—is a mask for the fear of death, since what the jealous lover fears is that there will not be time or space enough for himself. It is one of the peculiar splendors of *Othello* that we cannot understand Othello's belated jealousy without first understanding Iago's primal envy of Othello, which is at the hidden center of the drama.

II

Frank Kermode curiously says that "Iago's naturalist ethic ... is a wicked man's version of Montaigne," a judgment that Ben Jonson might have welcomed, but that I find alien to Shakespeare. Iago is not a naturalist but the fiercest version in all literature of an ideologue of the reductive fallacy, which can be defined as the belief that what is most real about any one of us is the worst thing that possibly could be true of us. "Tell me what she or he is really like," the reductionist keeps saying, and means: "Tell me the worst thing you can." Presumably the reductionist cannot bear to be deceived, and so becomes a professional at deception.

Iago is Othello's standard-bearer, a senior officer skilled and courageous in the field, as we have every reason to believe. "I am not what I am" is his chilling motto, and is endless to meditation. "I am that I am" is God's name in answer to the query of Moses, and reverberates darkly and antithetically in "I am not what I am." God will be where and when He will be, present or absent as is His choice. Iago is the spirit that will not be, the spirit of absence, a pure negativity. We know therefore from the start why Iago hates Othello, who is the largest presence, the fullest being in Iago's world, and particularly in battle. The hatred pretends to be empirical, but is ontological, and unquenchable in consequence. If Platonic eros is the desire for what one hasn't got, then Iago's hatred is the drive to destroy what one hasn't got. We shudder when the maddened Othello vows death to Desdemona as a "fair devil" and promotes Iago to be his lieutenant, for Iago superbly responds, "I am your own for ever," and means the reverse: "You too are now an absence."

Step by step, Iago falls into his own gap of being, changing as he hears himself plot, improvising a drama that must destroy the dramatist as well as his protagonists:

IAGO: And what's he then that says I play the villain,
When this advice is free I give, and honest,
Probal to thinking, and indeed the course
To win the Moor again? For 'tis most easy
Th' inclining Desdemona to subdue
In any honest suit; she's fram'd as fruitful
As the free elements. And then for her
To win the Moor, were['t] to renounce his baptism.
All seals and symbols of redeemed sin,
His soul is so enfetter'd to her love,
That she may make, unmake, do what she list,
Even as her appetite shall play the god
With his weak function. How am I then a villain,
To counsel Cassio to this parallel course,
Directly to his good? Divinity of hell!
When devils will the blackest sins put on,

They do suggest at first with heavenly shows,
As I do now; for whiles this honest fool
Plies Desdemona to repair his fortune,
And she for him pleads strongly to the Moor,
I'll pour this pestilence into his ear—
That she repeals him for her body's lust,
And by how much she strives to do him good,
She shall undo her credit with the Moor.
So will I turn her virtue into pitch,
And out of her own goodness make the net
That shall enmesh them all.

Harold C. Goddard called Iago a "moral pyromaniac," and we can hear Iago setting fire to himself throughout the play, but particularly in this speech. I think that Goddard, a profoundly imaginative critic, captured the essence of Iago when he saw that Iago was always at war, making every encounter, every moment, into an act of destruction. War is the ultimate reductive fallacy, since to kill your enemy you must believe the worst that can be believed about him. What changes in Iago as he listens to himself is that he loses perspective, because his rhetoric isolates by burning away context. Isolation, Freud tells us, is the compulsive's guarantee that the coherence of his thinking will be interrupted. Iago interposes intervals of monologue so as to defend himself against his own awareness of change in himself, and thus ironically intensifies his own change into the totally diabolic. As with Shakespeare's Richard III, Iago's monologues are swerves away from the Divine "I am that I am," past "I am not what I am," on to "I am not," negation mounting to an apotheosis.

The collapse of Othello is augmented in dignity and poignance when we gain our full awareness of Iago's achieved negativity, war everlasting. No critic need judge Othello to be stupid, for Othello does not incarnate war, being as he is a sane and honorable warrior. He is peculiarly vulnerable to Iago precisely because Iago is his standard-bearer, the protector of his colors and reputation in battle, pledged to die rather than allow the colors to be taken. His equivalent to Iago's monologues is a stirring elegy for the self, a farewell to war as a valid—because confined—occupation:

OTHELLO: I had been happy, if the general camp,
    Pioners and all, had tasted her sweet body,
    So I had nothing known. O now, for ever
    Farewell the tranquil mind! farewell content!
    Farewell the plumed troops and the big wars

That makes ambition virtue! O, farewell!
Farewell the neighing steed and the shrill trump,
The spirit-stirring drum, th' ear-piercing fife,
The royal banner, and all quality,
Pride, pomp, and circumstance of glorious war!
And O you mortal engines, whose rude throats
Th' immortal Jove's dread clamors counterfeit,
Farewell! Othello's occupation's gone.

"Pride, pomp, and circumstance of glorious war!" has yielded to Iago's incessant war against being. Othello, within his occupation's limits, has the greatness of the tragic hero. Iago breaks down those limits from within, from war's own camp, and so Othello has no chance. Had the attack come from the world outside war's dominion, Othello could have maintained some coherence, and gone down in the name of the purity of arms. Shakespeare, courting a poetics of pain, could not allow his hero that consolation.

Macbeth

Macbeth is the culminating figure in the sequence of what might be called Shakespeare's Grand Negations: Richard III, Iago, Edmund, Macbeth. He differs from his precursors in lacking their dark intellectuality, and their manipulative power over other selves. But he surpasses them in imagination, in its High Romantic sense, even though that is hardly a faculty in which they are deficient. His imagination is so strong that it exceeds even Hamlet's, so strong indeed that we can see that it is imagination, rather than ambition or the Witches, that victimizes and destroys Macbeth. The bloodiest tyrant and villain in Shakespeare, Macbeth nevertheless engages our imaginations precisely because he is so large a representation of the dangerous prevalence of the imagination. The tragedy *Macbeth* constitutes an implicit self-critique of the Shakespearean imagination, and therefore also of a crucial element in your own imagination, whoever you are.

Not even Hamlet dominates his play as Macbeth does; he speaks about one third of the text as we have it. Compared to him, the other figures in the drama take on a common grayness, except for Lady Macbeth, and she largely vanishes after the middle of Act III. No Shakespearean protagonist, again not even Hamlet, is revealed to us so inwardly as Macbeth. Shakespeare quite deliberately places us under a very paradoxical stress: we intimately accompany Macbeth in his interior journey, and yet we attempt to refuse all identity with Macbeth; an impossible refusal, since his imagination becomes our own. We are contaminated by Macbeth's fantasies; perhaps someday our critical instruments will be keen enough so that we will comprehend just how much Sigmund Freud's theories owe to precisely Macbethian contamination. I myself am inclined to place *The Tragedy of Macbeth*, foremost among Shakespeare's works, above even *Hamlet* and *Lear*, because of the unique power of contamination manifested by its protagonist's fantasy-making faculty. Everything that Macbeth says, particularly to himself, is notoriously memorable, yet I would assign a crucial function to a passage in Act I that defines the exact nature of Macbeth's imagination:

> Present fears
> Are less than horrible imaginings.
> My thought, whose murder yet is but fantastical,
> Shakes so my single state of man that function
> Is smothered in surmise, and nothing is
> But what is not.

What does Macbeth mean by "single" here? Perhaps "alone" or "unaided," perhaps "total," but either way the word indicates vulnerability to phantasmagoria. To smother function or thought's ordinary operation by surmise, which is anticipation but not action, is to be dominated by what might be called the proleptic imagination, which is Macbeth's great burden and his tragedy. Though the murder of Duncan is still a pure prolepsis, Macbeth has but to image an act or event and instantly he is on the other side of it, brooding retrospectively. The negations of Iago and Edmund were willed nihilisms, but Macbeth's imagination does the work of his will, so that "nothing is / But what is not." Macbeth represents an enormous enhancement of that element in us that allows us to see Shakespeare acted, whether in the theatre, or the mind's eye of the reader, without protesting or denying the illusion. It is not that Macbeth has faith in the imagination, but that he is enslaved to his version of fantasy. Brooding on Macduff's absence from court, Macbeth sums up his proleptic mode in one powerful couplet:

> Strange things I have in head that will to hand,
> Which must be acted ere they may be scanned.

He seems to know already that he seeks to murder every member of Macduff's family, yet he will not truly have the knowledge until the massacre is accomplished, as though the image in his head is wholly independent of his will. This is the burden of his great soliloquy at the start of Act I, Scene vii, with its Hamlet-like onset:

> If it were done when 'tis done, then 'twere well
> It were done quickly. If th'assassination
> Could trammel up the consequence, and catch,
> With his surcease, success; that but this blow
> Might be the be-all and the end-all—here,
> But here, upon this bank and shoal of time,
> We'd jump the life to come.

"Bank and shoal of time" is a brilliant trope, whether or not it is Shakespeare's, since "shoal" there is a scholarly emendation, and perhaps Shakespeare wrote "school," which would make "bank" into a school-bench. Scholars tell us also that "jump" here means "hazard," but I think Macbeth means both: to leap and to risk, and I suspect that Shakespeare actually wrote "shoal." The metaphor is superbly characteristic of precisely how Macbeth's imagination works, by leaping over present time and over a future act also, so as to land upon the other bank of time, looking back to the bank where he stood before action. The soliloquy ends with the same figuration, but now broken off by the entry of Lady Macbeth. Vaulting and overleaping, Macbeth's ambition, which is another name for the proleptic aspect of his imagination, falls upon the other side of his intent, which is to say, the other bank both of his aim and his meaning:

> I have no spur
> To prick the sides of my intent, but only
> Vaulting ambition, which o'erleaps itself
> And falls on th'other—

The intent is a horse all will, but Macbeth's imagination again falls on the other side of the will, and dominates the perpetually rapt protagonist, who is condemned always to be in a kind of trance or phantasmagoria that governs him, yet also is augmented by every action that he undertakes. Though Shakespeare doubtless gave full credence to his Witches, weird or wayward demiurges of the Gnostic cosmos of *Macbeth*, they may also be projections of Macbeth's own rapt state of prolepsis, his inability to control the temporal elements of his imagination. The Witches embody the temporal gap between what is imagined and what is done, so that they take the place of Macbeth's Will. We could not envision Iago or Edmund being sought out by the Witches, because Iago and Edmund will their own grand

negations, or indeed will to become grand negations of every value.
Macbeth imagines his negations, and becomes the grandest negation of
them all.

Why then do we sympathize with Macbeth's inwardness, in spite of
our own wills? He shares Hamlet's dark side, but is totally without
Hamlet's intellect. It is almost as though Shakespeare deliberately cut away
Hamlet's cognitive gifts while preserving Hamlet's sensibility in the
immensely powerful if purely involuntary imagination of Macbeth.
Hamlet interests us for reasons very different from why we interest ourselves; Macbeth precisely is interesting to us exactly as we are interesting,
in our own judgment. We know Macbeth's inwardness as we know our
own, but Hamlet's vast theatre of mind remains an abyss to us. Both
Macbeth and Lady Macbeth are well aware that in murdering Duncan they
are slaying the good father. We share their Oedipal intensity (which
becomes her madness) if not their guilt. The primal act of imagination, as
Freud had learned from Shakespeare, is the ambitious act of desiring the
father's death. The first part of Macbeth's appeal to us is his rapt state of
being or Oedipal ambition, but the second part, even more appealing, is his
power of representing an increasing state of being outraged, outraged by
time, by mortality, and by the equivocation of the fiend that lies like truth.

William Hazlitt shrewdly observed of Macbeth that: "His energy
springs from the anxiety and agitation of his mind." I would add that, as the
drama advances, the principal agitation is the energy of being outraged by
the baffling of expectations. Increasingly obsessed with time, Macbeth fears
becoming an actor who always misses his cue, and constantly learns that the
cues he was given are wrong. The energy that stems from an adroit representation of a state of being outraged is one that imbues us with a remarkable degree of sympathy. I recall watching a television film of Alec Guinness
playing the last days of Hitler, portrayed accurately as progressing to a
greater intensity of being outraged from start to end. One had to keep
recalling that this was a representation of Hitler in order to fight off an
involuntary sympathy. Our common fate is an outrage: each of us must die.
Shakespeare, implicating us in Macbeth's fate, profoundly associates the
proleptic imagination with the sense of being outraged, nowhere more than
in Macbeth's extraordinary refusal to mourn the death of his afflicted wife.
All of Western literature does not afford us an utterance so superbly outraged as this, or one that so abruptly jumps over every possible life to come:

> She should have died hereafter;
> There would have been a time for such a word.
> Tomorrow, and tomorrow, and tomorrow

Creeps in this petty pace from day to day,
To the last syllable of recorded time;
And all our yesterdays have lighted fools
The way to dusty death. Out, out, brief candle!
Life's but a walking shadow, a poor player
That struts and frets his hour upon the stage
And then is heard no more. It is a tale
Told by an idiot, full of sound and fury
Signifying nothing.

Dr. Samuel Johnson was so disturbed by this speech that initially he wished to emend "such a word" to "such a world." Upon reflection, he accepted "word," but interpreted it as meaning "intelligence," in the sense that we say we send "word" when we give intelligence. Macbeth, outraged yet refusing to mourn, perhaps begins with the distancing observation that his wife would have died sooner or later anyway, but then centers ironically upon the meaninglessness now, for him, of such a word as "hereafter," since he *knows* that quite literally there will be no tomorrow for him. In the grim music of the word "tomorrow" he hears his own horror of time, his proleptic imagining of all of remaining life, and not just for himself alone. Recorded time, history, will end with the last syllable of the word "tomorrow," but that will refer to a tomorrow that will not come. If all our yesterdays have existed to light "fools" (presumably meaning "victims") the way to a death that is only ourselves (Adam being created from the dust of red clay), then the brief candle of Lady Macbeth's life just as well has gone out. By the light of that candle, Shakespeare grants Macbeth an outraged but astonishing vision of life as an actor in a Shakespearean play, rather like *The Tragedy of Macbeth.* The best in this kind are but shadows, but life is not one of the best, being a bad actor, strutting and fretting away his performance, and lacking reverberation in the memories of the audience after they have left the theatre. Varying the figurative identification, Macbeth moves life's status from bad actor to bad drama or tale, composed by a professional jester or court fool, an idiot indulged in his idiocy. The story is either meaningless or a total negation, signifying nothing because there is nothing to signify. Theatrical metaphors are more fully appropriate for Shakespeare himself than for the tyrant Macbeth, we might think at first, but then we remember that Macbeth's peculiar imagination necessarily has made him into a poetic dramatist. Iago and Edmund, nihilistic dramatists, manipulated others, while Macbeth has manipulated himself, leaping over the present and the actions not yet taken into the scenes that followed the actions, as though they already had occurred.

Critics of Macbeth always have noted the terrible awe he provokes in us. Sublime in himself, the usurper also partakes in the dreadful sublimity of the apocalyptic cosmos of his drama. When Duncan is slain, lamentings are heard in the air, great winds blow, owls clamor through the night, and behave like hawks, killing falcons as if they were mice. And Duncan's horses break loose, warring against men, and then devour one another. It is as though the daemonic underworld of the Weird Sisters and Hecate had broken upwards into Duncan's realm, which in some sense they had done by helping to spur on the rapt Macbeth. Shakespeare's protagonist pays a fearful price for his sublimity, and yet as audience and readers we do not wish Macbeth to be otherwise than the grand negation he becomes. I think this is because Macbeth is not only a criticism of our imaginations, which are as guilty and Oedipal as his own, but also because Macbeth is Shakespeare's critique of his own tragic imagination, an imagination beyond guilt.

King Lear

In the long reaction against A.C. Bradley, we have been warned endlessly against meditating upon the girlhood of Shakespeare's heroines or brooding upon the earlier marital days of the Macbeths. Yet Shakespearean representation, as A.D. Nuttall observes, allows us to see aspects of reality we would not otherwise recognize. I would go beyond Nuttall to suggest that Shakespeare has molded both our sense of reality and our cognitive modes of apprehending that reality to a far greater degree than Homer or Plato, Montaigne or Nietzsche, Freud or Proust. Only the Bible rivals Shakespeare as an influence upon our sense of how human character, thinking, personality, ought to be imitated through, in, or by language. No Western writer shows less consciousness of belatedness than Shakespeare, yet his true precursor is not Marlowe but the Bible. *King Lear* as tragedy finds its only worthy forerunner in the Book of Job, to which John Holloway and Frank Kermode have compared it.

A comparison between the sufferings of Job and of Lear is likely to lead to some startling conclusions about the preternatural persuasiveness of Shakespearean representation, being as it is an art whose limits we have yet to discover. This art convinces us that Lear exposed to the storm, out on the heath, is a designedly Jobean figure. To be thrown from being king of Britain to a fugitive in the open, pelted by merciless weather, and betrayed by ungrateful daughters, is indeed an unpleasant fate, but is it truly Jobean? Job, after all, has experienced an even more dreadful sublimity: his sons, daughters, servants, sheep, camels, and houses all have been destroyed by Satanic fires, and his direct, physical torment far transcends Lear's, not to mention that he still suffers his wife, while we never do hear anything about Lear's queen, who amazingly brought forth monsters of the deep in Goneril and Regan, but also Cordelia, a soul in bliss. What would Lear's wife have said, had she accompanied her royal husband onto the heath?

> So went Satan forth from the presence of the LORD, and smote Job with sore boils from the sole of his foot unto his crown.
>
> And he took him a potsherd to scrape himself withal; and he sat down among the ashes.
>
> Then said his wife unto him, Dost thou still retain thine integrity? curse God, and die.

That Shakespeare intended his audience to see Job as the model for Lear's situation (though hardly for Lear himself) seems likely, on the basis of a pattern of allusions in the drama. An imagery that associates humans with worms, and with dust, is strikingly present in both works. Lear himself presumably thinks of Job when he desperately asserts, "I will be the pattern of all patience," a dreadful irony considering the king's ferociously impatient nature. Job is the righteous man handed over to the Accuser, but Lear is a blind king, who knows neither himself nor his daughters. Though Lear suffers the storm's fury, he is not Job-like either in his earlier sufferings (which he greatly magnifies) or in his relationship to the divine. It is another indication of Shakespeare's strong originality that he persuades us of the Jobean dignity and grandeur of Lear's first sufferings, even though to a considerable degree they are brought about by Lear himself, in sharp contrast to Job's absolute blamelessness. When Lear says that he is a man more sinned against than sinning, we tend to believe him, but is this really true at that point?

Only proleptically, as a prophecy, but again this is Shakespeare's astonishing originality, founded upon the representation of *impending change*, a change to be worked within Lear by his own listening to, and reflecting upon, what he himself speaks aloud in his increasing fury. He goes into the storm scene on the heath still screaming in anger, goes mad with that anger, and comes out of the storm with crucial change deeply in process within him, full of paternal love for the Fool and of concern for the supposed madman, Edgar impersonating Poor Tom. Lear's constant changes from then until the terrible end remain the most remarkable instance of a representation of a human transformation anywhere in imaginative literature.

But why did Shakespeare risk the paradigm of Job, since Lear, early and late, is so unlike Job, and since the play is anything but a theodicy? Milton remarked that the Book of Job was the rightful model for a "brief epic," such as his *Paradise Regained*, but in what sense can it be an appropriate model for a tragedy? Shakespeare may have been pondering his setting of *King Lear* in a Britain seven centuries before the time of Christ, a placement historically earlier than he attempted anywhere else, except for the Trojan War of *Troilus and Cressida*. *Lear* presumably is not a Christian play, though Cordelia is an eminently Christian personage, who says that she is about her father's business, in an overt allusion to the Gospel of Luke. But the Christian God and Jesus Christ are not relevant to the cosmos of *King Lear*. So appalling is the tragedy of this tragedy that Shakespeare shrewdly sets it before the Christian dispensation, in what he may have intuited was the time of Job. If *Macbeth* is Shakespeare's one full-scale venture into a Gnostic cosmos (and I think it was), then *King Lear* risks a more complete and catastrophic tragedy than anything in the genre before or since.

Job, rather oddly, ultimately receives the reward of his virtue; but Lear, purified and elevated, suffers instead the horror of Cordelia's murder by the underlings of Edmund. I think then that Shakespeare invoked the Book of Job in order to emphasize the absolute negativity of Lear's tragedy. Had Lear's wife been alive, she would have done well to emulate Job's wife, so as to advise her husband to curse God and die. Pragmatically, it would have been a better fate than the one Lear finally suffers in the play.

II

The Gloucester subplot may be said to work deliberately against Lear's Jobean sense of his own uniqueness as a sufferer; his tragedy will not be the one he desires, for it is not so much a tragedy of filial ingratitude as of a kind of apocalyptic nihilism, universal in its implications. We do not sympathize with Lear's immense curses, though they are increasingly related to his rising fear of madness, which is also his fear of a womanly nature rising up within him. Finally Lear's madness, like his curses, proceeds from his biblical sense of himself; desiring to be everything in himself, he fears greatly that he is nothing in himself. His obsession with his own blindness seems related to an aging vitalist's fear of impotence and so of mortality. Yet Lear is not just any old hero, nor even just a great king falling away into madness and death. Shakespeare allows him a diction more preternaturally eloquent than is spoken by anyone else in this or any other drama, and that evidently never will be matched again. Lear matters because his language is uniquely strong, and because we are persuaded that this splendor is wholly appropriate to him.

We can remark, following Nietzsche and Freud, that only one Western image participates neither in origin nor in end: the image of the father. Lear, more than Gloucester, more than any other figure even in Shakespeare, is *the* image of the father, the metaphor of paternal authority. Nature, in the drama, is both origin and end, mother and catastrophe, and it ought to be Lear's function to hold and safeguard the middle ground between the daemonic world and the realm of the gods. He fails, massively, and the ensuing tragedy engulfs an entire world, with a poignance unmatched in literature:

> *Enter* LEAR [*mad, crowned with weeds and flowers*].
>   But who comes here?
> The safer sense will ne'er accommodate
> His master thus.
> LEAR: No, they cannot touch me for [coining,] I am the King himself.
> EDG: O thou side-piercing sight!
> LEAR: Nature's above art in that respect. There's your press-money. That fellow handles his bow like a crow-keeper; draw me a clothier's yard. Look, look, a mouse! Peace, peace, this piece of toasted cheese will do't. There's my gauntlet, I'll prove it on a giant. Bring up the brown bills. O, well flown, bird! i' th' clout, i' th' clout—hewgh! Give the word.
> EDG: Sweet marjorum.
> LEAR: Pass.
> GLOU: I know that voice.
> LEAR: Ha! Goneril with a white beard? They flatter'd me like a dog, and told me I had the white hairs in my beard ere the black ones were there. To say "ay" and "no" to every thing that I said! "Ay," and "no" too, was no good divinity. When the rain came to wet me once, and the wind to make me chatter, when the thunder would not peace at my bidding, there I found 'em, there I smelt 'em out. Go to, they are not men o' their words: they told me I was every thing. 'Tis a lie, I am not ague-proof.
> GLOU: The trick of that voice I do well remember. Is't not the King?
> LEAR: Ay, every inch a king!
>   when I do stare, see how the subject quakes.

I pardon that man's life. What was thy cause?
Adultery?
Thou shalt not die. Die for adultery? No,
the wren goes to't, and the small gilded fly
does lecher in my sight.
Let copulation thrive; for gloucester's bastard son
was kinder to his father than my daughters
got 'tween the lawful sheets.
To't, luxury, pell-mell, for I lack soldiers.
Behold yond simp'ring dame,
whose face between her forks presages snow;
that minces virtue, and does shake the head
to hear of pleasure's name—
the fitchew nor the soiled horse goes to't
with a more riotous appetite.
Down from the waist they are centaurs,
though women all above;
but to the girdle do the gods inherit,
beneath is all the fiends': there's hell, there's darkness.
There is the sulphurous pit, burning, scalding,
Stench, consumption. Fie, fie, fie! pah, pah!
Give me an ounce of civet; good apothecary,
Sweeten my imagination. There's money for thee.

GLOU: O, let me kiss that hand!

LEAR: Let me wipe it first, it smells of mortality.

GLOU: O ruin'd piece of nature! this great world Shall so wear out
to nought. Dost thou know me?

LEAR: I remember thine eyes well enough. Dost thou squiny at
me? No, do thy worst, blind Cupid, I'll not love. Read thou
this challenge; mark but the penning of it.

GLOU: Were all thy letters suns, I could not see.

EDG: [*Aside*.] I would not take this from report; it is, And my heart
breaks at it.

LEAR: Read.

GLOU: What, with the case of eyes?

LEAR: O ho, are you there with me? No eyes in your head, nor no
money in your purse? Your eyes are in a heavy case, your
purse in a light, yet you see how this world goes.

GLOU: I see it feelingly.

LEAR: What, art mad? A man may see how this world goes with
no eyes. Look with thine ears; see how yond justice rails upon

yond simple thief. Hark in thine ear: change places, and
handy-dandy, which is the justice, which is the thief? Thou
hast seen a farmer's dog bark at a beggar?

GLOU: Ay, sir.

LEAR: And the creature run from the cur? There thou mightst
behold the great image of authority: a dog's obey'd in office.
Thou rascal beadle, hold thy bloody hand!
Why dost thou lash that whore? Strip thy own back,
Thou hotly lusts to use her in that kind
For which thou whip'st her. The usurer hangs the cozener.
Thorough tatter'd clothes [small] vices do appear;
Robes and furr'd gowns hide all. [Plate sin] with gold,
And the strong lance of justice hurtless breaks;
Arm it in rags, a pigmy's straw does pierce it.
None does offend, none, I say none, I'll able 'em.
Take that of me, my friend, who have the power
To seal th' accuser's lips. Get thee glass eyes,
And like a scurvy politician, seem
To see the things thou dost not. Now, now, now, now.
Pull off my boots; harder, harder—so.

EDG: [*Aside.*] O, matter and impertinency mix'd, Reason in madness!

LEAR: If thou wilt weep my fortunes, take my eyes.
I know thee well enough, thy name is Gloucester.
Thou must be patient; we came crying hither.
Thou know'st, the first time that we smell the air
We wawl and cry. I will preach to thee. Mark.

[LEAR *takes off his crown of weeds and flowers.*]

GLOU: Alack, alack the day!

LEAR: When we are born, we cry that we are come To this great
stage of fools.—

Kermode justly remarks of this scene that it is at once Shakespeare's
boldest effort of imagination and utterly lacking in merely *narrative* function. Indeed, it strictly lacks all function, and the tragedy does not need it.
We do not reason the need: poetic language never has gone further. Edgar,
who once pretended madness, begins by observing that "the safer sense" or
sane mind cannot accommodate itself to the vision of the ultimate paternal authority having gone mad. But "safer sense" here also refers to seeing,
and the entire scene is a vastation organized about the dual images of eye-
sight and of fatherhood, images linked yet also severed throughout the

Vastation: a laying waste

play. The sight that pierces Edgar's side is intolerable to a quiet hero whose only quest has been to preserve the image of his father's authority. His father, blinded Gloucester, recognizing authority by its voice, laments the mad king as nature's ruined masterpiece and prophesies that a similar madness will wear away the entire world into nothingness. The prophecy will be fulfilled in the drama's closing scene, but is deferred so that the reign of "reason in madness" or sight in blindness can be continued. Pathos transcends all limits in Lear's great and momentary breakthrough into sanity, as it cries out to Gloucester, and to all of us, "If thou wilt weep my fortune, take my eyes."

Hardly the pattern of all patience, Lear nevertheless has earned the convincing intensity of telling Gloucester, "Thou must be patient." What follows however is not Jobean but Shakespearean, perhaps even the essence of the drama's prophecy: "we came crying hither" and "When we are born, we cry that we are come / To this great stage of fools." The great theatrical trope encompasses every meaning the play crams into the word "fool": actor, moral being, idealist, child, dear one, madman, victim, truthteller. As Northrop Frye observes, the only characters in *King Lear* who are not fools are Edmund, Goneril, Regan, Cornwall, and their followers.

III

Lear's own Fool undergoes a subtle transformation as the drama burns on, from an oracle of forbidden wisdom to a frightened child, until at last he simply disappears, as though he blent into the identity of the dead Cordelia when the broken Lear cries out, "And my poor fool is hang'd!" Subtler still is the astonishing transformation of the most interesting consciousness in the play, the bastard Edmund, Shakespeare's most intensely theatrical villain, surpassing even Richard III and Iago. Edmund, as theatrical as Barabas, Marlowe's Jew of Malta, might almost be a sly portrait of Christopher Marlowe himself. As the purest and coolest Machiavel in stage history, at least until he knows he has received his death-wound, Edmund is both a remarkably antic and charming Satan, and a being with real self-knowledge, which makes him particularly dangerous in a world presided over by Lear, "who hath ever but slenderly known himself," as Regan remarks.

Edmund's mysterious and belated metamorphosis as the play nears its end, a movement from playing oneself to being oneself, turns upon his complex reactions to his own deathly musing: "Yet Edmund was beloved." It is peculiarly shocking and pathetic that his lovers were Goneril and Regan, monsters who proved their love by suicide and murder, or by victimage, but Shakespeare seems to have wished to give us a virtuoso display of his original art in changing character through the representation of a growing inwardness. Outrageously refreshing at his most evil (Edgar is a virtuous bore in contrast to him), Edmund is the most attractive of Jacobean hero-villains and inevitably captures both Goneril and Regan, evidently with singularly little effort. His dangerous attractiveness is one of the principal unexplored clues to the enigmas of Shakespeare's most sublime achievement. That Edmund has gusto, an exuberance befitting his role as natural son, is merely part of the given. His intelligence and will are more central to him, and darken the meanings of *King Lear*.

Wounded to death by Edgar, his brother, Edmund yields to fortune: "The wheel is come full circle, I am here." Where he is not is upon Lear's "wheel of fire," in a place of saving madness. Not only do Edmund and Lear exchange not a single word in the course of this vast drama, but it defies imagination to conceive of what they could say to one another. It is not only the intricacies of the double-plot that keep Edmund and Lear apart; they have no language in common. Frye points out that "nature" takes on antithetical meanings in regard to the other, in Lear and Edmund, and this can be expanded to the realization that Lear, despite all his faults, is incapable of guile, but Edmund is incapable of an honest passion of any kind. The lover of both Goneril and Regan, he is passive towards both, and is moved by their deaths only to reflect upon what was for him the extraordinary reality that anyone, however monstrous, ever should have loved him at all.

Why does he reform, however belatedly and ineffectually, since Cordelia is murdered anyway; what are we to make of his final turn towards the light? Edmund's first reaction towards the news of the deaths of Goneril and Regan is the grimly dispassionate, "I was contracted to them both; all three / Now marry in an instant," which identifies dying and marrying as a single act. In the actual moment of repentance, Edmund desperately says, "I pant for life. Some good I mean to do, / Despite of my own nature." This is not to say that nature no longer is his goddess, but rather that he is finally touched by images of connection or concern, be they as far apart as Edgar's care for Gloucester, or Goneril's and Regan's fiercely competitive lust for his own person.

I conclude by returning to my fanciful speculation that the Faustian Edmund is not only overtly Marlovian, but indeed may be Shakespeare's charmed but wary portrait of elements in Christopher Marlowe himself. Edmund represents the way not to go, and yet is the only figure in *King Lear* who is truly at home in its apocalyptic cosmos. The wheel comes full circle for him, but he has limned his nightpiece, and it was his best.

Antony and Cleopatra

Freud taught us that the therapy-of-therapies is not to invest too much libido in any single object whosoever. Antony at last refuses this wisdom and in consequence suffers what must be called an erotic tragedy, but then Cleopatra, who has spent her life exemplifying the same wisdom, suffers an erotic tragedy also, on Antony's account, one act of the drama more belatedly than he does. *The Tragedy of Antony and Cleopatra* is unique among Shakespeare's plays in that the tragedy's doubleness, equal in both man and woman as it was with Romeo and Juliet, takes place between equally titanic personages. Each truly is all but everything in himself and herself, and *knows* it, and neither fears that he or she is really nothing in himself or herself, or nothing without the other. Both consciously play many parts, and yet also *are* those other parts. Both are adept at playing themselves, yet also at being themselves. Like Falstaff and Hamlet, they are supreme personalities, major wits, grand counter-Machiavels (though overmatched by Octavian, greatest of Machiavels), and supreme consciousnesses. They fall in love with one another, resist and betray the love repeatedly, but finally yield to it and are destroyed by it, in order fully to fulfill their allied natures. More even than the death of Hamlet, we react to their suicides as a human triumph and as a release for ourselves. But why? And how?

The crucial originality here is to have represented two great personalities, the Herculean hero proper and a woman of infinite guile and resource, in their overwhelming decline and mingled ruin. A destruction through authentic and mutual love becomes an aesthetic redemption precisely because love's shadow is ruin. We have no representations of this kind before Shakespeare, since a Euripidean vision of erotic ruin, as in the *Medea*, permits no aesthetic redemption, while Virgil's Dido, like Medea, is a solitary sufferer. Antony and Cleopatra repeatedly betray one another, and betray themselves, yet these betrayals are forgiven by them and by us, since they become phases of apotheosis that release the sparks of grandeur even as the lamps are shattered.

From act 4, scene 14, through to the end of the play, we hear something wonderfully original even for Shakespeare, a great dying fall, the release of a new music. It begins with the dialogue between Antony and his marvelously named, devoted follower, Eros:

ANTONY. Eros, thou yet behold'st me?
EROS. 						Ay, noble lord.
ANTONY. Sometime we see a cloud that's dragonish,

> A vapor sometime like a bear or lion,
> A [tower'd] citadel, a pendant rock,
> A forked mountain, or blue promontory
> With trees upon't that nod unto the world,
> And mock our eyes with air. Thou hast seen these signs,
> They are black vesper's pageants.
>
> EROS.   Ay, my lord.
> ANTONY. That which is now a horse, even with a thought
>   The rack dislimns, and makes it indistinct
>   As water is in water.
> EROS.   It does, my lord.
> ANTONY. My good knave Eros, now thy captain is
>   Even such a body. Here I am Antony,
>   Yet cannot hold this visible shape, my knave.
>   I made these wars for Egypt, and the Queen,
>   Whose heart I thought I had, for she had mine—
>   Which whilst it was mine had annex'd unto't
>   A million more (now lost)—she, Eros, has
>   Pack'd cards with Caesar's, and false-play'd my glory
>   Unto an enemy's triumph.
>   Nay, weep not, gentle Eros, there is left us
>   Ourselves to end ourselves.

There is a deliberate touch of the cloud-watching Hamlet in Antony here, but with Hamlet's parodistic savagery modulated into a gentleness that befits the transmutation of the charismatic hero into a self transcendent consciousness, almost beyond the consolations of farewell. The grandeur of this transformation is enhanced when Antony receives the false tidings Cleopatra sends of her supposed death, with his name her last utterance:

> Unarm, Eros, the long day's task is done,
> And we must sleep.

The answering chorus to that splendor is Cleopatra's, when he dies in her arms:

> The crown o'th'earth doth melt. My lord!
> O, wither'd is the garland of the war,
> The soldier's pole is fall'n! Young boys and girls
> Are level now with men; the odds is gone,

And there is nothing left remarkable
Beneath the visiting moon.

Antony touches the Sublime as he prepares to die, but Cleopatra's lament for a lost Sublime is the prelude to a greater sublimity, which is to be wholly her own. She is herself a great actress, so that the difficulty in playing her, for any actress, is quite extraordinary. And though she certainly loved Antony, it is inevitable that, like any great actress, she must love herself all but apocalyptically. Antony has a largeness about him surpassing any other Shakespearean hero except for Hamlet; he is an ultimate version of the charismatic leader, loved and followed because his palpable glory can be shared, in some degree, since he is also magnificently generous. But Shakespeare shrewdly ends him with one whole act of the play to go, and retrospectively we see that the drama is as much Cleopatra's as the two parts of *Henry IV* are Falstaff's.

Remarkable as Antony is in himself, he interests us primarily because he has the splendor that makes him as much a catastrophe for Cleopatra as she is for him. Cleopatra is in love with his exuberance, with the preternatural vitality that impresses even Octavian. But she knows, as we do, that Antony lacks her infinite variety. Their love, in Freudian terms, is not narcissistic but anaclitic; they are propped upon one another, cosmological beings who are likely to be bored by anyone else, by any personality neither their own nor one another's. Antony is Cleopatra's only true match and yet he is not her equal, which may be the most crucial or deepest meaning of the play. An imaginative being in that he moves the imagination of others, he is simply not an imaginer of her stature. He need not play himself, he is Herculean. Cleopatra ceases to play herself only when she is transmuted by his death and its aftermath, and we cannot be sure, even then, that she is not both performing and simultaneously becoming that more transcendent self. Strangely like the dying Hamlet in this single respect, she suggests, at the end, that she stands upon a new threshold of being:

I am fire and air; my other elements
I give to baser life.

Is she no longer the earth of Egypt, or the water of the Nile? We have not exactly thought of her as a devoted mother, despite her children by Julius Caesar and by Antony, but in her dying dialogue with Charmian she transmutes the asps, first into her baby, and then apparently into an Antony she might have brought to birth, as in some sense indeed she did:

CHARMIAN. O eastern star!
CLEOPATRA.   Peace, peace!
Dost thou not see my baby at my breast,
    That sucks the nurse asleep?
CHARMIAN. O, break! O, break!
CLEOPATRA. As sweet as balm, as soft as air, as gentle—O
    Antony!—Nay, I will take thee too:
        [*Applying another asp to her arm.*]
    What should I stay—   *Dies.*

As Lear dies, Kent cries out "Break, heart, I prithee break!" even as
Charmian does here, not wishing upon the rack of this tough world to
stretch Cleopatra out longer. When Antony's men find him wounded to
death, they lament that "the star is fall'n," and that "time is at his period."
Charmian's "O eastern star!" associates one dying lover with the other,
even as her echo of Kent suggests that the dying Empress of the East is in
something like the innocence of Lear's madness. Cleopatra is sucked to
sleep as a mother is by a child, or a woman by a lover, and dies in such
peace that Octavian, of all men, is moved to the ultimate tribute:

        she looks like sleep,
As she would catch another Antony
In her strong toil of grace.

Bewildering us by her final manifestation of her infinite variety,
Cleopatra dies into a beyond, a Sublime where actress never trod.

Coriolanus

William Hazlitt, writing in 1816, gave us what seems to me the most
provocative criticism that Shakespeare's Coriolanus has received.
Beginning with the observation that the play was "a storehouse of political
commonplaces," Hazlitt sadly observed that Shakespeare, unlike himself,
seemed a man of the Right, if only because "the cause of the people is
indeed but little calculated as a subject for poetry." It might be salutary if
many of our contemporary students of literature, who wish to make of it
an instrument for social change, would meditate upon Hazlitt's profound
reflections on poetry's love of power:

The language of poetry naturally falls in with the language of
power. The imagination is an exaggerating and exclusive faculty:

it takes from one thing to add to another: it accumulates circumstances together to give the greatest possible effect to a favourite object. The understanding is a dividing and measuring faculty, it judges of things not according to their immediate impression on the mind, but according to their relations to one another. The one is a monopolising faculty, which seeks the greatest quantity of present excitement by inequality and disproportion; the other is a distributive faculty, which seeks the greatest quantity of ultimate good, by justice and proportion. The one is an aristocratical, the other a republican faculty. The principle of poetry is a very anti-levelling principle. It aims at effect, it exists by contrast. It admits of no medium. It is everything by excess. It rises above the ordinary standard of sufferings and crimes. It presents a dazzling appearance. It shows its head turretted, crowned, and crested. Its front is gilt and blood-stained. Before it "it carries noise, and behind it leaves tears." It has its altars and its victims, sacrifices, human sacrifices. Kings, priests, nobles, are its train-bearers, tyrants and slaves its executioners.— "Carnage is its daughter."—Poetry is right-royal. It puts the individual for the species, the one above the infinite many, might before right. A lion hunting a flock of sheep or a herd of wild asses is a more poetical object than they; and we even take part with the lordly beast, because our vanity or some other feeling makes us disposed to place ourselves in the situation of the strongest party. So we feel some concern for the poor citizens of Rome when they meet together to compare their wants and grievances, till Coriolanus comes in and with blows and big words drives this set of "poor rats," this rascal scum, to their homes and beggary before him. There is nothing heroical in a multitude of miserable rogues not wishing to be starved, or complaining that they are like to be so; but when a single man comes forward to brave their cries and to make them submit to the last indignities, from mere pride and self-will, our admiration of his prowess is immediately converted into contempt for their pusillanimity. The insolence of power is stronger than the plea of necessity. The tame submission to usurped authority or even the natural resistance to it has nothing to excite or flatter the imagination: it is the assumption of a right to insult or oppress others that carries an imposing air of superiority with it. We had rather be the oppressor than the oppressed. The love of power in ourselves and the admiration of it in others are both natural to man: the one makes him a tyrant, the other a slave.

Even I initially resist the dark implications of Hazlitt's crucial insight: "The principle of poetry is a very anti-levelling principle." Wallace Stevens, who like Hazlitt and Nietzsche took the lion as the emblem of poetry, tells us that poetry is a destructive force: "The lion sleeps in the sun ... / It could kill a man." Hazlitt, an unreconstructed Jacobin, writes with the authority of the strongest literary critic that the European Left has yet produced. I prefer him to T.S. Eliot on *Coriolanus*, not just because Eliot writes with the grain politically, as it were, and Hazlitt against it, but because the Romantic critic also understands the drama's family romance better than the poet of *The Waste Land* does.

Eliot certainly was fonder of Coriolanus than Hazlitt could find it in himself to be. I cannot quarrel with Hazlitt's account of the Roman hero's motivations: "Coriolanus complains of the fickleness of the people: yet, the instant he cannot gratify his pride and obstinacy at their expense, he turns his arms against his country." When Volumnia cries out for the pestilence to strike all trades and occupations in Rome, because they have defied her son, Hazlitt allows himself a splendidly mordant comment:

This is but natural: it is but natural for a mother to have more regard for her son than for a whole city; but then the city should be left to take some care of itself. The care of the state cannot, we here see, be safely entrusted to maternal affection, or to the domestic charities of high life. The great have private feelings of their own, to which the interests of humanity and justice must courtesy. Their interests are so far from being the same as those of the community, that they are in direct and necessary opposition to them; their power is at the expense of our weakness; their riches of our poverty; their pride of our degradation; their splendour of our wretchedness; their tyranny of our servitude. If they had the superior knowledge ascribed to them (which they have not) it would only render them so much more formidable; and from Gods would convert them into Devils. The whole dramatic moral of *Coriolanus* is that those who have little shall have less, and that those who have much shall take all that others have left. The people are poor; therefore they ought to be starved. They are slaves; therefore they ought to be beaten. They work hard; therefore they ought to be treated like beasts of burden. They are ignorant; therefore they ought not to be allowed to feel that they want food, or clothing, or rest, that they are enslaved, oppressed, and miserable. This is the logic of the imagination and the passions; which seek to aggrandize what excites admiration and to heap contempt on misery, to raise power into tyranny, and to make tyranny absolute; to thrust down that which is low still lower, and to make wretches desperate: to exalt magistrates into kings, kings into gods; to degrade subjects to the rank of slaves, and slaves to the condition of brutes. The history of mankind is a romance, a mask, a tragedy, constructed upon the principles of *poetical justice*; it is a noble or royal hunt, in which what is sport to the few is death to the many, and in which the spectators halloo and encourage the strong to set upon the weak, and cry havoc in the chase though they do not share in the spoil. We may depend upon it that what men delight to read in books, they will put in practice in reality.

Poetical justice is not political or social justice, because it ensues from the royal hunt of the imagination. Hazlitt is not concerned that this should be so; poetry and power marry one another. His proper concern, as a literary critic who would die for social change if he could, is that we protect ourselves, not against literature, but against those who would make a wrong because literal use of the poetics of power. Shrewd as Hazlitt's political insight is, his best insight into the play comes when he contrasts the attitudes toward Coriolanus of Volumnia, his mother, and Virgilia, his wife: "The one is only anxious for his honour; the other is fearful for his life." Glory indeed is Volumnia's obsession; Shakespeare makes her Homeric, a sort of female Achilles, while Coriolanus is more like Virgil's Turnus (as Howard Felperin notes), which may be why his wife is named Virgilia. What is most problematical in *Coriolanus* is the hero's relationship to his fierce mother, a relationship unique in Shakespeare.

II

Volumnia hardly bears discussion, once we have seen that she would be at home wearing armor in *The Iliad*. She is about as sympathetic as the Greek heroes in Shakespeare's *Troilus and Cressida*. Coriolanus himself sustains endless analysis and meditation; even the question of our sympathy for him is forever open. Neither a beast nor a god, he is a great soldier, far greater even than Antony or Othello. Indeed, to call him merely a great soldier seems quite inadequate. He is a one-man army, unique and pure, a sport of nurture rather than of nature, a dreadful monument to his mother's remorseless drive, her will-to-power. Perhaps he resembles Spenser's Talus, the iron man, more even than he suggests Virgil's Turnus. He has no military weaknesses, and no civilian strengths. Politically he is a walking and breathing disaster, in a play that persistently imposes politics upon him. The play would fail if Coriolanus were totally unsympathetic to us, and clearly the play is very strong, though its virtues do not make less weird Eliot's celebrated judgment that *Hamlet* was an aesthetic failure, while *Coriolanus* was Shakespeare's best tragedy. Hamlet contains us, while Coriolanus does not even contain himself. As several critics have remarked, he is a kind of baby Mars, and is very nearly empty, a moral void. How can a baby nullity possibly be a tragic hero?

For Frank Kermode, *Coriolanus* is a tragedy of ideas, but Kermode is unable to tell us what the ideas are, and though he calls Coriolanus a great man, he also does not tell us in just what that greatness consists. I may be unjust to Kermode if the crucial idea turns out to be solipsism and if the greatness of Coriolanus is in his imperfect solipsism which cannot become perfect so long as Volumnia is alive. But solipsism, perfect or not, constitutes greatness in a poet, rather than in a tragic hero. Milton's Satan is an almost perfect solipsist, and that, rather than his splendid wickedness, is why he is a heroic villain and not the hero of a cosmic tragedy. Satan is a great poet, almost the archetype of the modern strong poet (as I have written elsewhere). Coriolanus has no imagination and is no poet at all, except when he provokes his own catastrophe.

Kenneth Burke's *Coriolanus* is a tragedy of the grotesque, which I translate as meaning that politics and the grotesque are one and the same, and that seems fair and true enough. Coriolanus is to Burke a master of invective, rather like Shakespeare's Timon, and the wielder of invective makes a convincing tragic scapegoat. That gives us still the question of this hero's eminence; is he more than a great (and prideful) killing machine? A.D. Nuttall, in his admirable study of Shakespearean mimesis, finds the warrior's aristocratic spirit to be both large and shallow, "at one and same time a sort of Titan and a baby." But how can we get at the Titanism, or is it actually a mockery of the old giants, so that Coriolanus is merely a prophecy of General George Patton? Nuttall shrewdly takes away everything he gives Coriolanus, whose "character is one of great pathos," but: "The pathos lies in the fact that he has no inside." Again, Nuttall salutes Coriolanus for one moment of "true Stoic grandeur," when he replies to banishment with: "I banish you." Nuttall then adds that we see a red-faced child in a temper tantrum. As Nuttall says, this is superb mimesis, but can we greatly care what happens to such a hero? In Homer, the answer would be affirmative, since Achilles is at least as much a spoiled child as Coriolanus is. Yet Achilles is a poet also, a powerful imagination brooding bitterly upon its own mortality, and so we care what happens to him. His greatness is convincing not just because others reflect it to us, but because his eloquence is universally persuasive.

Harold C. Goddard, the most generous and perceptive of all Shakespearean critics, finds the one fault of Coriolanus to be that he "lacks unconsciousness of his virtue." Less generously, we could label Coriolanus an instance of "Mars as narcissist," rather than Goddard's "proud idealist" who is entirely a victim of his virago of a mother. Perhaps the ambivalence that Coriolanus provokes in us can be set aside if we contemplate his heroic death scene, wholly appropriate for a tragic protagonist in Shakespeare:

CORIOLANUS: Hear'st thou, Mars?
AUFIDIUS: Name not the god, thou boy of tears!
CORIOLANUS: Ha?
AUFIDIUS: No more.
CORIOLANUS: Measureless liar, thou hast made my heart
    Too great for what contains it. "Boy"? O slave!
    Pardon me, lords, 'tis the first time that ever
    I was forc'd to scold. Your judgments, my grave lords,
    Must give this cur the lie; and his own notion—
    Who wears my stripes impress'd upon him, that
    Must bear my beating to his grave—shall join
    To thrust the lie unto him.
1. LORD: Peace both, and hear me speak.
CORIOLANUS: Cut me to pieces, Volsces, men and lads,
    Stain all your edges on me. "Boy," false hound!
    If you have writ your annals true, 'tis there
    That, like an eagle in a dove-cote, I
    [Flutter'd] your Volscians in Corioles.
    Alone I did it. "Boy"!
AUFIDIUS: Why, noble lords,
    Will you be put in mind of his blind fortune,
    Which was your shame, by this unholy braggart,
    'Fore your own eyes and ears?
ALL CONSPIRATORS: Let him die for't.
ALL PEOPLE: Tear him to pieces! Do it presently!—
    He kill'd my son!—My daughter!—He kill'd
    my cousin Marcus!—
    He kill'd my father!
2. LORD: Peace ho! no outrage, peace!
    The man is noble, and his fame folds in
    This orb o' th' earth. His last offenses to us
    Shall have judicious hearing. Stand, Aufidius,
    And trouble not the peace.

CORIOLANUS: O that I had him,
    With six Aufidiuses, or more, his tribe,
    To use my lawful sword!
AUFIDIUS: Insolent villain!
ALL CONSPIRATORS: Kill, kill, kill, kill, kill him!
    Draw the Conspirators, and kills Martius, who falls.

This is Coriolanus at his worst and at his best, with the extremes not
to be disentangled. His triple repetition of "Boy" reflects his fury both at
Aufidius's insolence and at his own subservience to his mother, whose boy
he now knows he will never cease to be. Yet his vision of himself as an eagle
fluttering his enemies' dove-cotes raises his legitimate pride to an ecstasy
in which we share, and we are captured by his exultant and accurate "Alone
I did it." There is his tragedy, and his grandeur: "Alone I did it." If they
have writ their annals true, then he is content to be cut to pieces by them.
His death is tragic because it is a *sparagmos*, not Orphic, but not the death
of Turnus either. What is torn apart is the last representative of the heroism that fights alone and wins alone, and that can find no place in the world
of the commonal and the communal.

THE HISTORIES

Shakespeare's greatest history play is the ten-act drama constituted by *King
Henry IV—Parts One and Two*. Judged as a single work, this vast Falstaffiad
is one of Shakespeare's major achievements, akin to *Antony and Cleopatra*,
As You Like It, *Twelfth Night*, *Measure for Measure*, and *The Winter's Tale*.
The four high tragedies—*Hamlet*, *Othello*, *King Lear*, and *Macbeth*—stand
a little apart, in their own cosmos, as does *The Tempest*. The Falstaffiad is
at the center of Shakespeare's work, and its superb protagonist, Sir John
Falstaff, rivals Shakespeare's other triumphs in the invention of the human:
Hamlet, Rosalind, Iago, Lear, Macbeth, Cleopatra.

Criticism, particularly in our century, is frequently both inaccurate
and unkind about Falstaff. That is because the brilliant and uncanny wit
outfaces and outrages his undertakers. He also buries them. Falstaff is so
large a form of life and thought that all of us have trouble catching up with
him. He confounds our expectations, and calls our compromises into question.

Falstaff's vitality, his battle-cry being: "Give me life," is the most crucial of his attributes, but his intelligence is endless, and matches his exuberance. Nearly everything he says rewards much pondering, for he
beholds reality, and not the shams that mock it. Sir John long since has

seen through the "honor" for which Hotspur and Prince Hal compete. Falstaff may be an outrageous Socrates, but so was Socrates. Sir John's other affinities are with Cervantes's Sancho Panza and with Rabelais's Panurge, and most closely with Chaucer's Wife of Bath. Heroic vitalists all, these abide as images of gusto in its highest form, allied to wisdom and to laughter.

Aligned against Falstaff are the state and time, and the state, in the guise of the newly crowned Henry V, will destroy him. Though legions of scholars have acclaimed this destruction, their sentiments are not Shakespeare's. Shakespeare carefully excluded Falstaff from *Henry V*, except for Mistress Quickly's poignant description of Sir John's deathbed scene. Can we imagine King Henry V eloquently saluting his "happy few" if Falstaff were among them, bottle of sack in his holster?

In his darker moments, Falstaff is haunted by the parable of Lazarus the leper and a purple-clad glutton who refuses him food and water (Luke 16:19–26). This is a parable of rejection, first of Lazarus by the wealthy glutton, and then of the glutton by Abraham, who takes Lazarus into his bosom while refusing to aid the stingy rich man, who burns in hell. Falstaff's three allusions to this parable reveal his own fear of rejection by Hal, an apprehension that is realized when Falstaff kneels to the purple-clad newly crowned Henry V, and is denounced and exiled. Shakespeare's answer comes in Mistress Quickly's declaration that the deceased Falstaff is "in Arthur's bosom," a clear displacement of Abraham's bosom.

A.C. Bradley, nearly a century ago, made the definitive comment upon the sublime Falstaff:

> And, therefore, we praise him, we laud him, for he offends none but the virtuous, and denies that life is real or life is earnest, and delivers us from the apprehension of such nightmares, and lifts us into the atmosphere of perfect freedom.

Henry IV, Parts 1 and 2

Falstaff is to the world of the histories what Shylock is to the comedies and Hamlet to the tragedies: *the* problematical representation. Falstaff, Shylock, Hamlet put to us the question: precisely how does Shakespearean representation differ from anything before it, and how has it overdetermined our expectations of representation ever since?

The fortunes of Falstaff in scholarship and criticism have been endlessly dismal, and I will not resume them here. I prefer Harold Goddard on Falstaff to any other commentator, and yet I am aware that Goddard appears to have sentimentalized and even idealized Falstaff. I would say better that than the endless litany absurdly patronizing Falstaff as Vice, Parasite, Fool, Braggart Soldier, Corrupt Glutton, Seducer of Youth, Cowardly Liar, and everything else that would not earn the greatest wit in all literature an honorary degree at Yale or a place on the board of the Ford Foundation.

Falstaff, I will venture, in Shakespeare rather than in Verdi, is precisely what Nietzsche tragically attempted yet failed to represent in his Zarathustra: a person without a superego, or should I say, Socrates without the *daimon*. Perhaps even better, Falstaff is not the Sancho Panza of Cervantes, but the exemplary figure of Kafka's parable "The Truth about Sancho Panza." Kafka's Sancho Panza, a free man, has diverted his *daimon* from him by many nightly feedings of chivalric romances (it would be science fiction nowadays). Diverted from Sancho, his true object, the *daimon* becomes the harmless Don Quixote, whose mishaps prove edifying entertainment for the "philosophic" Sancho, who proceeds to follow his errant *daimon*, out of a sense of responsibility. Falstaff's "failure," if it can be termed that, is that he fell in love, not with his own *daimon*, but with his bad son, Hal, who all too truly is Bolingbroke's son. The witty knight should have diverted his own *daimon* with Shakespearean comedies, and philosophically have followed the *daimon* off to the forest of Arden.

Falstaff is neither good enough nor bad enough to flourish in the world of the histories. But then he is necessarily beyond, not only good and evil, but cause and effect as well. A greater monist than the young Milton, Falstaff plays at dualism partly in order to mock all dualisms, whether Christian, Platonic, or even the Freudian dualism that he both anticipates and in some sense refutes.

Falstaff provoked the best of all critics, Dr. Johnson, into the judgment that "he has nothing in him that can be esteemed." George Bernard Shaw, perhaps out of envy, called Falstaff "a besotted and disgusting old wretch." Yet Falstaff's sole rival in Shakespeare is Hamlet; no one else, as Oscar Wilde noted, has so comprehensive a consciousness. Representation itself changed permanently because of Hamlet and Falstaff. I begin with my personal favorite among all of Falstaff's remarks, if only because I plagiarize it daily:

> O, thou has damnable iteration, and art indeed able to corrupt a saint. Thou hast done much harm upon me, Hal, God forgive thee for it! Before I knew thee, Hal, I knew nothing, and now am I, if a man should speak truly, little better than one of the wicked.

W.H. Auden, whose Falstaff essentially was Verdi's, believed the knight to be "a comic symbol for the supernatural order of charity" and thus a displacement of Christ into the world of wit. The charm of this reading, though considerable, neglects Falstaff's grandest quality, his immanence. He is as immanent a representation as Hamlet is transcendent. Better than any formulation of Freud's, Falstaff perpetually shows us that the ego indeed is always a bodily ego. And the bodily ego is always vulnerable, and Hal indeed has done much harm upon it, and will do far worse, and will need forgiveness, though no sensitive audience ever will forgive him. Falstaff, like Hamlet, and like Lear's Fool, does speak truly, and Falstaff remains, despite Hal, rather better than one of the wicked, or the good.

For what is supreme immanence in what might be called the order of representation? This is another way of asking: is not Falstaff, like Hamlet, so original a representation that he originates much of what we know or expect about representation? We cannot see how original Falstaff is because Falstaff *contains* us; we do not contain him. And though we love Falstaff, he does not need our love any more than Hamlet does. His sorrow is that he loves Hal rather more than Hamlet loves Ophelia, or even Gertrude. The Hamlet of act 5 is past loving anyone, but that is a gift (if it is a gift) resulting from transcendence. If you dwell wholly in this world, and if you are, as Falstaff is, a *pervasive* entity, or as Freud would say, "a strong egoism," then you must begin to love, as Freud also says, in order that you may not fall ill. But what if your strong egoism is not afflicted by any ego-ideal, what if you are never watched, or watched over, by what is above the ego? Falstaff is *not* subject to a power that watches, discovers, and criticizes all his intentions. Falstaff, except for his single and misplaced love, is free, is freedom itself, because he seems free of the superego.

II

Why does Falstaff (and not his parody in *The Merry Wives of Windsor*) pervade histories rather than comedies? To begin is to be free, and you cannot begin freshly in comedy any more than you can in tragedy. Both genres are family romances, at least in Shakespeare. History in Shakespeare is hardly the genre of freedom for kings and nobles, but it is for Falstaff. How and why? Falstaff is of course his own mother and his own father, begotten out of wit by caprice. Ideally he wants nothing except the audience, which he always has; who could watch anyone else on stage when Ralph Richardson was playing Falstaff? Not so ideally, he evidently wants the love of a son, and invests in Hal, the impossible object. But primarily he has what he must have, the audience's fascination with the ultimate image of freedom. His percursor in Shakespeare is not Puck or Bottom, but Faulconbridge the Bastard in *The Life and Death of King John*. Each has a way of providing a daemonic chorus that renders silly all royal and noble squabbles and intrigues. The Bastard in *John*, forthright like his father Richard the Lion Heart, is not a wicked wit, but his truth-telling brutally prophesies Falstaffs function.

There are very nearly as many Falstaffs as there are critics, which probably is as it should be. These proliferating Falstaffs tend either to be degraded or idealized, again perhaps inevitably. One of the most ambiguous Falstaffs was created by the late Sir William Empson: "He is the scandalous upper-class man whose behavior embarrasses his class and thereby pleases the lower class in the audience, as an 'exposure.'" To Empson, Falstaff also was both nationalist and Machiavel, "and he had a dangerous amount of power." Empson shared the hint of Wyndham Lewis that Falstaff was homosexual, and so presumably lusted (doubtless in vain) after Hal. To complete this portrait, Empson added that Falstaff, being both an aristocrat and a mob leader, was "a familiar dangerous type," a sort of Alcibiades one presumes.

Confronted by so ambiguous a Falstaff, I return to the sublime knight's rhetoric, which I read very differently, since Falstaff's power seems to me not at all a matter of class, sexuality, politics, or nationalism. Power it is: sublime pathos, *potentia*, the drive for life, more life, at every and any cost. I will propose that Falstaff is neither a noble synecdoche nor a grand hyperbole, but rather a metalepsis or far-fetcher, to use Puttenham's term. To exist without a super ego is to be a solar trajectory, an ever-early brightness, which Nietzsche's Zarathustra, in his bathos, failed to be. "Try to live as though it were morning," Nietzsche advises. Falstaff does not need the advice, as we discover when we first encounter him:

FALSTAFF: Now, Hal, what time of day is it, lad?
PRINCE: Thou art so fat-witted with drinking of old sack, and unbuttoning thee after supper, and sleeping upon benches after noon, that thou hast forgotten to demand that truly which thou wouldest truly know. What a devil hast thou to do with the time of the day? unless hours were cups of sack, and minutes capons, and clocks the tongues of bawds, and dials the signs of leaping-houses, and the blessed sun himself a fair hot wench in flame-color'd taffata; I see no reason why thou shouldst be so superfluous to demand the time of the day.

I take it that wit here remains with Falstaff, who is not only witty in himself but the cause of wit in his ephebe, Prince Hal, who mocks his teacher, but in the teacher's own exuberant manner and mode. Perhaps there is a double meaning when Falstaff opens his reply with: "Indeed, you come near me now, Hal," since near is as close as the Prince is capable of, when he imitates the master. Master of what? is the crucial question, generally answered so badly. To take up the stance of most Shakespeare scholars is to associate Falstaff with "such inordinate and low desires, / Such poor, such bare, such lewd, such mean attempts, / Such barren pleasures, rude society." I quote King Henry the Fourth, aggrieved usurper, whose description of Falstaff's aura is hardly recognizable to the audience. We recognize rather: "Counterfeit? I lie, I am no counterfeit. To die is to be a counterfeit, for he is but the counterfeit of a man who hath not the life of a man; but to counterfeit dying, when a man thereby liveth, is to be no counterfeit, but the true and perfect image of life indeed." As Falstaff rightly says, he has saved his life by counterfeiting death, and presumably the moralizing critics would be delighted had the unrespectable knight been butchered by Douglas, "that hot termagant Scot."

The true and perfect image of life, Falstaff, confirms his truth and perfection by counterfeiting dying and so evading death. Though he is given to parodying Puritan preachers, Falstaff has an authentic obsession with the dreadful parable of the rich man and Lazarus in Luke 16:19ff. A certain rich man, a purple-clad glutton, is contrasted with the beggar Lazarus, who desired "to be fed with the crumbs which fell from the rich man's table; moreover the dogs came and licked his sores." Both glutton and beggar die, but Lazarus is carried into Abraham's bosom, and the purple glutton into hell, from which he cries vainly for Lazarus to come and cool his tongue. Falstaff stares at Bardolph, his Knight of the Burning Lamp, and affirms, "I never see thy face but I think upon hell-fire and Dives that liv'd in purple; for there he is in his robes, burning, burning." Confronting his hundred and fifty tattered prodigals, as he marches them off to be food for powder, Falstaff calls them "slaves as ragged as Lazarus in the painted cloth, where the glutton's dogs lick'd his sores." In *Henry IV, Part 2*, Falstaff's first speech again returns to this fearful text, as he cries out against one who denies him credit: "Let him be damn'd like the glutton! Pray God his tongue be hotter!" Despite the ironies abounding in Falstaff the glutton invoking Dives, Shakespeare reverses the New Testament, and Falstaff ends, like Lazarus, in Abraham's bosom, according to the convincing testimony of Mistress Quickly in *Henry V*, where Arthur Britishly replaces Abraham:

BARDOLPH: Would I were with him, wheresome'er he is, either in
     heaven or in hell!
HOSTESS: Nay sure, he's not in hell; he's in Arthur's bosom, if ever
     man went to Arthur's bosom. 'A made a finer end, and went
     away and it had been any christom child.

In dying, Falstaff is a newly baptized child, innocent of all stain. The
pattern of allusions to Luke suggests a crossing over, with the rejected
Falstaff a poor Lazarus upon his knees in front of Dives wearing the royal
purple of Henry V. To a moralizing critic this is outrageous, but
Shakespeare does stranger tricks with biblical texts. Juxtapose the two
moments:

FALSTAFF: My King, my Jove! I speak to thee, my heart!
KING: I know thee not, old man, fall to thy prayers.
     How ill white hairs becomes a fool and jester!
     I have long dreamt of such a kind of man,
     So surfeit-swell'd, so old, and so profane;
     But being awak'd, I do despise my dream.

And here is Abraham, refusing to let Lazarus come to comfort the
"clothed in purple" Dives:

And beside all this, between us and you there is a great gulf fixed:
so that they which would pass from hence to you cannot; neither
can they pass to us, that would come from thence.

Wherever Henry V is, he is not in Arthur's bosom, with the rejected
Falstaff.

III

I suggest that Shakespearean representation in the histories indeed
demands our understanding of what Shakespeare did to history, in contrast
to what his contemporaries did. Standard scholarly views of literary history, and all Marxist reductions of literature and history alike, have the curious allied trait of working very well for, say, Thomas Dekker, but being
absurdly irrelevant for Shakespeare. Falstaff and the Tudor theory of king-
ship? Falstaff and surplus value? I would prefer Falstaff and Nietzsche's
vision of the use and abuse of history for life, if it were not that Falstaff triumphs precisely where the Overman fails. One can read Freud on our

discomfort in culture backwards, and get somewhere close to Falstaff, but the problem again is that Falstaff triumphs precisely where Freud denies that triumph is possible. With Falstaff as with Hamlet (and, perhaps, with Cleopatra) Shakespearean representation is so self-begotten and so influential that we can apprehend it only by seeing that it originates us. We cannot judge a mode of representation that has overdetermined our ideas of representation. Like only a few other authors—the Yahwist, Chaucer, Cervantes, Tolstoy—Shakespeare calls recent critiques of literary representation severely into doubt. Jacob, the Pardoner, Sancho Panza, Hadji Murad: it seems absurd to call them figures of rhetoric, let alone to see Falstaff, Hamlet, Shylock, Cleopatra as tropes of ethos and/or of pathos. Falstaff is not language but diction, the product of Shakespeare's will over language, a will that changes characters through and by what they say. Most simply, Falstaff is not how meaning is renewed, but rather how meaning gets started.

Falstaff is so profoundly original a representation because most truly he represents the essence of invention, which is the essence of poetry. He is a perpetual catastrophe, a continuous transference, a universal family romance. If Hamlet is beyond us and beyond our need of him, so that we require our introjection of Horatio, so as to identify ourselves with Horatio's love for Hamlet, then Falstaff too is beyond us. But in the Falstaffian beyonding, as it were, in what I think we must call the Falstaffian sublimity, we are never permitted by Shakespeare to identify ourselves with the Prince's ambivalent affection for Falstaff. Future monarchs have no friends, only followers, and Falstaff, the man without a superego, is no one's follower. Freud never speculated as to what a person without a superego would be like, perhaps because that had been the dangerous prophecy of Nietzsche's Zarathustra. Is there not some sense in which Falstaff's whole being implicitly says to us, "The wisest among you is also merely a conflict and a hybrid between plant and phantom. But do I bid you become phantoms or plants?" Historical critics who call Falstaff a phantom, and moral critics who judge Falstaff to be a plant, can be left to be answered by Sir John himself. Even in his debased form, in *The Merry Wives of Windsor*, he crushes them thus:

> Have I liv'd to stand at the taunt of one that makes fritters of English? This is enough to be the decay of lust and late-walking through the realm.

But most of all Falstaff is a reproach to all critics who seek to demystify mimesis, whether by Marxist or deconstructionist dialectics. Like

Hamlet, Falstaff is a super-mimesis, and so compels us to see aspects of reality we otherwise could never apprehend. Marx would teach us what he calls "the appropriation of human reality" and so the appropriation also of human suffering. Nietzsche and his deconstructionist descendants would teach us the necessary irony of failure in every attempt to represent human reality. Falstaff, being more of an original, teaches us himself. "No, that's certain, I am not a double man; but if I be not Jack Falstaff, then am I a Jack." A double man is either a phantom or two men, and a man who is two men might as well be a plant. Sir John is Jack Falstaff; it is the Prince who is a Jack or rascal, and so are Falstaff's moralizing critics. We are in no position then to judge Falstaff or to assess him as a representation of reality. Hamlet is too dispassionate even to want to contain us. Falstaff is passionate and challenges us not to bore him, if he is to deign to represent us.

Richard III

> Why, I, in this weak piping time of peace,
> Have no delight to pass away the time,
> Unless to see my shadow in the sun
> And descant on mine own deformity.
> And therefore, since I cannot prove a lover
> To entertain these fair well-spoken days,
> I am determined to prove a villain
> And hate the idle pleasures of these days.
> (1.1.24–31)

The opening ferocity of Richard, still duke of Gloucester, in *The Tragedy of Richard the Third* is hardly more than a fresh starting point for the development of the Elizabethan and Jacobean hero-villain after Marlowe, and yet it seems to transform Tamburlaine and Barabas utterly. Richard's peculiarly self-conscious pleasure in his own audacity is crossed by the sense of what it means to see one's own deformed shadow in the sun. We are closer already not only to Edmund and Iago than to Barabas, but especially closer to Webster's Lodovico who so sublimely says: "I limn'd this nightpiece and it was my best." Except for Iago, nothing seems farther advanced in this desperate mode than Webster's Bosola:

>   O direful misprision!
> I will not imitate things glorious
> No more than base: I'll be mine own example.—
> On, on, and look thou represent, for silence,

The thing thou bear'st.
(5.4.87–91)

Iago is beyond even this denial of representation, because he does will silence:

Demand me nothing; what you know, you know:
From this time forth I never will speak word.
(5.2.303–4)

Iago is no hero-villain, and no shift of perspective will make him into one. Pragmatically, the authentic hero-villain in Shakespeare might be judged to be Hamlet, but no audience would agree. Macbeth could justify the description, except that the cosmos of his drama is too estranged from any normative representation for the term hero-villain to have its oxymoronic coherence. Richard and Edmund would appear to be the models, beyond Marlowe, that could have inspired Webster and his fellows, but Edmund is too uncanny and superb a representation to provoke emulation. That returns us to Richard:

Was ever woman in this humor woo'd?
Was ever woman in this humor won?
I'll have her, but I will not keep her long.
What? I, that kill'd her husband and his father,
To take her in her heart's extremest hate,
With curses in her mouth, tears in her eyes,
The bleeding witness of my hatred by,
    Having God, her conscience, and these bars against me,
And I no friends to back my suit [at all]
But the plain devil and dissembling looks?
And yet to win her! All the world to nothing!
Hah!
Hath she forgot already that brave prince,
Edward, her lord, whom I, some three months since,
Stabb'd in my angry mood at Tewksbury?
A sweeter and a lovelier gentleman,
Fram'd in the prodigality of nature—
Young, valiant, wise, and (no doubt) right royal—
The spacious world cannot again afford.
And will she yet abase her eyes on me,
That cropp'd the golden prime of this sweet prince

And made her widow to a woeful bed?
On me, whose all not equals Edward's moi'ty?
On me, that halts and am misshapen thus?
My dukedom to a beggarly denier,
I do mistake my person all this while!
Upon my life, she finds (although I cannot)
Myself to be a marv'llous proper man.
I'll be at charges for a looking-glass,
And entertain a score or two of tailors
To study fashions to adorn my body:
Since I am crept in favor with myself,
I will maintain it with some little cost.
But first I'll turn yon fellow in his grave,
And then return lamenting to my love.
Shine out, fair sun, till I have bought a glass,
That I may see my shadow as I pass.
(1.2.227–63)

Richard's only earlier delight was "to see my shadow in the sun / And descant on mine own deformity." His savage delight in the success of his own manipulative rhetoric now transforms his earlier trope into the exultant command: "Shine out, fair sun, till I have bought a glass, / That I may see my shadow as I pass." That transformation is the formula for interpreting the Jacobean hero-villain and his varied progeny: Milton's Satan, the Poet in Shelley's *Alastor*, Wordsworth's Oswald in *The Borderers*, Byron's Manfred and Cain, Browning's Childe Roland, Tennyson's Ulysses, Melville's Captain Ahab, Hawthorne's Chillingworth, down to Nathanael West's Shrike in *Miss Lonelyhearts*, who perhaps ends the tradition. The manipulative, highly self-conscious, obsessed hero-villain, whether Machiavellian plotter or hater, idealistic quester, ruined or not, moves himself from being the passive sufferer of his own moral and/or physical deformity to becoming a highly active melodramatist. Instead of standing in the light of nature to observe his own shadow, and then have to take his own deformity as subject, he rather commands nature to throw its light upon his own glass of representation, so that his own shadow will be visible only for an instant as he passes on to the triumph of his will over others.

Richard II

There is a general agreement that Shakespeare represents Richard II as a kind of spoiled adolescent (in our terms, not Shakespeare's, since adolescence is a later invention sometimes ascribed to Rousseau). I suspect it might be better to term Shakespeare's Richard II an almost perfect solipsist. He is certainly, as everyone sees, an astonishing poet and a very bad king. The puzzle of the play, to me, is why Richard II is so sympathetic. I do not mean dramatic sympathy, such as we extend to Macbeth, overwhelmed as we are by his intense inwardness. Macbeth is anything but humanly sympathetic. Richard II is, despite his self-pity, his petulance, and a veritable hoard of other bad qualities.

Northrop Frye eloquently calls Richard's "overreacting imagination that sketches the whole course of a future development before anyone else has had time to figure out the present one" a weakness. Pragmatically this is a weakness because it makes Richard doom-eager, but it also renders him curiously attractive, particularly in contrast to the usurper, Bolingbroke. Harold Goddard, whose readings of Shakespeare never leave me, termed Richard "a man of unusual, though perverted, gifts," the principal perversions being sentimentalism and narcissism. Since Shakespeare's most original quality, in my judgment, was the representation of change through a character's self-overhearing, I would call Richard II the first major manifestation of that originality, and I suspect that is why he moves us to a very troubled sympathy. He is indeed a mimesis that compels more of reality to divulge itself than we could have seen without him.

A.D. Nuttall, in his remarkable *A New Mimesis*, the best study of Shakespeare's representation of reality, also emphasizes Richard II's proleptic stance towards his own catastrophe:

> Richard II is plagued not so much by Bolingbroke as by his own capacity for conceptual anticipation: Bolingbroke does not force Richard from the throne, he moves into spaces successively vacated, with elaborately conscious art, by Richard.

A Freudian reading would find Richard an instance of "moral masochism," the collapse of the ego before the superego, sometimes related to strongly manifested bisexuality. But Freud seems to me a codification of Shakespeare, so that a Shakespearean reading of Freud is more enlightening, and shows us that moral masochism is a theatrical tendency in which the ego dramatizes its doom-eagerness in order to achieve a priority in self-destructiveness, so as to anticipate the severity of the shadows of early and abandoned object-affections. Richard II assists at his own crucifixion because he desires a firstness in the exposure of a reality that he knows he cannot master. His perverse, final trace of the royal is to be strong only in his own overthrow.

Since Richard is the anointed king as well as much the most interesting personage in his drama, we are compelled to take his poetry very seriously indeed. There is no one else in Shakespeare's dramas up through 1595 who is anything like his imaginative equal. Had Shakespeare died in 1595, then Richard would have been his principal study in a dramatic consciousness, with Shylock, Falstaff, Rosalind, and Hamlet still to come in the five years subsequent. Until the advent of Hamlet, there is nothing like Richard's eloquence in Shakespearean verse. The edge of that eloquence first troubles us when Richard first despairs:

No matter where—of comfort no man speak:
Let's talk of graves, of worms, and epitaphs,
Make dust our paper, and with rainy eyes
Write sorrow on the bosom of the earth.
Let's choose executors and talk of wills;
And yet not so, for what can we bequeath
Save our deposed bodies to the ground?
Our lands, our lives, and all are Bullingbrook's,
And nothing can we call our own but death,
And that small model of the barren earth
Which serves as paste and cover to our bones.
For God's sake let us sit upon the ground
And tell sad stories of the death of kings:
How some have been depos'd, some slain in war,
Some haunted by the ghosts they have deposed,
Some poisoned by their wives, some sleeping kill'd,
All murthered—for within the hollow crown
That rounds the mortal temples of a king
Keeps Death his court, and there the antic sits,
Scoffing his state and grinning at his pomp,
Allowing him a breath, a little scene,
To monarchize, be fear'd, and kill with looks,
Infusing him with self and vain conceit,
As if this flesh which walls about our life
Were brass impregnable; and humor'd thus,
Comes at the last and with a little pin
Bores thorough his castle wall, and farewell king!
Cover your heads, and mock not flesh and blood
With solemn reverence, throw away respect,
Tradition, form, and ceremonious duty,
For you have but mistook me all this while.

I live with bread like you, feel want,
Taste grief, need friends: subjected thus,
How can you say to me I am a king?

It is an astonishing outburst, and Richard is crucially changed by it.
We may not like him any the better for it, but he is highly conscious of the
gap between his royal legitimacy and the luxuriance of his despair. His
sense of "the king's two bodies" is more dialectical than that doctrine
should allow. Shakespeare's sense of it is very clear; you can celebrate
England and its soil if the rightful king is in power, however inadequate he
is, but the celebration turns sour if a usurper, however capable, reigns.
Richard is both his own victim, or rather the victim of his own imagination, and the sacrifice that becomes inevitable when the distance between
the king as he should be and the actual legitimate monarch becomes too
great. The shock of his own increasing consciousness of that distance is
what changes Richard from a rapacious and blustering weakling into a self-
parodying ritual victim. In this change, Richard does not acquire any
human dignity, but he does begin to incarnate an extraordinary aesthetic
dignity, both lyrical and dramatic. I think he becomes Shakespeare's first
implicit experiment in representation, which is to risk identifying poetry
and a national ritual sacrifice. The risk is not that Richard will fail to be
persuasive, but that he will put poetry and its powers of representation into
question.

His rhetoric of pleasurable despair is more than oxymoronic, and
enforces the lesson that Nietzsche learned from the poets; what makes representation memorable is pleasurable pain, rather than painful plea sure. I
know of many readers and students who agree with Dr. Samuel Johnson in
his judgment that *Richard II* "is not finished at last with the happy force of
some other of his tragedies, nor can be said much to affect the passions, or
enlarge the understanding." Yet even these recalcitrants thrill to the justly
famous cadences of "For God's sake let us sit upon the ground / And tell
sad stories of the death of kings." I think of Hart Crane's marvelous variation upon this in *Voyages VI*:

Waiting, afire, what name, unspoke,
I cannot claim: let thy waves rear
More savage than the death of kings,
Some splintered garland for the seer.

Crane shrewdly interprets Shakespeare as associating the death of
kings and the splintering of poetic wreaths. Dr. Johnson, best of critics, was

too unmoved by *Richard II* to achieve an accurate sense of the king's transformation:

> It seems to be the design of the poet to raise Richard to esteem in
> his fall, and consequently to interest the reader in his favour. He
> gives him only passive fortitude, the virtue of a confessor rather
> than of a king. In his prosperity we saw him imperious and
> oppressive, but in his distress he is wise, patient, and pious.

In his fall, Richard is not wise but eloquent, not patient but driving towards death, not pious but a kind of Christ-parody. His wounded narcissism is augmented by the turning of his aggressivity against himself, and he overgoes Marlowe's Edward II as a rhetorician of self-pity:

> They shall be satisfied. I'll read enough,
> When I do see the very book indeed
> Where all my sins are writ, and that's myself.
> Give me that glass, and therein will I read.
> No deeper wrinkles yet? Hath sorrow struck
> So many blows upon this face of mine,
> And made no deeper wounds? O flatt'ring glass,
> Like to my followers in prosperity,
> Thou dost beguile me! Was this face the face
> That every day under his household roof
> Did keep ten thousand men? Was this the face
> That like the sun, did make beholders wink?
> Is this the face which fac'd so many follies,
> That was at last out-fac'd by Bullingbrook?
> A brittle glory shineth in this face,
> As brittle as the glory is the face,
> [*Dashes the glass against the ground.*]
> For there it is, crack'd in an hundred shivers.
> Mark, silent king, the moral of this sport,
> How soon my sorrow hath destroy'd my face.

The outrageous parody of Marlowe's Faustus celebrating Helen is scarcely an accident in a play that subsumes Marlowe's *Edward II*. By associating Richard with two of Marlowe's antiheroes, Shakespeare suggests a likeness between his Richard and the self-destructive, narcissistic great poet who was Shakespeare's closest precursor. It may seem fantastic to suggest that the aura of Christopher Marlowe seeps into the rhetoric and psychology of Richard II, but this was a complex trick that Shakespeare was to play again. The fine symbolic gesture of dashing the mirror to pieces is wholly appropriate for the Marlovian protagonists, and for Christopher Marlowe's own fate. Here as elsewhere Shakespeare is warning himself (and us) that Marlowe's way was not to be taken up.

Formally, *Richard II* is a tragedy, as Johnson took it to be, but it is the tragedy of a self-indulgent poet rather than the fall of a great king. The dashing of the glass is also the destruction of the legitimate royal countenance, yet when Richard is murdered we do not experience the shock of a monarch dying. Hamlet, who never ascends a throne, dies more than royally, but Richard's apparent courage when he kills the attendants is precisely what Goddard called it: "the reflex action of a man without self-control in the presence of death." There is aesthetic dignity in Richard's rhetoric of decline and fall, but not in the actual way that he dies. It is the death of the poet who has not matured into the possession and representation of wisdom.

THE ROMANCES

An unfortunate critical tradition, now too prevalent to be overthrown, has named this fourfold of late Shakespearean dramas his "romances." Actually very different from one another, they are essentially comedies, perhaps tragi-comedies. Though all of them have visionary elements, none is as extreme as *A Midsummer Night's Dream* or *Macbeth* in relying upon the supernatural. Because these "late romances" have the misleading reputation as being works of an ultimate reconciliation, they tend to be inadequately performed, with their cosmic ethos thrown away, that being the particular fate now of *The Tempest*.

Pericles, the earliest of these plays, essentially is a pageant or processional, while *Cymbeline* seems to me an extravagant self-parody, in which Shakespeare recalls earlier triumphs largely to mock them. *The Winter's Tale* is even more a knowing illusion, at once a passionate celebration of eros, and a paean to the horrible glories of sexual jealousy. Though *The Tempest* is now widely acted and written about as a post-colonial farce, it seems to me Shakespeare's comic version of the Faust story, with Prospero supplanting Marlowe's Dr. Faustus, and Ariel taking the place of the Marlovian Mephistopheles.

Once we regard these four plays as comedies or tragi-comedies, their supposed common features and themes tend to vanish. Shakespeare, a naturally comic genius even in *Hamlet* and in *Antony and Cleopatra*, is furthest from comedy in *Othello* and *Macbeth*. *King Lear*, most tragic of tragedies, is also wildly grotesque, transcending the limits of laughter in the Fool's apocalyptic ironies. Shakespeare returns greatly to comedy in *The Winter's Tale* and *The Tempest*, as much triumphs of irony and wit as are *As You Like It* and *Twelfth Night*, or in a darker mode, *Measure for Measure*. Once you realize that Caliban, despite his cowardly poignance, is a comic villain and not a heroic West Indian Freedom Fighter, then the laughter of *The Tempest* returns, though this humor is now in political exile from our stages.

What matters most about these misnamed "romances" is their greatest strength, invention, which Dr. Johnson rightly considered the essence of poetry. The brothel scenes in *Pericles* juxtapose the impregnable Marina with the amiably bewildered bawds, who want only to get on with their business, mixing pleasure and profit with venereal illness and casual death. *Cymbeline*, which obsessively cannot cease from Shakespearean self-parody, nevertheless centers upon Imogen, who joins Rosalind, Portia, and Helena, as one of the playwright's most delightful and humanly impressive women. *The Winter's Tale* is most memorable for its contraries, the murderous insanity of Leontes's sexual jealousy, and the loving splendor of his daughter, Perdita, a new Proserpina renewing the fertility of the earth. Add Autolycus, sublime singer of thievery, and you have a world of interest and value manifested in a new kind of comedy.

That comedy, which as yet we scarcely understand, triumphs in *The Tempest*, in the contrast between Prospero and his enemies, and in the more radical disjunction between Prospero's ally, Ariel, and his outcast adopted child, Caliban. Politicizing *The Tempest* has merely obscured its comic splendor, but Shakespeare, greatest of entertainers as of poets, never can be obscured for long.

The Tempest

The Tempest is not a mystery play, offering a secret insight into human finalities; act 5 of *Hamlet* is closer to that. Perhaps *The Tempest* does turn ironically upon Shakespeare's conscious farewell to his dramatic art, but such an irony or allegory does not enhance the play's meanings. I sometimes think *The Tempest* was the first significant drama in which not much happens, beyond its protagonist's abandonment of his scheme of justified revenge precisely when he has all his enemies in his power. Most explanations of Prospero's refusal to take revenge reduce to the formulaic observation: "That's the way things turn out in Shakespeare's late romances." Let us move again towards the question: why does Prospero not gratify himself by fulfilling his revenge?

The originality of representation in *The Tempest* embraces only Prospero, the supernatural Ariel, compounded of fire and air, and the preternatural Caliban, compounded of earth and water. Unlike *The Winter's Tale*, *The Tempest* contrives to be a romance of the marvelous without ever being outrageous; the Shakespearean exuberance expresses itself here by cheerfully discarding any semblance of a plot.

Prospero, who is almost always sympathetic as Miranda's father, is dubiously fair to Ariel, and almost too grimly censorious towards the wretched Caliban. His peculiar severity towards Ferdinand also darkens him. But only this split, between loving father and puritanical hermeticist, makes Prospero truly interesting. He does not move our imagination as Ariel does, and Ariel, a kind of revised Puck, is less original a representation than Caliban is. Caliban does not run off with the play, as Barnardine does in *Measure for Measure*, but he makes us wonder how much humanity Prospero has sacrificed in exchange for hermetic knowledge and wisdom.

Caliban is uncanny to us, in precisely Freud's sense of "the uncanny." Something long estranged from us, yet still familiar, returns from repression in Caliban. We can be repelled by Caliban's degradation and by his deformity, but like Prospero we have to acknowledge that Caliban is somehow ours, not to be repudiated. It is not clear to me whether Caliban is meant to be wholly human, as there is something amphibian about him, and his mother Sycorax, like the weird sisters in *Macbeth*, has her preternatural aspects. What is certain is that Caliban has aesthetic dignity, and that the play is not wholly Prospero's only because of him. You could replace Ariel by various sprites (though not without loss), but you would not have *The Tempest* if you removed Caliban.

Why Shakespeare called the play *The Tempest* I cannot understand. Perhaps he should have called it *Prospero* or even *Prospero and Caliban*. Though the "names of the actors" describes Caliban as a "savage and deformed slave," I have never known any reader or theatergoer who could regard that as an adequate account of what may be Shakespeare's most deeply troubling single representation after Shylock. Robert Browning's Caliban, in the great monologue "Caliban upon Setebos," seems to me the most remarkable interpretation yet ventured, surpassing all overt literary criticism, and so I will employ it here as an aid, while yielding to all those who would caution me that Browning's Caliban is not Shakespeare's. Yes, but whose Caliban is?

Prospero forgives his enemies (and evidently will pardon Caliban because he achieves a complex stance that hovers between the disinterestedness of the Hamlet of act 5, and a kind of hermetic detachment from his own powers, perhaps because he sees that even those are dominated by a temporal ebb and flow. But there is also a subtle sense in which Prospero has been deeply wounded by his failure to raise up a higher Caliban, even as Caliban is palpably hurt (in many senses) by Prospero. Their relations, throughout the play, are not less than dreadful and wound us also, as they seem to have wounded Browning, judging by his Caliban's meditation:

> Himself peeped late, eyed Prosper at his books
> Careless and lofty, lord now of the isle:
> Vexed, 'stiched a book of broad leaves, arrow-shaped,
> Wrote thereon, he knows what, prodigious words;
> Has peeled a wand and called it by a name;
> Weareth at whiles for an enchanter's robe
> The eyed skin of a supple oncelot;
> And hath an ounce sleeker than youngling mole,
> A four-legged serpent he makes cower and couch,
> Now snarl, now hold its breath and mind his eye,
> And saith she is Miranda and my wife:
> 'Keeps for his Ariel a tall pouch-bill crane
> He bids go wade for fish and straight disgorge;
> Also a sea-beast, lumpish, which he snared,
> Blinded the eyes of, and brought somewhat tame,
> And split its toe-webs, and now pens the drudge
> In a hole o' the rock and calls him Caliban;
> A bitter heart that bides its time and bites.
> 'Plays thus at being Prosper in a way,
> Taketh his mirth with make-believes: so He.
> (ll. 150–69)

That lumpish sea-beast, "a bitter heart that bides its time and bites," is the tortured plaything of a sick child, embittered by having been cast out by a foster father. As a slave, Shakespeare's Caliban is rhetorically defiant, but his curses are his only weapon. Since he has not inherited his mother's powers, Caliban's curses are in vain, and yet they have the capacity to provoke Prospero and Miranda, as in the first scene where the three appear together:

> PROSPERO: Come on,
>   We'll visit Caliban my slave, who never
>   Yields us kind answer.
> MIRANDA: 'Tis a villain, sir,

I do not love to look on.

PROSPERO: But as 'tis,
　　We cannot miss him. He does make our fire,
　　Fetch in our wood, and serves in offices
　　That profit us. What ho! slave! Caliban!
　　Thou earth, thou! speak.

CALIBAN: (*Within.*)   There's wood enough within.

PROSPERO: Come forth, I say, there's other business for thee.
　　Come, thou tortoise, when?

Enter ARIEL *like a water-nymph.*

　　Fine apparition! My quaint Ariel,
　　Hark in thine ear.

ARIEL: My lord, it shall be done.   *Exit.*

PROSPERO: Thou poisonous slave, got by the devil himself
　　Upon thy wicked dam, come forth!

Enter CALIBAN.

CALIBAN: As wicked dew as e'er my mother brush'd
　　With raven's feather from unwholesome fen
　　Drop on you both! A south-west blow on ye,
　　And blister you all o'er!

PROSPERO: For this, be sure, to-night thou shalt have cramps,
　　Side-stitches, that shall pen thy breath up; urchins
　　Shall, for that vast of night that they may work,
　　All exercise on thee; thou shalt be pinch'd
　　As thick as honeycomb, each pinch more stinging
　　Than bees that made 'em.

CALIBAN: I must eat my dinner.
　　This island's mine by Sycorax my mother,
　　Which thou tak'st from me. When thou cam'st first,
　　Thou strok'st me and made much of me, wouldst give me
　　Water with berries in't, and teach me how
　　To name the bigger light, and how the less,
　　That burn by day and night; and then I lov'd thee
　　And show'd thee all the qualities o' th' isle,
　　The fresh springs, brine-pits, barren place and fertile.
　　Curs'd be I that did so! All the charms
　　Of Sycorax, toads, beetles, bats, light on you!

For I am all the subjects that you have,
Which first was mine own king; and here you sty me
In this hard rock, whiles you do keep from me
The rest o' th' island.

PROSPERO: Thou most lying slave,
Whom stripes may move, not kindness! I have us'd thee
(Filth as thou art) with human care, and lodg'd thee
In mine own cell, till thou didst seek to violate
The honor of my child.

CALIBAN: O ho, O ho, wouldst had been done!
Thou didst prevent me; I had peopled else
This isle with Calibans.

MIRANDA: Abhorred slave,
Which any print of goodness wilt not take,
Being capable of all ill! I pitied thee,
Took pains to make thee speak, taught thee each hour
One thing or other. When thou didst not, savage,
Know thine own meaning, but wouldst gabble like
A thing most brutish, I endow'd thy purposes
With words that made them known. But thy vild race
(Though thou didst learn) had that in't which good natures
Could not abide to be with; therefore wast thou
Deservedly confin'd into this rock,
Who hadst deserv'd more than a prison.

CALIBAN: You taught me language, and my profit on't
Is, I know how to curse. The red-plague rid you
For learning me your language!

PROSPERO: Hag-seed, hence!
Fetch us in fuel, and be quick, thou'rt best,
To answer other business. Shrug'st thou, malice?
If thou neglect'st, or dost unwillingly
What I command, I'll rack thee with old cramps,
Fill all thy bones with aches, make thee roar
That beasts shall tremble at thy din.

CALIBAN: No, pray thee.
[*Aside.*] I must obey. His art is of such pow'r,
It would control my dam's god, Setebos,
And make a vassal of him.

PROSPERO: So, slave, hence!   *Exit Caliban.*
(1.2.307–74)

Is it, as some would say, that our resentment of Prospero and Miranda here and our sympathy (to a degree) with Caliban, are as irrelevant as a preference for Shylock over Portia? I do not think so, since Shylock is a grotesque bogeyman rather than an original representation, while Caliban, though grotesque, is immensely original. You can New Historicize Caliban if you wish, but a discourse on Caliban and the Bermudas trade is about as helpful as a neo-Marxist analysis of Falstaff and surplus value, or a Lacanian-feminist exegesis of the difference between Rosalind and Celia. Caliban's peculiar balance of character and personality is as unique as Falstaff's and Rosalind's, though far more difficult to describe. But Prospero's balance also yields reluctantly to our descriptions, as if more than his white magic is beyond us. Prospero never loses his anger or sense of outrage in regard to Caliban, and surely some guilt attaches to the magus, who sought to make Caliban into what he could not become and then went on punishing Caliban merely for being himself, Caliban, a man of his own island and its nature, and not at all a candidate for hermetic transformations. Caliban can be controlled and chastised by Prospero's magical art, but he is recalcitrant, and holds on to the strange dignity of being Caliban, although endlessly insulted by everyone who speaks to him in the play.

Alas, that dignity vanishes in the presence of the jester Trinculo and the drunken Stephano, with whom Caliban attempts to replace Prospero as master. The immense puzzle of Shakespeare's vision of Caliban is enhanced when the slave's most beautiful speech comes in the grotesque context of his seeking to soothe the fears of Trinculo and Stephano which are caused by the music of the invisible Ariel:

> Be not afeard, the isle is full of noises,
> Sounds, and sweet airs, that give delight and hurt not.
> Sometimes a thousand twangling instruments
> Will hum about mine ears; and sometime voices,
> That if I then had wak'd after long sleep,
> Will make me sleep again, and then in dreaming,
> The clouds methought would open, and show riches
> Ready to drop upon me, that when I wak'd
> I cried to dream again.
> (3.2.135–43)

This exquisite pathos is Caliban's finest moment, and exposes the sensibility that Prospero presumably hoped to develop, before Caliban's attempted rape of Miranda. The bitterest lines in the play come in Prospero's Jehovah-like reflections upon his fallen creature:

A devil, a born devil, on whose nature
Nurture can never stick; on whom my pains,
Humanely taken, all, all lost, quite lost;
And as with age his body uglier grows,
So his mind cankers. I will plague them all,
Even to roaring.
(4.1.88–93)

This could be Milton's God, Schoolmaster of Souls, fulminating at the opening of *Paradise Lost*, book 3. True, Prospero turns to the rarer action of forgiveness and promises Caliban he yet will receive pardon and Caliban promises to "seek for grace." Yet Shakespeare was uninterested in defining that grace; he does not even tell us if Caliban will remain alone on the island in freedom, or whether he is to accompany Prospero to Milan, a weird prospect for the son of Sycorax. All that Prospero promises himself in Milan is a retirement "where / Every third thought shall be my grave." We want Caliban to be left behind in what is, after all, his own place, but Shakespeare neither indulges nor denies our desires. If Prospero is at last a kind of benign Iago (an impossible oxymoron), then Caliban's recalcitrances finally look like an idiosyncratic rebellion of actor against playwright, creature against demiurge. A warm monster is dramatically more sympathetic than a cold magus, but that simplistic difference does not explain away the enigma of Caliban. I suspect that Prospero forgives his enemies because he understands, better than we can, the mystery of time. His magic reduces to what Nietzsche called the will's revenge against time, and against time's "it was." Caliban, who need not fear time, and who hates Prospero's books of magic, perhaps represents finally time's revenge against all those who conjure with books.

The Winter's Tale

Winter's tales, then and now, tend to be wild chronicles, fantastic stories told by the fireside. Once accounted a comedy, Shakespeare's *The Winter's Tale* is now considered a romance, together with *Pericles* and *Cymbeline* before it and *The Tempest* beyond it. Granted that the comedy of one era is hardly that of another, it would still be difficult to think of *The Winter's Tale* as a comedy. Yet we think of *Measure for Measure* as a comedy (a "problem play" is not a genre), and there are dark affinities between it and *The Winter's Tale*. In *The Winter's Tale* everything again is beyond absurdity, ranging from a spectacularly unexpected, paranoid jealousy and murderousness to the resurrection of the statue as the living Hermione. The

Shakespeare who writes *The Winter's Tale* might almost be Anthony Burgess's Shakespeare in *Nothing like the Sun* and *Enderby's Dark Lady*. This is an overtly outrageous Shakespeare, deliberately provoking to fury his empirical friend and rival, Ben Jonson, by giving Bohemia a sea-coast.

On that spurious coast poor Antigonus exits, pursued by a bear, in a stage direction worthy of Groucho Marx. As with *Measure for Measure*, all that matters is the staging of a fantastic story, an entertainment so designed that it allows for a totally original and most powerful meditation upon death in *Measure for Measure*, and in *The Winter's Tale* allows for the pastoral phantasmagoria of act 4 and for our enchantment by Perdita. Perdita, I will venture, is the play, the goddess Flora incarnated in a personality so fresh and winning that reality cannot hold out against her. She is everything in herself, while happily not needing to know it, whereas Leontes moves towards madness because he fears that he is nothing in himself, a fear which he projects upon everyone and everything else:

> Is whispering nothing?
> Is leaning cheek to cheek? is meeting noses?
> Kissing with inside lip? stopping the career
> Of laughter with a sigh (a note infallible
> Of breaking honesty)? horsing foot on foot?
> Skulking in corners? wishing clocks more swift?
> Hours, minutes? noon, midnight? and all eyes
> Blind with the pin and web but theirs, theirs only,
> That would unseen be wicked? Is this nothing?
> Why then the world and all that's in't is nothing,
> The covering sky is nothing, Bohemia nothing,
> My wife is nothing, nor nothing have these nothings,
> If this be nothing.

One dozen rhetorical questions, followed by six assertions of total nihilism, is an astonishing structure for a speech, yet marvelously appropriate for a descent through sudden and wholly irrational jealousy into the death drive. Othello has Iago, but Leontes has nothing:

> Affection! thy intention stabs the centre.
> Thou dost make possible things not so held,
> Communicat'st with dreams (how can this be?),
> With what's unreal thou co-active art,
> And fellow'st nothing. Then 'tis very credent
> Thou mayst co-join with something, and thou dost

(And that beyond commission), and I find it
(And that to the infection of my brains
And hard'ning of my brows).

Hallett Smith, in the very useful *Riverside Shakespeare*, reads "affection" here not as "desire" but as Leontes' own jealousy. Probably both readings are right, since Leontes' projected jealousy is also his own unruly desire, a return of repressed bisexuality, with its deep need for betrayal. Shakespeare's beautiful irony is that "affection" here is meant by Leontes as the sexual drive of the supposed lovers, yet manifestly projects his own murderous jealousy. For a romance to begin with a paranoid siege of jealousy is profoundly appropriate, and demonstrates Shakespeare to be Proust's (and Freud's) largest precursor. *The Winter's Tale*, even as a title, becomes a story of projected jealousy and its antidote, whose name is Perdita.

II

Even Shakespeare has nothing else as ecstatic as act 4 of *The Winter's Tale*, which has established one of the limits of literature as an art. Autolycus is one kind of splendor, setting the context by bold contrast to "an art / Which does mend Nature—change it rather; but / The art itself is Nature." That art is Perdita's nature, and becomes Florizel's:

PER:　　　　　　　　　　O Proserpina,
　　For the flow'rs now, that, frighted, thou let'st fall
　　From Dis's waggon! daffadils,
　　That come before the swallow dares, and take
　　The winds of March with beauty; violets, dim,
　　But sweeter than the lids of Juno's eyes,
　　Or Cytherea's breath; pale primeroses,
　　That die unmarried, ere they can behold
　　Bright Phoebus in his strength (a malady
　　Most incident to maids); bold oxlips, and
　　The crown imperial; lilies of all kinds
　　(The flow'r-de-luce being one). O, these I lack,
　　To make you garlands of, and my sweet friend,
　　To strew him o'er and o'er!
FLO:　　　　　　　　　　What? like a corse?
PER: No, like a bank, for love to lie and play on;
　　Not like a corse; or if—not to be buried,

But quick and in mine arms. Come, take your flow'rs.
Methinks I play as I have seen them do
In Whitsun pastorals. Sure this robe of mine
Does change my disposition.

FLO: What you do
Still betters what is done. When you speak, sweet,
I'ld have you do it ever; when you sing,
I'ld have you buy and sell so; so give alms;
Pray so; and for the ord'ring your affairs,
To sing them too. When you do dance, I wish you
A wave o' th' sea, that you might ever do
Nothing but that; move still, still so,
And own no other function. Each your doing
(So singular in each particular)
Crowns what you are doing in the present deeds,
That all your acts are queens.

One sees why Florizel might take the risk of "a wild dedication of yourselves / To unpath'd waters, undream'd shores." Rosalie Colie usefully traced some of the Shakespearean originalities in regard to pastoral conventions here. I myself would emphasize how little really any conventions of pastoral suit either Perdita's art-exalted nature or Florizel's as he is influenced by her. Perdita incants more like a mortal goddess, Flora, than like an earthly maiden, while the inspired Florizel celebrates her like an Elizabethan John Keats. It takes an extraordinary effort to keep in mind that Perdita is invoking absent flowers, rather than actual, natural presences. Those "daffadils, violets, primeroses, oxlips, lilies" are not seasonal, due to Proserpina's failure of nerve, and so Perdita's great declaration is a kind of litany of negations, and yet makes a wholly positive effect, upon the audience as upon her lover. When she cries out, with marvelous boldness: "Come, take your flowers," she substitutes her own body for the floral tribute she has conveyed only through its absence. Startled as she herself is by her unaccustomed and only apparent lack of modesty, she provokes Florizel's ecstatic defense of her ontological goodness, as it were. I can think of no comparable praise by a lover to his beloved, anywhere in Western literature since the song that was Solomon's.

The deepest aesthetic puzzle (and strength) of *The Winter's Tale* remains its extraordinary originality, striking even for Shakespeare. In a drama where everything is incongruous, everything works together to conclude in a new mode of congruity:

If this be magic, let it be an art
Lawful as eating.

If eating has become yet another art that itself is Nature, then we
tremble on the verge of an aesthetic that, by magic, will consume Nature.
Jealousy will vanish away, and with it our darkest tendency, which is to
react to any declaration that we are alive, by hooting at it, like an old tale.
The Winter's Tale evidently exists to tell us that, it appears, we live, though
yet we speak not.

Ben Jonson

(1572–1637)

BEN JONSON, SHAKESPEARE'S FRIEND AND RIVAL, OWED HIS START AS A dramatist to Shakespeare's generosity in bringing Jonson to the notice of the Lord Chamberlain's Men, Shakespeare's players, in 1598. Jonson, pugnacious and furiously learned, from 1599 on asserted himself to become almost the anti-Shakespeare in his dramas. In effect, Jonson challenged Shakespeare for the heritage of Christopher Marlowe. There is considerable irony in this, since Marlowe had no comic invention, while Jonson survives now only for his comedies, *Volpone* and *The Alchemist* in particular. T.S. Eliot shrewdly saw Jonson as Marlowe's continuator, which is peculiarly true in the sense that Marlowe's characters all are cartoons, and Jonson's, when successful, all are caricatures. The disasters of Jonson's *Sejanus*, his major tragedy, and of *Catiline*, his later attempt to outdo Shakespeare in Roman tragedy, are instructive, despite the noble obfuscations of Eliot, which are sublimely mistaken:

> The creation of a work of art, we will say the creation of a character in a drama, consists in the process of transfusion of the personality, or, in a deeper sense, the life, of the author into the character. This is a very different matter from the orthodox creation in one's own image. The ways in which the passions and desires of the creator may be satisfied in the work of art are complex and devious. In a painter they may take the form of a predilection for certain colours, tones, or lightings; in a writer the original impulse may be even more strangely transmuted. Now, we may say with Mr. Gregory Smith that Falstaff or a score of Shakespeare's characters have a "third dimension" that Jonson's have not. This will mean, not that Shakespeare's spring from the feelings or

imagination and Jonson's from the intellect or invention; they have equally an emotional source; but that Shakespeare's represent a more complex tissue of feelings and desires, as well as a more supple, a more susceptible temperament. Falstaff is not only the roast Manningtree ox with the pudding in his belly; he also "grows old," and, finally, his nose is as sharp as a pen. He was perhaps the *satisfaction* of more, and of more complicated feelings; and perhaps he was, as the great tragic characters must have been, the offspring of deeper, less apprehensible feelings: deeper, but not necessarily stronger or more intense, than those of Jonson. It is obvious that the spring of the difference is not the difference between feeling and thought, or superior insight, superior perception, on the part of Shakespeare, but his susceptibility to a greater range of emotion, and emotion deeper and more obscure. But his characters are no more "alive" than are the characters of Jonson.

What *are* "deeper, but not necessarily stronger or more intense" feelings? Unless Eliot (who despised Freud) intends another disparagement of depth psychology, he evades coherence here. Are Falstaff and Cleopatra, Hamlet and Iago, Lear and Macbeth really no more "alive" than Volpone and Mosca, Morose and Truewit, Subtle and Sir Epicure Mammon?

Jonson, like Marlowe, does not attempt to give us representations of human inwardness. Marlowe overwhelms us with rhetorical splendor, while Jonson's satirical comedy also employs stunning eloquence rather than insights into the mysteries of personality. At their best, roles in Jonson are ideograms. In his Prologue to *Cynthia's Revels*, Jonson said that his kind of play "affords/ Words above action: matter, above words." This is directed against Shakespeare, who lacked "matter," in Jonson's sense of moral instruction. And yet the matter of Jonson's "comical satires"—*Every Man Out of His Humor, Cynthia's Revels*, and *Poetaster*—essentially is Jonson's self-love, and his assertion that he alone is the Poet. Time, despite T.S. Eliot's neo-classical last stand, has settled the matter. We stage and read *Twelfth Night*, and not *Cynthia's Revels*.

Canonization is now an absurdly abused process, but is simply a question of just how much time we any of us have. I enjoy *Cynthia's Revels*, such as it is, but it is food for specialists. The California School system now insists upon multiculturalism, but by this it is not meant that students are to read *The Tale of Genji* and *Don Quixote*, but rather recent works of Japanese-American and Hispanic-American origin. If we were all to live three hundred years, rather than seventy-five, this might be admirable. If not, not.

The best account of the wit-combat between Shakespeare and Jonson is in *Shakespeare and The Poets' War* by James P. Bednarz (2001). Bednarz demonstrates Shakespeare's counter-measures against Jonson in *As You Like It*, *Twelfth Night*, and *Troilus and Cressida*, comedies that deftly satirize the satirical Jonson.

Ben Jonson is a great lyric and reflective poet, but he achieves the heights as a dramatic poet only in *Volpone* and *The Alchemist*, where the critique of Shakespeare is very indirect. Jonson satirizes sexual desire, and the satire is without limits. Shakespeare both satirizes and exalts desire in his comedies through *Twelfth Night*, and then turns against it (though with ironic reservations) in the final comedies: *Troilus and Cressida*, *All's Well that Ends Well*, and *Measure for Measure*. Jonson, who could not get away from Shakespeare in tragedy—his attempt to write a rival *Richard III* was abandoned—created a mode of comedy that was all his own, and that clearly possesses a moral purpose. Shakespeare happily fled from Jonsonian moral purposes, as they were antithetical to any adequately complex vision of Eros. Shakespeare, like Marlowe, was an Ovidian poet; Jonson preferred Horace. And yet, by temperament, Jonson was exuberant and vehement, "burly Ben." His masterpiece is *Volpone*, which is—akin to Shakespeare's twenty or so triumphs—still rammed with life.

Volpone

Jonson's magnificent vehemence carries him over to Volpone's side, in defiance of Jonsonian moral theory. Not that Volpone (and the plebeian Mosca even more so) is not hideously punished. He—like Mosca—is outrageously overpunished, which may be Jonson's self-punishment for the imaginative introjection of his greatest creation. Perhaps Jonson is chastising us also, knowing that we too would delight in Volpone. The representation of gusto, when worked with Jonson's power, becomes a gusto that captivates us, so that it scarcely matters if we remember how wicked Volpone is supposed to be. Massively aware of this paradox, distrusting the theatrical while creating Volpone as a genius of theatricality, Jonson takes moral revenge upon Volpone, the audience, and even himself. The imagination wishes to be indulged, and delights in being deceived. No playgoer or reader wishes to see Volpone's deceptions fail, and our delight is surely Jonson's delight also.

Robert M. Adams has some shrewd comments upon what I suppose we might want to call Jonson's ambivalences towards the theater:

> The tone of punishment and correction runs through a lot of Jonson's dramatic work; there are passages which don't come far

short of suggesting that he thought the work itself a form of correction, if not punishment, for the audience: "physic of the mind" was one of his terms.

Jonson might have observed that he was following Aristotle's precepts, yet a "physic of the mind" does seem stronger than a catharsis. You tend to receive worse than you (badly) merit in Jonson, and that hardly purges you of fear. It is something of a mystery anyway why Jonson believed Volpone and Mosca needed to be so severely punished. Except for his exasperated attempt to rape Celia, Volpone preys only upon those who deserve to be fleeced, and thus defrauds only the fraudulent. Nor does Jonson represent Volpone's failed lust for Celia as being without its own imaginative opulence. As with Sir Epicure Mammon in *The Alchemist*, we hear in Volpone's mad eloquence the equivocal splendor of a depraved will corrupting imagination to its own purposes:

> CELIA: Some serene blast me, or dire lightning strike
>   This my offending face!
> VOLPONE: Why droops my Celia?
>   Thou hast, in place of a base husband, found
>   A worthy lover: use thy fortune well,
>   With secrecy and pleasure. See, behold,
>   What thou art queen of; not in expectation,
>   As I feed others: but possessed and crowned.
>   See here a rope of pearl; and each, more orient
>   Than that the brave Egyptian queen caroused:
>   Dissolve and drink them. See, a carbuncle
>   May put out both the eyes of our St. Mark;
>   A diamond, would have bought Lollia Paulina,
>   When she came in like star-light, hid with jewels,
>   That were the spoils of provinces; take these,
>   And wear, and lose them: yet remains an earring
>   To purchase them again, and this whole state.
>   A gem but worth a private patrimony,
>   Is nothing: we will eat such at a meal.
>   The heads of parrots, tongues of nightingales,
>   The brains of peacocks, and of ostriches,
>   Shall be our food: and, could we get the phoenix,
>   Though nature lost her kind, she were our dish.
> CELIA: Good sir, these things might move a mind affected
>   With such delights; but I, whose innocence

Is all I can think wealthy, or worth th'enjoying,
And which, once lost, I have nought to lose beyond it,
Cannot be taken with these sensual baits:
If you have conscience—

VOLPONE: 'Tis the beggar's virtue;
If thou hast wisdom, hear me, Celia.
Thy baths shall be the juice of gilly-flowers,
Spirit of roses, and of violets,
The milk of unicorns, and panthers' breath
Gathered in bags, and mixed with Cretan wines.
Our drink shall be preparéd gold and amber;
Which we will take, until my roof whirl around
With the vertigo: and my dwarf shall dance,
My eunich sing, my fool make up the antic,
Whilst we, in changèd shapes, act Ovid's tales,
Thou, like Europa now, and I like Jove,
Then I like Mars, and thou like Erycine:
So, of the rest, till we have quite run through,
And wearied all the fables of the gods.
Then will I have thee in more modern forms,
Attiréd like some sprightly dame of France,
Brave Tuscan lady, or proud Spanish beauty;
Sometimes, unto the Persian Sophy's wife,
Or the Grand Signor's mistress; and, for change,
To one of our most artful courtesans,
Or some quick Negro, or cold Russian;
And I will meet thee in as many shapes:
Where we may so transfuse our wandering souls
Out at our lips, and score up sums of pleasures.

It is difficult to believe that Jonson did not admire the superb audacity of Volpone's hyperboles, which out-Marlowe Marlowe. "Could we get the phoenix,/ Though nature lost her kind, she were our dish," is particularly fine, as that firebird, mythical and immortal, is always present only in one incarnation at any single moment. Heroic in the bravura of his lust, the Ovidian Volpone charms us by the delicious zeal with which he envisions Celia's changes of costume. Sir Epicure Mammon holds on always in my memory for his energetic "here's the rich Peru," but Volpone is positively endearing as he gets carried away in transports of voluptuousness, and bursts into strains of Catullus in his exuberance:

Come, my Celia, let us prove,
While we can, the sports of love,
Time will not be ours for ever,
He, at length, our good will sever;
Spend not then his gifts in vain:
Suns that set may rise again;
But if once we lose this light,
'Tis with us perpetual night.
Why should we defer our joys?
Fame and rumor are but toys.
Cannot we delude the eyes
Of a few poor household spies?
Or his easier ears beguile,
Thus removéd by our wile?—
'Tis no sin love's fruits to steal;
But the sweet thefts to reveal,
To be taken, to be seen,
These have crimes accounted been.

Jonas Barish, moved by his depth of Jonsonian scholarship to a
Jonsonian moralizing, reads Volpone's Ovidian and Catullan allusions as
evidence that: "Folly, vanity, lust, have been, are, will be. At any given
moment their practitioners are legion, and often interchangeable." Yes,
and doubtless Jonson would have been gratified, but what about the verve,
wit, lyric force, and intoxicating eloquence with which Jonson has
endowed Volpone? Foolish and vain lusters may be interchangeable, but
whom would you get if you gave up Volpone? We are again in the paradox
of Jonson's theatrical art at its most extraordinary, which brings Volpone
back to delight us after he has been so cruelly sentenced:

[VOLPONE comes forward]
The seasoning of a play is the applause.
Now, though the fox be punished by the laws,
He yet doth hope, there is no suffering due,
For any fact which he hath done 'gainst you;
If there be, censure him; here he doubtful stands:
If not, fare jovially, and clap your hands. [Exit]
THE END

Where can we find the Jonsonian ambivalence in this? Volpone indeed
has done nothing except entertain us, richly beyond most rivals. Barish

strongly remarks that when Jonson imposes a terrible punishment upon Volpone, we feel betrayed. I would use a darker word, and say that we are outraged, though we grant that Volpone is outrageous. Jonson's moral aesthetic was not quite what he thought it to be. His savage relish in Volpone's tricks is also a savage relish for the stage, and so also a savage appreciation for the savagery of his audience.

John Webster

(c. 1580-1632)

The Duchess of Malfi

THOUGH THE CENTRAL TRADITION OF THE HERO-VILLAIN GOES DIRECTLY
from Shakespeare through Milton on to the High Romantics and their
heirs, we might be puzzled at certain strains in Browning, Tennyson,
Hawthorne, and Melville, if we had not read John Webster's two astonishing plays, *The White Devil* and *The Duchess of Malfi*. Russell Fraser memorably caught Webster's curious link to Marlowe, whom he otherwise
scarcely resembles:

> His violent protagonists are memorable as they are endowed with
> the same amoral energy with which Barabas and Tamburlaine and
> Mortimer are endowed. Unlike these Marlovian heroes or hero-
> villains, they do not speak to us—quoting from Michael Drayton's
> tribute to Marlowe—of "brave translunary things," rather of the
> charnel house and the grisly business appurtenant to it.

Here is the death scene of Flamineo, and of his sister, Vittoria
Corombona, in *The White Devil*:

> VIT. COR. Oh, my greatest sin lay in my blood!
>   Now my blood pays for't.
> FLAM.   Thou'rt a noble sister!
>   I love thee now. If woman do breed man,
>   She ought to teach him manhood. Fare thee well.
>   Know, many glorious women that are famed
>   For masculine virtue have been vicious,

> Only a happier silence did betide them.
> She hath no faults who hath the art to hide them.

VIT. COR. My soul, like to a ship in a black storm,
> Is driven I know not whither.

FLAM.   Then cast anchor.
> Prosperity doth bewitch men, seeming clear,
> But seas do laugh, show white, when rocks are near.
> We cease to grieve, cease to be fortune's slaves,
> Nay, cease to die, by dying. Art thou gone?
> And thou so near the bottom? False report,
> Which says that women vie with the nine Muses
> For nine tough durable lives! I do not look
> Who went before, nor who shall follow me;
> No, at myself I will begin and end.
> While we look up to heaven, we confound
> Knowledge with knowledge. Oh, I am in a mist!

VIT. COR. Oh, happy they that never saw the court,
> Nor ever knew great men but by report!

                                        VITTORIA dies.

FLAM. I recover like a spent taper, for a flash,
> And instantly go out.
> Let all that belong to great men remember the
> old wives' tradition, to be like the lions i' the
> Tower on Candlemas-day: to mourn if the sun
> shine, for fear of the pitiful remainder of
> winter to come.
> 'Tis well yet there's some goodness in my death;
> My life was a black charnel. I have caught
> An everlasting cold; I have lost my voice
> Most irrecoverably. Farewell, glorious villains!
> This busy trade of life appears most vain,
> Since rest breeds rest where all seek pain by pain.
> Let no harsh flattering bells resound my knell;
> Strike, thunder, and strike loud, to my farewell!

                                        Dies.

Vittoria Corombona rides her black ship to Hell without final knowledge, but Flamineo is a knower, a Machiavel in the high Marlovian sense,
which has its Gnostic aspect. By beginning and ending "at myself,"
Flaminio seeks to avoid a final agon between his self-knowledge and a rival
Christian knowledge: "While we look up to heaven, we confound /

Knowledge with knowledge." And yet, Flamineo cries out: "Oh, I am in a mist!", which is what it is to the confounded, and perhaps leads to the self-epitaph: "My life was a black charnel." The mist appears also in the death speech of a greater hero-villain than Flamineo, Bosola in *The Duchess of Malfi*:

> In a mist; I know not how;
> Such a mistake as I have often seen
> In a play. Oh, I am gone.
> We are only like dead walls, or vaulted graves
> That ruined, yields no echo. Fare you well;
> It may be pain, but no harm to me to die
> In so good a quarrel. Oh, this gloomy world,
> In what shadow, or deep pit of darkness
> Doth womanish and fearful mankind live?
> Let worthy minds ne'er stagger in distrust
> To suffer death or shame for what is just.
> Mine is another voyage.
>
> *Dies.*

Bosola's final vision is of the cosmic emptiness, what the Gnostics called the *kenoma*, into which we have been thrown: "a shadow, or deep pit of darkness." When Bosola dies, saying: "Mine is another voyage," he may mean simply that he is not suffering death for what is just, unlike those who have "worthy minds." But this is Bosola, master of direful misprision, whose motto is: "I will not imitate things glorious, / No more than base; I'll be mine own example." This repudiation of any just representation of essential nature is also a Gnostic repudiation of nature, in favor of an anti-thetical quest: "On, on: and look thou represent, for silence, / The thing thou bearest." What Bosola both carries and endures, and so represents, by a kind of super-mimesis, is that dark quest, whose admonition, "on, on" summons one to the final phrase: "Mine is another voyage." As antitheti-cal quester, Bosola prophesies Milton's Satan voyaging through Chaos towards the New World of Eden, and all those destructive intensities of wandering self-consciousness from Wordsworth's Solitary through the Poet of *Alastor* on to their culmination in the hero-villain who recites the great dramatic monologue, "Childe Roland to the Dark Tower Came":

> Burningly it came on me all at once,
> This was the place! those two hills on the right,
> Crouched like two bulls locked horn in horn in fight;

While to the left, a tall scalped mountain ... Dunce,
Dotard, a-dozing at the very nonce,
    After a life spent training for the sight!

What in the midst lay but the Tower itself?
    The round squat turret, blind as the fool's heart,
    Built of brown stone, without a counterpart
In the whole world. The tempest's mocking elf
Points to the shipman thus the unseen shelf
    He strikes on, only when the timbers start.

Not see? because of night perhaps?—why, day
    Came back again for that! before it left,
    The dying sunset kindled through a cleft:
The hills, like giants at a hunting, lay,
Chin upon hand, to see the game at bay,—
    'Now stab and end the creature—to the heft!'

The Machiavel spends a life training for the sight, and yet is self-betrayed, because he is self-condemned to be "blind as the fool's heart." He will see, at the last, and he will know, and yet all that he will see and know are the lost adventurers his peers, who like him have come upon the Dark Tower unaware. The Jacobean hero-villain, at the end, touches the limit of manipulative self-knowledge, and in touching that limit gives birth to the High Romantic self-consciousness which we cannot evade, and which remains the affliction of our Post-modernism, so-called, as it was of every Modernism, from Milton to our present moment.

Molière

(1622-1673)

Dom Juan

AFTER SHAKESPEARE, MOLIÈRE, MORE THAN RACINE, DISPUTES IBSEN'S
eminence as the prime creator of European drama. The best starting-point
for regarding Molière I learned long ago from Jacques Guicharnaud: our
lives are romances, farces, disgraces so that we have to embrace bad faith
lest we doubt ourselves.

Is that the inner drama of Molière's *Dom Juan*? I myself dissent from
the two readings of *Dom Juan* elsewhere, but then I have never encountered an interpretation, or a performance of *Dom Juan* that persuaded me.
Molière, who played the role of Sganarelle, got into more than his usual
trouble with moralists, both secular and religious, with this ambiguous
drama. In conjunction with *Tartuffe*, *Dom Juan* cost Molière the last sacrament and an unsanctified burial. During the playwright-actor's life, he suffered threats and consequent anxieties, though his great patron, the Sun-
King, Louis XIV, protected him to a considerable degree.

Goethe delighted in *Dom Juan*, as in the rest of Molière, and one sees
why: Molière's irony is already Goethean. Dom Juan is hardly the free spirit he presents himself as being. Anticipating Bryon's Don Juan as well as
Goethe's Faust, Molière's Dom Juan is remarkably passive: his career has
become accidental, though he continues to run for election (as it were) to
the eminence of Super-Seducer, and he seeks votes everywhere, as though
he doubts his own mythic status. Though he proclaims his autonomy, he
himself belies it, since to maintain yourself as a living legend is a considerable exhaustion. Entropy threatens the Great Lover, and yet he persists,
though with increasing irony. He knows that he acts in a contradictory
fashion, but exults in the uniqueness of what he does. At the same time, he

shows less and less interest in enjoying his female victims, if "enjoyment" is at all an accurate category in regard to his erotic project.

Molière, subtle and deep beyond devising, makes Dom Juan the most sympathetic figure in the play, certainly more so than the tricky Sganarelle. And yet the dramatist limits our sympathy: the diabolic seducer is not at all diabolic, and endlessly suffers the cost of confirmation. If I were directing the play, I would find a Bill Clinton look-alike for the role of Dom Juan (I should say that I voted twice for Clinton, and wish I could help elect him for a third time). There can be no rest for Dom Juan, for he is the victim of his myth, and he would become the equivalent of an aging rock-star or ex-president if he fortunately did not achieve a sublime punishment at play's end.

Dom Juan's entire project is blasphemous, not because of its dubious sexuality, but because God is the ultimate rival, the more successful seducer. The pragmatic enmity of God, the greater celebrity, is what redeems the hero-villain from nihilism, and confers aesthetic dignity upon him. Nowhere else in Molière does anyone die; Shakespearean deaths on stage were considered barbarous by most of the French. When Juan is swallowed up by hellfire, we have a unique moment in French theater, up to that time. But *Dom Juan* is a singular play: what genre is it? Molière transgresses the limits of comedy in this work, as though he had become impatient with the conditions set for his exercise of his art.

II

Dom Juan cannot change, but then nobody in Molière can change, a condition in which they have more in common with Dante's characters than with Shakespeare's. But Dante knows the truth; Molière knows only that truth is evasive and elusive, while Shakespeare is too intellectually large and imaginatively wealthy to allow much relevance to truth.

What is the truth about Alceste in that most exuberant of all non-Shakespearean comedies, *The Misanthrope*? He is the most complex character in Molière, who acted the part, whereas he avoided the role of Dom Juan, just as he played Orgon rather than Tartuffe. In some respects, Alceste is a comic Hamlet, but then so is Hamlet. There are large differences: Hamlet has a considerable sense of humor, is as fierce towards himself as he is severe to others, and is too great to risk an absurd quest. And yet Alceste is a strenuous satirist, like Hamlet, and like Hamlet he has the aesthetic dignity of being authentically outraged by his society's corruption. Molière again bruises the limits of comedy by giving us a hero both impossibly absurd and yet admirable, who resists all moralization you might be tempted to turn against him.

Perhaps Alceste fails as a lover, but so does Hamlet. No great satirist has survived marriage, and Alceste's greatness is almost too palpable for comedy, however outrageously he speaks and behaves. It is totally inaccurate to pair him with Dom Juan, because Alceste does not solicit your favor nor ask you to confirm his metaphysical existence by your suffrage. Eric Bentley shrewdly notes that *The Misanthrope* is an exception to all theatrical rules, just as *Hamlet* is. Alceste's ideas matter a great deal, like Hamlet's and Molière goes against his own dramatic wisdom in allowing Alceste's mind to transcend the world of the play. Falstaff is so witty that the two parts of *Henry IV* cannot contain him, but Shakespeare knew that to allow Falstaff into *Henry V* would destroy that play. Alceste flees the salon, into whatever metaphorical solitude, because his passionate will threatens the play's ability to sustain itself as comedy.

Le Misanthrope

Critics have pondered the "philosophical implications" of *Le Misanthrope*, which makes as uneasy as the traditions of considering *Hamlet*, two thirds of a century earlier, a philosophical play.

Does not *Le Misanthrope*, as much as *Hamlet*, test the limits of the satirist as dramatic protagonist? Both truthtellers pragmatically are their own worse enemies. Both men are apocalyptic idealists who malform what they touch. But Alceste is no more a fool than Hamlet is. Neither tragedy nor comedy can sustain a satirist at its center. A melancholic of great intellectual power is a profound trouble to stage representation.

The merciless honesty shared by Hamlet and Alceste is a socially destructive agent. Shakespeare has no inhibitions as to Hamlet's destructiveness: Elsinore is devastated, with Horatio its one survivor. But Molière writes for a divided audience, under the protection of the Sun King. Something of Alceste's farcical coloring is a defensive device on Molière's part.

Still, that understates both the greatness of Alceste and Molière's need to ward that greatness off. Like Hamlet, Alceste asks the audience for nothing. In a sense, both characters ask their creators for nothing, but Shakespeare loves Hamlet, and Molière does not dare to love Alceste.

Jacques Guicharnaud, wisest of all Molière's critics, tells us to remember that for Molière, we are all essentially vice. How far is that from Alceste's view? Or from Hamlet's?

Molière was a notorious cuckold. In Shakespeare, there is an anxiety of cuckoldry, though I assume (contra James Joyce) that Anne Hathaway, distant and unregarded, was not the cause. I long to see *Le Misanthrope* played with Alceste given full sympathy, though theatrical convention is against me.

John Gay

(1685-1732)

The Beggar's Opera

WILLIAM EMPSON, WITH AMIABLE IRONY, SAID OF *THE BEGGAR'S OPERA* that its glory was "to give itself so wholeheartedly to vulgarization." The acute word there is "wholeheartedly," and that is the truer glory of John Gay's durable opera, ancestor of Gilbert and Sullivan and of Brecht's *Threepenny Opera*. It is so wholehearted a work (like the rest of Gay) that it runs off and away from Gay's utmost intentions and very nearly becomes an artistic heterocosm, a little world of its own, endlessly cheerful, yet always shadowed by betrayal, the pox, and the gallows. Martin Price finds in the "ironic flexibility and detachment" of Gay a precise anticipation of Brecht's celebrated "alienation effect," and Gay indeed is much more complex in his design and stance than the Marxist Brecht chose to be.

The Beggar's Opera is a benign first cousin of *The Dunciad* and *A Tale of a Tub*, and, though a "Newgate pastoral," remains a kind of pastoral, as Empson classically demonstrated: "It is [the] clash and identification of the refined, the universal, and the low that is the whole point of the pastoral." Mock-pastoral, in Empson's vision, fostered a code of independence. Rereading *The Beggar's Opera*, after listening to a good recorded performance of it, oppresses me rather (it is the only oppression involved) with a sense of how dependent everyone in Gay's world truly is, where you escape no consequence of your actions, whether illegal or immoral, except in the grand and unlikely reprieve that the Beggar-poet is obliged to grant. Lockit, Peachum, Macheath, Filch, the gang, are not less dependent upon the underworld system and economy than are Mrs. Peachum, Polly, Lucy, Diana Trapes, and those eight vivid whores of whom Jenny Diver is the most interesting. Everyone is splendidly capable of hanging everyone else, no man is far from the gallows and no woman from transportation. Yet the marvelous good humor, zest for life, general high spirits, and fantastic bravura are unmatched in literature between Villon and Babel's *Tales of Odessa*. Like Villon and Babel, Gay has a clear sense of the abyss and knows well that his dance of life is always just a step away from a dance of death.

Gay's sense of the absurd owes something to his good friends Swift and Pope, but his sense of potential punishment or anxious expectations is essentially his own. Technically Peachum is the opera's villain, and Macheath its hero, but they agree upon everything that matters, have the same values and the same fatalism. Peachum, being older and wiser, plays it safer; Macheath is the more overt gambler and knows himself to be compulsive about women. What they share most crucially is a knowledge manifested, to a lesser degree, by everyone else in the opera. To keep going in a dangerous existence (and this opera intends to teach us that all existence is dangerous), you require a rhetoric of self-justification and indeed self-exaltation. You need never misrepresent your motives, whether to yourself or to others, but you must elevate your language when you apply it to your own status or function in the economy, psychic or social. That rhetorical elevation need not be assigned to others, though that is the true division between Peachum and Macheath. Peachum and Mrs. Peachum rarely address Polly without calling her a slut or hussy, and Lockit does as well with Lucy. Macheath, in everything he says to his gang or his women, is as nobly rhetorical as the hero of romance he knows himself not to be.

Polly and Lucy, as Martin Price remarks, are necessarily their father's daughters and are quite formidable women, as Macheath discovers. If the gallant captain truly loves anyone in the opera, she appears to be Jenny Diver, who betrays him as a lowlife Cleopatra should, with style and without regret. Gay, never forgetting that his genre was operatic satire, declined to develop any of his women (or men, for that matter) more complexly than his plot required. Yet there is a curious wistfulness in Macheath. Gay clearly felt the attractions with which he had endowed the feckless mock-aristocratic highwayman, but he had the aesthetic restraint to circumscribe his own sympathy and so keep our sympathy for Macheath from becoming at all serious.

Still, Macheath is no Mack the Knife, just as Peachum is finally too engaging, in his gusto and mercenary intensity, to be less than a good-natured satire upon Walpole, who had the wit to attend, just once, and to call for an encore at the right moment. Gay swerved from Macheath at the right moment, since to execute the hero would have ruined the opera, despite the Beggar-poet's call for "strict poetical justice." Peachum and Lockit are indeed, as Macheath says, infamous scoundrels, but we don't want them hanged anymore than we want to see Macheath hanged. In his farewell to representatives of the gang, Macheath is on the edge of turning comic opera into tragicomedy, when he tells his men, "look well to yourselves, for in all probability you may live some months longer." We prefer Peachum's opening aria:

> Through all the employments of life,
>   Each neighbour abuses his brother;
> Whore and rogue they call husband and wife:
>   All professions be-rogue one another.
> The priest calls the lawyer a cheat,
>   The lawyer be-knaves the divine;
> And the statesman, because he's so great,
>   Thinks his trade as honest as mine.

That is Gay's true note: exuberantly outrageous and faithful to the reality principle that governs the opera, without, however, abandoning itself to that principle. The highest praise I can render Gay is that he returns us to Shakespeare's Falstaff and Falstaff's cosmos. Peachum is no Falstaff and Macheath no Hotspur, but Falstaff's vision of reality (though not his awesome wit) is revived in *The Beggar's Opera*.

Henrik Ibsen

(1828–1906)

MY FAVORITE PLAYS BY IBSEN WOULD INCLUDE *BRAND* AND THE EPIC *Emperor and Galilean*, as well as *Peer Gynt* and *Hedda Gabler*. Though Previously I had been baffled by Brian Johnston's (*The Ibsen Cycle*) insistence on the close parallel between Hegel's *Phenomenology of Mind* and Ibsen's final twelve plays, Johnston indeed does demonstrate that Ibsen's work fits very well into the Hegelian vision of tragedy. Whether or not this resulted from the direct influences upon Ibsen, like Shakespeare and Hegel, Ibsen is a world-visionary who works on a vast scale. Parallels between the three necessarily abound.

Brand and the Emperor Julian are Ibsen's most heroic characters, yet they are hero-villains in the Shakespearean mode. This doubleness applies still more strongly to Hedda Gabler, and to later figures like Solness and Rubek. For Thomas Van Laan, Hedda Gabler is a version of Shakespeare's Cleopatra; I would add Iago to the mix. The Ibsenite hero-villains, like the Shakespearean, are trollish or daemonic; the great exception is Peer Gynt, whose comic genius (like Falstaff's), redeems him from most taints of trollishness. The Emperor Julian has his Macbeth-aspect, but Peer is a natural man, and amiable scamp who may behave like a hero-villain, but who charms himself, his fellow-characters, and the audience into forgiving everything. Call Peer Gynt, like Ibsen himself, a borderline troll, but far gentler than his fiercer creator. For Ibsen's true self-portrait, we can turn to Hedda Gabler, a worth rival of Shakespeare's Cleopatra.

Brand and *Hedda Gabler*

Ibsen's vast range is allied to his uncanny ability to transcend genre; in both respects he is like Shakespeare, the dominant though frequently hidden influence upon his work. Shakespeare wrote his 38 (or so) plays in a quarter century; Ibsen composed for 50 years, and gave us 25 plays. His masterpieces, in my judgment, include *Brand, Peer Gynt, Emperor* and *Galilean*, in the period 1865–1873, with *Hedda Gabler* as a great postlude in 1890. *Peer Gynt* and *Hedda Gabler* retain their popularity, but do not seem so frequently performed as what are taken to be Ibsen's "social dramas": *A Doll's House, Ghosts, An Enemy of the People, The Wild Duck*, and the earlier *Pillars of Society*. His final period, after he turned sixty, gave us four great visionary plays: *The Lady from the Sea, The Master Builder, John Gabriel Borkman*, and *When We Dead Awaken*. Yet all of Ibsen is visionary drama; he inherited Shakespeare's invention of the human, characters capable of overhearing themselves, and his mastery of inwardness is second only to Shakespeare's. I will confine myself, in this Introduction, to brief accounts of only two plays: *Brand* and *Hedda Gabler*, or rather to the two sublime characters who give their names to these dramas.

Ibsen, who could be caustic, had a powerful aversion to Strindberg. "I have always liked storms," he wrote in a letter to his sister, a fondness that helps explain his purchase of a large portrait of Strindberg, which he hung on the wall of his study. Under the baleful gaze of his enemy, whom he considered "delightfully mad," Ibsen was spurred on to even more exuberance in his final plays, *John Gabriel Borkman* and the apocalyptic *When We Dead Awaken*. Earlier, in response to *Hedda Gabler*, where he found himself portrayed as Lovberg, the poet inspired to suicide by the demonic Hedda, Strindberg expressed his own fury:

> It seems to me that Ibsen realizes that I shall inherit the crown when he is finished. He hates me mentally.... And now the decrepit old troll seems to hand me the revolver! ... I shall survive him and many others, and the day *The Father* kills *Hedda Gabler*, I shall stick the gun in the old troll's neck.

The wild Strindberg was more overtly trollish than the socially conforming Ibsen, but Strindberg accurately diagnosed his unwelcome precursor as an "old troll." Trolls are not easy to define, particularly when they are thoroughly mixed into the human. If you think of the later Freudian myth of the rival drives of love and death, Eros and Thanatos, you get close to human trollishness. Ibsen's trollish figures are both doom-eager and desperate for more life; they are Ibsen's Shakespearean energies personified. Thomas Van Laan traces Hedda Gabler's debt to Shakespeare's Cleopatra, and on the level of deliberate allusion, that is definitely correct. But the deeper, more implicit model for Hedda is "honest Iago," the most

trollish of all Shakespearean characters. Ibsen once told an interviewer
that: "There must be troll in what I write," and one can wonder if he ever
fully enjoyed the apparent Shakespearean detachment that he cultivated.
No one should miss either the troll in Ibsen himself, or the presence of
Ibsen in Brand, Hedda Gabler, Peer Gynt, and all their fellow protagonists. Perhaps Falstaff and Hamlet each had a link to Shakespeare's own
personality and character, but such a surmise can only be imaginative.
Ibsen is not Shakespeare; the dramatist of the great trolls was as late
Romantic as they were: vitalistic, close to nihilistic, determined to turn life
into the true work of art.

Brand speaks of "the poem of my life"; if he is a man of God, that god
seems more Dionysus than Yahweh. Guilt, to a Dionysiac hero, has nothing to do with Original Sin, but rather reflects a failure to sustain ecstasy.
Compromising in any way, with anything or anyone, is totally alien to
Brand. He seeks only the Sublime, which he calls God, yet other names
(including Brand's own) seem more accurate. Destroying the lives of those
one loves best is hardly a path to God. Brand's capacity for suffering seems
infinite, but why need he immerse those who care most for him in suffering that they cannot sustain? Ibsen is aware that *Brand* is not a "religious
drama"; Brand, according to the dramatist, could also have been a sculptor
or politician. W.H. Auden strongly disagreed. Himself a Kierkegaardian,
Auden regarded Brand as an Apostle, someone who knows only "that he is
called upon to forsake everything he has been, to venture into an unknown
and probably unpleasant future." One can wonder if Auden was correct in
so assimilating Brand to Kierkegaard's difficult question of "becoming a
Christian" in a country ostensibly already Christian. Auden himself points
to the clear Nietzschean elements in Brand's exaltation of the will. If Brand
is an Apostle, then the message he carries was given to him by the god
Dionysus, who in one of his aspects is something of a troll.

II

Brand fascinates, though he also alienates himself from us. Even as he
beholds the avalanche coming down upon him, he cries out to God:
"Answer!" We shudder at the sublimity of the Brandian will, and yet we are
not allowed to sympathize with Brand. Hedda Gabler, even more fascinating, powerfully provokes something of the same dramatic sympathy that
Iago inspires in us. Hedda is the greatest figure in all Ibsen, possibly
because she is Ibsen. "Men and women don't belong in the same century,"
the playwright enigmatically remarked. I think Ibsen would have said the
same of the twentieth century, or the twenty-first, or any whatsoever.

As a demon or half-troll, Hedda emulates Iago by writing a tragic farce in which she and the other protagonists are caught in the net of her devisings. Oscar Wilde, accurate always, said he "felt pity and terror, as though the play had been Greek." Just as deftly, Wilde could have added: "or *Othello*." Hedda, who fears boring herself to death, finds Iago's cure for *ennui*: murder (or ruin) your fellow characters. Ibsen's marvelous woman shoots herself in the forehead, in the mode of Iago affirming: "from this time forth I never shall speak word," as he prepares to die silently under torture. Both Hedda and Iago are sublime solipsists, dramatists of the self at the expense of all others. And both are too grand for our mere disapproval. They stimulate our fear and our pity, as do Brand and Solness and so many of Ibsen's titans. The exception is Peer Gynt, who escapes into comedy.

Oscar Wilde

(1854–1900)

OSCAR WILDE FIRST PUBLISHED A BOOK IN 1881, AND AFTER MORE THAN A hundred years literary opinion has converged in the judgment that Wilde, as Borges asserts, was almost always right. This rightness, which transcends wit, is now seen as central to the importance of being Oscar. Daily my mail brings me bad poetry, printed and unprinted, and daily I murmur to myself Wilde's apothegm: "All bad poetry springs from genuine feeling." Arthur Symons, like Wilde a disciple of Walter Pater, reviewed the Paterian *Intentions* of Wilde with this exquisite summary: "He is conscious of the charm of graceful echoes, and is always original in his quotations." Symons understood that Wilde, even as playwright and as storyteller, was essentially a critic, just as Pater's fictions were primarily criticism.

Wilde began as a poet, and alas was and always remained quite a bad poet. An admirer of *The Ballad of Reading Gaol* should read the poem side-by-side with *The Ancient Mariner*, in order to see precisely its crippling failure to experience an anxiety of influence. Of course, Ruskin and Pater also began as poets, but then wisely gave it up almost immediately, unlike Matthew Arnold who waited a little too long. It is deeply unfortunate that the young Wilde gave the world this poem about Mazzini:

> He is not dead, the immemorial Fates
> Forbid it, and the closing shears refrain,
> Lift up your heads, ye everlasting gates!
> Ye argent clarions sound a loftier strain!
> For the vile thing he hated lurks within
> Its sombre house, alone with God and memories of sin.

This dreadful travesty and amalgam of Shelley, Swinburne, the Bible,

Milton and whatnot, is typical of Wilde's verse, and opened him to many attacks which became particularly nasty in America during his notorious lecture tour of 1882. Thomas Wentworth Higginson, whom we remember as Emily Dickinson's amiable and uncomprehending "Mentor," made a public attack upon Wilde's poetic immorality which expanded into an accusation of cowardice for not taking part in the Irish national struggle: "Is it manhood for her gifted sons to stay at home and help work out the problem; or to cross the Atlantic and pose in ladies' boudoirs or write prurient poems which their hostesses must discreetly ignore?" The force of Higginson's rhetoric evaporates for us when we remember that the burly Wilde was no coward, physical or moral, and also when we remember that Higginson, with his customary blindness, linked Wilde to Walt Whitman's work as a wound-dresser in the Washington, D.C. Civil War hospitals: "I am one of many to whom Whitman's 'Drum-Taps' have always sounded as hollow as the instrument they counterfeit." Why, Higginson demanded, had not Whitman's admirable physique gone into battle with the Union armies? A Civil War hero himself, Higginson would have had no scruples about hurling the middle-aged bard and idler into battle. We can credit W.B. Yeats with more insight into Wilde, let alone into Whitman, than Higginson displayed, since Yeats insisted that Wilde was essentially a man of action displaced into a man of letters. In some curious sense, there is a sickness-unto-action in Wilde's life and work, a masked despair that led him to the borders of that realm of fantasy the Victorians called "nonsense" literature, the cosmos of Edward Lear. Lionel Trilling aptly located Wilde's masterpiece, *The Importance of Being Earnest*, in that world, and it seems to me never far from Wilde's work. The metaphysical despair of ever knowing or speaking truth Wilde probably absorbed from his nearest precursor, Walter Pater, whose "Sebastian Van Storck" in *Imaginary Portraits* is a major depiction of intellectual despair. Wilde, deliberately less subtle than his evasive master, Pater, speaks out directly through his mouthpiece, Algernon, in the original, four-act version of *The Importance of Being Earnest*:

> My experience of life is that whenever one tells a lie one is corroborated on every side. When one tells the truth one is left in a very lonely and painful position, and no one believes a word one says.

Wilde's most profound single work is "The Decay of Lying: An Observation," an essay in what now would be called literary theory brilliantly cast in dialogue form. Vivian, speaking for Wilde, rejects what passes for lying in mere politicians:

They never rise beyond the level of misrepresentation, and actually condescend to prove, to discuss, to argue. How different from the temper of the true liar, with his frank, fearless statements, his superb irresponsibility, his healthy, natural disdain of proof of any kind! After all, what is a fine lie? Simply that which is its own evidence. If a man is sufficiently unimaginative to produce evidence in support of a lie, he might just as well speak the truth at once.

Lying then is opposed to misrepresentation, because aesthetic lying is a kind of supermimesis, and is set, not against truth or reality, but against time, and antithetically against time's slave, nature. As Vivian remarks: "Nothing is more evident than that Nature Hates Mind. Thinking is the most unhealthy thing in the world, and people die of it just as they die of any other disease. Fortunately, in England at any rate, thought is not catching." Nature's redemption can come only through imitating art. We can believe that Wilde's deathbed conversion to the Church was simply a reaffirmation of his lifelong belief that Christ was an artist, not in Wilde a frivolous belief but an heretical one, indeed an aesthetic version of Gnosticism. Hence Wilde's preference for the Fourth Gospel, which he shrewdly regarded as Gnostic:

> While in reading the Gospels—particularly that of St. John himself, or whatever early Gnostic took his name and mantle—I see the continual assertion of the imagination as the basis of all spiritual and material life, I see also that to Christ imagination was simply a form of love, and that to him love was lord in the fullest meaning of the phrase.

This is Wilde speaking out of the depths, in *De Profundis*, the epistle addressed to Lord Alfred Douglas from Reading Gaol. G. Wilson Knight, startlingly linking Wilde and Christ, hints that the ideology of Wilde's homosexuality was its dominant element, involving the raising of love to the high realm of aesthetic contemplation. Without disputing Knight (or Wilde), one can observe that such an elevation is more like Pater than Plato, more like the lying against time that is the privileged moment than the lying against mortality that is the realm of the timeless Ideas. As Pater's most dangerous disciple, Wilde literalizes Pater's valorization of perception over nature, of impression over description.

II

Wilde stands between Pater and Yeats, between a doctrine of momentary aesthetic ecstasies, phantasmagoric hard gemlike flames, and a vision of lyric simplification through aesthetic intensity, what Yeats called the Condition of Fire. Pater, and not Lord Alfred Douglas, was Wilde's disaster, as Yeats knew and intimated. Though his immediate sources were in Ruskin, Swinburne and the Pre-Raphaelites, Pater's sensibility went back to the Keats of the "Ode on Melancholy." Wilde, High Romantic in every way, nevertheless did not have a Romantic sensibility, which is why his verse, derived from all of the Romantics, is so hopelessly inadequate. As a sensibility, Wilde is a fantastic version of Congreve and Sheridan and Goldsmith; an Anglo-Irish wit wandering in the regions of Lewis Carroll, W.S. Gilbert, and Edward Lear, to repeat Trilling's insight again. Nonsense is the truest rejection of mere nature, and the strongest program for compelling nature to cease imitating itself and to imitate art instead. Wilde's theory of criticism achieves magnificence when it extravagantly leaps over sense into the cognitive phantasmagoria of a true theory of the lie, an escape from time into the fantasy of interpretation:

> I know that you are fond of Japanese things. Now, do you really imagine that the Japanese people, as they are presented to us in art, have any existence? If you do, you have never understood Japanese art at all. The Japanese people are the deliberate self-conscious creation of certain individual artists. If you set a picture by Hokusai, or Hokkei, or any of the great native painters, beside a real Japanese gentleman or lady, you will see that there is not the slightest resemblance between them. The actual people who live in Japan are not unlike the general run of English people; that is to say, they are extremely commonplace, and have nothing extraordinary or curious about them. In fact the whole of Japan is a pure invention. There is no such country, there are no such people. One of our most charming painters went recently to the Land of the Chrysanthemum in the foolish hope of seeing the Japanese. All he saw, all he had a chance of painting, were a few lanterns and some fans.

In fact the whole of Japan is a pure invention. There is no such country, there are no such people. That is certainly one of the grand critical epiphanies, one of those privileged moments that alone make criticism memorable. Japan momentarily becomes one with that far and wide land where the Jumblies live, where the Pobble who has no toes and the Dong with a luminous nose dwell together. It is also the land of the Canon Chasuble and Miss Prism and Lady Bracknell, the land of cucumber sandwiches where Wilde deserved and desired to live. Call it, surprisingly enough, what Wilde called it, the land of the highest Criticism:

> ... I would say that the highest Criticism, being the purest form of personal impression, is in its way more creative than creation, as it has least reference to any standard external to itself, and is, in fact, its own reason for existing, and, as the Greeks would put it, in itself, and to itself, an end. Certainly, it is never trammelled by any shackles of verisimilitude. No ignoble considerations of probability, that cowardly concession to the tedious repetitions of domestic or public life, affect it ever. One may appeal from fiction unto fact. But from the soul there is no appeal.

Call this Wilde's credo, or as Richard Ellmann, his crucial scholar, words it, "The Critic as Artist as Wilde." It leads to an even finer declaration, which catches the whole movement from Ruskin and Pater through Wilde and on to Yeats and Wallace Stevens in their critical essays:

> That is what the highest criticism really is, the record of one's own soul. It is more fascinating than history, as it is concerned simply with oneself. It is more delightful than philosophy, as its subject is concrete and not abstract, real and not vague. It is the only civilized form of autobiography, as it deals not with the events, but with the thoughts of one's life; not with life's physical accidents of deed or circumstance, but with the spiritual moods and imaginative passions of the mind.

The only civilized form of autobiography: I know of no better description of authentic criticism. What we want from a critic is not ideology and not method, not philosophy and not history, not theology and not linguistics, not semiotics and not technique, not feminism and not sociology, but precisely the moods and passions of cognition, of imagining, of the life of the spirit. If you want Marx and Hegel, Heidegger and Lacan and their revisionists, then take them, but if you want literary criticism, then turn to Hazlitt and Ruskin, to Pater and Wilde. Wilde's unique gift is the mode of wit by which he warns us against falling into careless habits of accuracy, and by which he instructs us that the primary aim of the critic is to see the object as in itself it really is not.

III

Why then did Wilde rush to social destruction? On February 14, 1895, *The Importance of Being Earnest* opened in London, only six weeks after the opening of *An Ideal Husband*. Wilde was forty-one, in the full possession of his talents and his health. On February 28, he found the Marquis of Queensberry's card waiting for him at the Albemarle Club, with its illiterate, nasty address "To Oscar Wilde, posing as a somdomite [*sic*]," in which the weird touch of "posing" failed to amuse him. His note of that day to his close friend Robert Ross has an uncharacteristic tone of hysteria:

Bosie's father has left a card at my club with hideous words on it. I don't see anything now but a criminal prosecution. My whole life seems ruined by this man. The tower of ivory is assailed by the foul thing. On the sand is my life spilt. I don't know what to do.

Had he done nothing he would not have found himself, less than three months later, sentenced to two years' hard labor. Richard Ellmann speaks of Wilde's "usual cycle which ran from scapegrace to scapegoat," and presumably Ellmann's forthcoming biography will explain that compulsion. Whatever its psychopathology, or even its psychopoetics, its most salient quality seems to be a vertigo-inducing speed. Freud presumably would have found in it the economics of moral masochism, the need for punishment. Yeats subtly interpreted it as due to the frustrations of a man who should have spent himself in action, military or political. One remembers Lady Bracknell remarking of Jack's and Algernon's father that, "The General was essentially a man of peace, except in his domestic life," an observation that perhaps precludes any vision of Wilde in battle or in political strife. The economic problem of masochism doubtless had its place within Wilde, but few moralists hated pain more than Wilde, and nothing even in Wilde surpasses the moral beauty of the closing pages of "The Soul of Man under Socialism":

Pain is not the ultimate mode of perfection. It is merely provisional and a protest. It has reference to wrong, unhealthy, unjust surroundings. When the wrong, and the disease, and the injustice are removed, it will have no further place. It will have done its work. It was a great work, but it is almost over. Its sphere lessens every day.

   Nor will man miss it. For what man has sought for is, indeed, neither pain nor pleasure, but simply Life. [Wilde's italics]

We remember, reading this, that Wilde was Ruskin's disciple as well as Pater's. Ruskin's credo, as phrased in *Unto This Last*, is the prophetic basis for Wilde's social vision:

There is no wealth but Life—Life, including all its powers of love, of joy, and of admiration. That country is the richest which nourishes the greatest number of noble and happy human beings.

Why then was the author of "The Soul of Man under Socialism" and of *The Importance of Being Earnest so* doom-eager? His best poem was not in verse, but is the extraordinary prose-poem of 1893, "The Disciple":

When Narcissus died the pool of his pleasure changed from a cup of sweet waters into a cup of salt tears, and the Oreads came weeping through the woodland that they might sing to the pool and give it comfort.

And when they saw that the pool had changed from a cup of sweet waters into a cup of salt tears, they loosened the green tresses of their hair and cried to the pool and said, 'We do not wonder that you should mourn in this manner for Narcissus, so beautiful was he.'

'But was Narcissus beautiful?' said the pool.

'Who should know better than you?' answered the Oreads. 'Us did he ever pass by, but you he sought for, and would lie on your banks and look down at you, and in the mirror of your waters he would mirror his own beauty.'

And the pool answered, 'But I loved Narcissus because, as he lay on my banks and looked down at me, in the mirror of his eyes I saw ever my own beauty mirrored.'

Kierkegaard might have called this "The Case of the Contemporary Disciple Doubled." Narcissus never saw the pool, nor the pool Narcissus, but at least the pool mourns him. Wilde's despair transcended even his humane wit, and could not be healed by the critical spirit or by the marvelous rightness of his perceptions and sensations.

The Importance of Being Earnest

I recall writing that, in Lady Augusta Bracknell's rolling periods, Oscar Wilde fused the rhetorical prose styles of Dr. Samuel Johnson and Shakespeare's Sir John Falstaff. "Rise, sir, from this semirecumbent posture. It is most indecorous." competes with: "Human life is everywhere a condition where much is to be endured and little to be enjoyed." And again with: "O thou hast damnable iteration and art indeed able to corrupt a saint. Thou hast done much harm upon me, Hal, God forgive you for it! Before I knew thee, Hal, I knew nothing and now to speak truly am I become little better than one of the wicked." Falstaff is the most elaborate, Johnson the most severe, Bracknell the most outrageous, but all are outrageous enough, and none accepts any demurral.

From her first entrance, Lady Bracknell is on the attack, a dreadnought firing from all turrets:

> Good afternoon, dear Algernon, I hope you are behaving quite well.

She proceeds to disapprove, massively, of the mythical invalid, Bunbury, Algernon's excuse for getting away on country junkets:

> Well, I must say, Algernon, that I think it is high time that Mr. Bunbury made up his mind whether he was going to live or die. This shilly-shallying with the question is absurd.

In some respects, Lady Augusta Bracknell is an ironic prophecy of the Conservative Prime Minister, Dame Margaret Thatcher, iron field marshal of the British victory over the Argentines in the Falklands War. One can see Lady Bracknell in the role, perhaps with Groucho Marx as her adjutant, since heroic farce is her mode. The finest Lady Bracknell I have seen is Dame Edith Evans, in the splendid Anthony Asquith film that features also Michael Redgrave and Margaret Rutherford. Dame Edith played the role as it must be performed, with Wagnerian severity and frowning high seriousness.

Lady Bracknell, a Sublime monster, in some respects is larger than the play, just as the dread Juno is too gigantic a menace even for the *Aeneid*. When I think of Oscar Wilde's work, I always first recall *Earnest*, and then cheer myself up by rolling forth various grand pronouncements of the magnificent Augusta. Wilde said of his greatest play: "It is written by a butterfly for butterflies," which is also very cheering. If Lady Bracknell, in full flight, is a butterfly, then we are listening to an iron butterfly:

> To lose one parent, Mr. Worthing, may be regarded as a misfortune; to lose both looks like carelessness. I dislike arguments of

any kind. They are always vulgar, and often convincing. The General was essentially a man of peace, except in his domestic life.

Lady Bracknell's is the voice of authority, that is to say of social authority, and therefore madness. Her lunacy is founded upon a solipsism so absolute as to be very nearly without rival:

Come, dear, we have already missed five, if not six, trains. To miss any more might expose us to comment on the platform.

I join my friend Camille Paglia in my passion for this truly gorgeous expression of solipsism. Lady Bracknell's greatness is that she would not comprehend that no one on the platform possibly could know how many trains she had missed, since she cannot conceive of her absence, but only of her overwhelming presence.

George Bernard Shaw

(1856-1950)

"WITH THE SINGLE EXCEPTION OF HOMER THERE IS NO EMINENT WRITER, not even Sir Walter Scott, whom I despise so entirely as I despise Shakespear when I measure my mind against his." Shaw, obsessive polemicist, would write anything, even that unfortunate sentence. No critic would wish to measure Shaw's mind against Shakespeare's, particularly since originality was hardly Shaw's strength. Shavian ideas are quarried from Schopenhauer, Nietzsche, Ibsen, Wagner, Ruskin, Samuel Butler, Shelley, Carlyle, Marx (more or less), William Morris, Lamarck, Bergson—the list could be extended. Though an intellectual dramatist, Shaw essentially popularized the concepts and images of others. He continues to hold the stage and might appear to have earned his reputation of being the principal writer of English comic drama since Shakespeare. Yet his limitations are disconcerting, and the experience of rereading even his most famous plays, after many years away from them, is disappointingly mixed. They are much more than period pieces, but they hardly seem to be for all time. No single comedy by Shaw matches Wilde's *Importance of Being Earnest* or the tragic farces of Beckett.

Eric Bentley best demonstrated that Shaw viewed himself as a prose prophet in direct succession to Carlyle, Ruskin, and Morris. This is the Shaw of the prefaces, of *Essays in Fabian Socialism*, of *Doctors' Delusions*, *Crude Criminology*, *Sham Education*. Only the prefaces to the plays are still read, and of course they are not really prefaces to the plays. They expound Shaw's very odd personal religion, the rather cold worship of Creative Evolution. Of this religion, one can say that it is no more bizarre than most, and less distasteful than many, but it is still quite grotesque. To judge religions by aesthetic criteria may seem perverse, but what others are relevant for poems, plays, stories, novels, personal essays? By any aesthetic standard,

Shaw's heretical faith is considerably less interesting or impressive than D.H. Lawrence's barbaric vitalism in *The Plumed Serpent* or even Thomas Hardy's negative homage to the Immanent Will in *The Dynasts*.

G.K. Chesterton, in his book on Shaw (1909), observed that the heroine of *Major Barbara*

> ends by suggesting that she will serve God without personal hope, so that she may owe nothing to God and He owe everything to her. It does not seem to strike her that if God owes everything to her He is not God. These things affect me merely as tedious perversions of a phrase. It is as if you said, "I will never have a father unless I have begotten him."

"He who is willing to do the work gives birth to his own father," Kierkegaard wrote, and Nietzsche mused: "If one hasn't had a good father, then it is necessary to invent one." Shaw was neither a Darwinian nor a Freudian and I think he was a bad Nietzschean, who had misread rather weakly the sage of *Zarathustra*. But in his life he had suffered an inadequate father and certainly he was willing to do the work. Like his own Major Barbara, he wished to have a God who would owe everything to G.B.S. That requires a writer to possess superb mythopoeic powers, and fortunately for Shaw his greatest literary strength was as an inventor of new myths. Shaw endures in a high literary sense and remains eminently readable as well as actable because of his mythmaking faculty, a power he shared with Blake and Shelley, Wagner and Ibsen. He was not a stylist, not a thinker, not a psychologist, and utterly lacked even an iota of the uncanny Shakespearean ability to represent character and personality with overwhelming persuasiveness. His dialogue is marred by his garrulous tendencies, and the way he embodied his ideas is too often wearisomely simplistic. And yet his dramas linger in us because his beings transcend their inadequate status as representations of the human, with which he was hopelessly impatient anyway. They suggest something more obsessive than daily life, something that moves and has its being in the cosmos we learn to call Shavian, a comic version of Schopenhauer's terrible world dominated by the remorseless Will to Live.

As a critic, Shaw was genial only where he was not menaced, and he felt deeply menaced by the Aesthetic vision, of which his Socialism never quite got free. Like Oscar Wilde and Wilde's mentor Walter Pater, Shaw was the direct descendant of Ruskin, and his animus against Wilde and Pater reflects the anxiety of an ambitious son toward rival claimants to a heritage. Pater insisted upon style, as did Wilde, and Shaw has no style to speak of, not much more, say, than Eugene O'Neill. Reviewing Wilde's *An Ideal Husband* on January 12, 1895, for Frank Harris's *Saturday Review*, Shaw was both generous and just:

> Mr. Wilde, an arch-artist, is so colossally lazy that he trifles even with the work by which an artist escapes work. He distils the very quintessence, and gets as product plays which are so unapproachably playful that they are the delight of every playgoer with twopenn'orth of brains.

A month later, confronted by *The Importance of Being Earnest: A Trivial Comedy for Serious People*, Shaw lost his composure, his generosity, and his sense of critical justice:

> I cannot say that I greatly cared for The Importance of Being Earnest. It amused me, of course; but unless comedy touches me as well as amuses me, it leaves me with a sense of having wasted my evening. I go to the theatre to be moved to laughter, not to be tickled or bustled into it; and that is why, though I laugh as much as anybody at a farcical comedy, I am out of spirits before the end of the second act, and out of temper before the end of the third, my miserable mechanical laughter intensifying these symptoms at every outburst. If the public ever becomes intelligent enough to know when it is really enjoying itself and when it is not, there will be an end of farcical comedy. Now in The Importance of Being Earnest there is plenty of this rib-tickling: for instance, the lies, the deceptions, the cross purposes, the sham mourning, the christening of the two grown-up men, the muffin eating, and so forth. These could only have been raised from the farcical plane by making them occur to characters who had, like Don Quixote, convinced us of their reality and obtained some hold on our sympathy. But that unfortunate moment of Gilbertism breaks our belief in the humanity of the play.

Would it be possible to have a sillier critical reaction to the most delightful comic drama in English since Shakespeare? Twenty-three years later, Shaw wrote a letter (if it is that) to Frank Harris, published by Harris in his *Life of Wilde* (1918), and then reprinted by Shaw in his *Pen Portraits and Reviews*. Again Wilde was an artist of "stupendous laziness," and again was indicted, this time after his death, for heartlessness:

Our sixth meeting, the only other one I can remember, was the one at the Cafe Royal. On that occasion he was not too preoccupied with his danger to be disgusted with me because I, who had praised his first plays handsomely, had turned traitor over The Importance of Being Earnest. Clever as it was, it was his first really heartless play. In the others the chivalry of the eighteenth-century Irishman and the romance of the disciple of Théophile Gautier (Oscar was old-fashioned in the Irish way, except as a critic of morals) not only gave a certain kindness and gallantry to the serious passages and to the handling of the women, but provided that proximity of emotion without which laughter, however irresistible, is destructive and sinister. In The Importance of Being Earnest this had vanished; and the play, though extremely funny, was essentially hateful. I had no idea that Oscar was going to the dogs, and that this represented a real degeneracy produced by his debaucheries. I thought he was still developing; and I hazarded the unhappy guess that The Importance of Being Earnest was in idea a young work written or projected long before under the influence of Gilbert and furbished up for Alexander as a potboiler. At the Cafe Royal that day I calmly asked him whether I was not right. He indignantly repudiated my guess, and said loftily (the only time he ever tried on me the attitude he took to John Gray and his more abject disciples) that he was disappointed in me. I suppose I said, "Then what on earth has happened to you?" but I recollect nothing more on that subject except that we did not quarrel over it.

Shaw remains unique in finding *The Importance of Being Earnest* (of all plays!) "essentially hateful." A clue to this astonishing reaction can be found in Shaw's outraged response to Max Beerbohm's review of *Man and Superman*, as expressed in his letter to Beerbohm, on September 15, 1903:

You idiot, do you suppose I don't know my own powers? I tell you in this book as plainly as the thing can be told, that the reason Bunyan reached such a pitch of mastery in literary art (and knew it) whilst poor Pater could never get beyond a nerveless amateur affectation which had not even the common workaday quality of vulgar journalism (and, alas! didn't know it, though he died of his own futility), was that it was life or death with the tinker to make people understand his message and see his vision, whilst Pater had neither message nor vision & only wanted to cultivate style, with the result that of the two attempts I have made to read him the first broke down at the tenth sentence & the second at the first. Pater took a genteel walk up Parnassus: Bunyan fled from the wrath to come: that explains the difference in their pace & in the length they covered.

Poor Pater is dragged in and beaten up because he was the apostle of style, while Bunyan is summoned up supposedly as the model for Shaw, who also has a message and a vision. It is a little difficult to associate *The Pilgrim's Progress* with *Man and Superman*, but one can suspect shrewdly that Pater here is a surrogate for Wilde, who had achieved an absolute comic music of perfect style and stance in *The Importance of Being Earnest*. Shavians become indignant at the comparison, but Shaw does poorly when one reads side by side any of the *Fabian Essays* and Wilde's extraordinary essay "The Soul of Man under Socialism." Something even darker happens when we juxtapose *Man and Superman* with *The Importance of Being Earnest*, but then Shaw is not unique in not being able to survive such a comparison.

Man and Superman

Everything about *Man and Superman*, paradoxical as the play was to begin with, now seems almost absurdly problematical. The very title cannot mean (any more) what Shaw doubtless intended it to mean: the Superman of Nietzsche, Zarathustra, the heroic vitalist who prophesies the next phase of Creative Evolution, the next resting place of that cold God, the Life Force. Nietzsche's Zarathustra, as Shaw blandly chose never to see, is a god-man who is free of what Freud came to call the Over-I (superego), the shadow or spectre of bad conscience that hovers above each separate self. But Shaw's Superman is simply Bunyan's Pilgrim writ large and brought (supposedly) up to date, Shaw being about as much an immoralist as Bunyan.

Nietzsche transvalued all values (perhaps) or tried to (in some moods), and at the least developed an extraordinary perspectivism that really does call every stance—rhetorical, cosmological, psychological—into question. Shaw was interested neither in rhetoric (which he dismissed as Paterian "style") nor in psychology (Associationist or Freudian), and his cosmological speculations, though mythologically powerful, are informed primarily by his post-Ruskinian and only quasi-Marxist political economics. His Fabian socialism marries the British Protestant or Evangelical sensibility (Bunyan, Carlyle, Ruskin) to philosophical speculation that might transcend Darwinian-Freudian scientism (Schopenhauer, Lamarck, Nietzsche, Bergson). Such a sensibility is moral and indeed Puritanical, so that Shaw always remained in spirit very close to Carlyle rather than to Nietzsche (who despised Carlyle and loved Emerson for his slyly immoralistic Self-Reliance). Shaw's Superman, alas, in consequence looks a lot more like Thomas Carlyle crying out "work, for the night cometh in which no man can work" than he does like Zarathustra-Nietzsche urging us: "Try to live as though it were morning."

In Shaw's defense, he took from the Nietzschean metaphor of the Superman what he most needed of it: a political and therefore literal reading, in which the Superman is nothing but what Shaw called "a general raising of human character through the deliberate cultivation and endowment of democratic virtue without consideration of property or class." That is a boring idealization, from an aesthetic or epistemological perspective, but pragmatically it is indeed what we most require and never will attain, which is why doubtless we must perish as a civilization. Such a consideration, fortunately, has nothing to do with *Man and Superman* as a farce and a sexual comedy, or with its glory, the extraordinary inserted drama of dialectic and mythology, "Don Juan in Hell," certainly the outstanding instance of a play-within-a-play from Shakespeare to Pirandello.

The preface to *Man and Superman* is a dedicatory epistle to the drama critic Arthur Bingham Walkley and is a piece of Shavian outrageousness, particularly in promising far more than the play can begin to deliver. Shakespeare, perpetual origin of Shavian aesthetic anxiety, is associated with Dickens as being obsessed with the world's diversities rather than its unities. Consequently, they are irreligious, anarchical, nihilistic, apolitical, and their human figures are lacking in will. Against them, Shaw ranges Bunyan, Nietzsche, and himself—the artist-philosophers! Shakespeare did not understand virtue and courage, which is the province of the artist-philosophers.

The shrewdest reply one could make to Shaw is to contrast Shakespeare's Falstaff (whom Shaw praises) to Nietzsche's Zarathustra. Which is the Superman, embodiment of the drive to live, person free of the superego? Hamlet, to Shaw, is an inadequate Don Juan, since he is famously irresolute. The sadness is that the Don Juan we will see debating the Devil in Hell is only (at best) a wistful impersonation of Hamlet, who remains the West's paradigm of intellectuality even as Falstaff abides forever as its paradigm of wit.

Yet this epistle commencing *Man and Superman* is one of Shaw's grandest performances, reminding us of how soundly he trained as a Hyde Park soapbox orator, a splendid preparation for a polemical playwright of ideas. In the midst of his perpetual advertisements for himself, he utters a poignant credo:

> Now you cannot say this of the works of the artist-philosophers. You cannot say it, for instance, of The Pilgrim's Progress. Put your Shakespearian hero and coward, Henry V and Pistol or Parolles, beside Mr Valiant and Mr Fearing, and you have a sudden revelation of the abyss that lies between the fashionable author who could see nothing in the world but personal aims and the tragedy of their disappointment or the comedy of their incongruity, and the field preacher who achieved virtue and courage by identifying himself with the purpose of the world as he understood it. The contrast is enormous: Bunyan's coward stirs your blood more than Shakespear's hero, who actually leaves you cold and secretly hostile. You suddenly see that Shakespear, with all his flashes and divinations, never understood virtue and courage, never conceived how any man who was not a fool could, like Bunyan's hero, look back from the brink of the river of death over the strife and labor of his pilgrimage, and say "yet do I not repent me"; or, with the panache of a millionaire, bequeath "my sword to him that shall succeed me in my pilgrimage, and my courage and skill to him that can get it." This is the true joy in life, the being used for a purpose recognized by yourself as a mighty one; the being thoroughly worn out before you are thrown on the scrap heap; the being a force of Nature instead of a feverish selfish little clod of ailments and grievances complaining that the world will not devote itself to making you happy. And also the only real tragedy in life is the being used by personally minded men for purposes which you recognize to be base. All the rest is at worst mere misfortune or mortality: this alone is misery, slavery, hell on earth; and the revolt against it is the only force that offers a man's work to the poor artist, whom our personally minded rich people would so willingly employ as pandar, buffoon, beauty monger, sentimentalizer and the like.

Shakespeare then is not a prophet or at least does not himself suffer personally the burden of his prophecy. Bunyan and Shaw are prophets, and if they suffer, then also they experience the "true joy in life ... the being a force of Nature." The passage has in it the accent of Carlyle, except that Carlyle rendered it with more gusto in his sublimely outrageous style, and Carlyle (not being in direct competition with Shakespeare) set Shakespeare first among the artist-prophets, higher even than Goethe. We are moved by Shaw, yet he has not the rhetorical power to overwhelm us (however dubiously) as Carlyle sometimes does.

Why has Shaw, of all dramatists, written a play about Don Juan Tenorio, or John Tanner, as he is called in *Man and Superman*? And in what way is the bumbling Tanner, cravenly fleeing the Life Force that is Ann Whitefield, a Don Juan? A crafty ironist, Shaw knows that all Don Juans, whether literary or experiential, are anything but audacious seducers. Poor Tanner is a relatively deliberate Shavian self-parody, and is all too clearly an Edwardian gentleman, a pillar of society, and very much a Puritan. He is all superego, and from the start is Ann's destined victim, her proper and inevitable husband, the father of her children. She will let him go on talking; she acts, and that is the end of it. The true Don Juan does not like women, which is why he needs so many of them. Tanner adores and needs Ann, though perhaps he will never know how early on the adoration and the need commenced in him.

Don Juan, as Shaw revises the myth, is Faust (whom Shaw calls the Don's cousin). He is the enemy of God, in direct descent from Faust's ancestor, Simon Magus the first Gnostic, who took the cognomen of Faustus ("the favored one") when he moved his campaign of charlatanry to Rome. Shaw's Don Juan is Prometheus as well as Faust, and so is an enemy not so much of God as of Jehovah (Shelley's Jupiter in *Prometheus Unbound*) the sky-tyrant, the deity of finance capitalism, repressive sexual morality, and institutional or historical Christianity.

It is manifest that *Man and Superman* does not have a Faustian or Promethean hero in the absurdly inadequate though amiable John Tanner. Tanner is, as Eric Bentley economically observes, a fool and a windbag, all-too-human rather than Don Juan Tenorio the Superman. But Shaw gives him a great dream: "Don Juan in Hell." Again Bentley is incisive: "Take away the episode in hell, and Shaw has written an anti-intellectual comedy." I would go a touch further and say: "Take away the episode in hell, and Shaw has written a very unfunny comedy." Though it can be directed and acted effectively, most of the play singularly lacks wit; its paradoxes are sadly obvious. But the paradoxes of "Don Juan in Hell" continue to delight and disturb, as in the contrast between the erotic philosophies of Don Juan and the Statue:

> DON JUAN: I learnt it by experience: When I was on earth, and
> made those proposals to ladies which, though universally con-
> demned, have made me so interesting a hero of legend, I was
> not infrequently met in some such way as this. The lady

would say that she would countenance my advances, provided they were honorable. On inquiring what that proviso meant, I found that it meant that I proposed to get possession of her property if she had any, or to undertake her support for life if she had not; that I desired her continual companionship, counsel, and conversation to the end of my days, and would take a most solemn oath to be always enraptured by them: above all, that I would turn my back on all other women for ever for her sake. I did not object to these conditions because they were exorbitant and inhuman: it was their extraordinary irrelevance that prostrated me. I invariably replied with perfect frankness that I had never dreamt of any of these things; that unless the lady's character and intellect were equal or superior to my own, her conversation must degrade and her counsel mislead me; that her constant companionship might, for all I knew, become intolerably tedious to me; that I could not answer for my feelings for a week in advance, much less to the end of my life; that to cut me off from all natural and unconstrained intercourse with half my fellowcreatures would narrow and warp me if I submitted to it, and, if not, would bring me under the curse of clandestinity; that, finally, my proposals to her were wholly unconnected with any of these matters, and were the outcome of a perfectly simple impulse of my manhood towards her womanhood.

ANA: You mean that it was an immoral impulse.

DON JUAN: Nature, my dear lady, is what you call immoral. I blush for it; but I cannot help it. Nature is a pandar, Time a wrecker, and Death a murderer. I have always preferred to stand up to those facts and build institutions on their recognition. You prefer to propitiate the three devils by proclaiming their chastity, their thrift, and their loving kindness; and to base your institutions on these flatteries. Is it any wonder that the institutions do not work smoothly?

THE STATUE: What used the ladies to say, Juan?

DON JUAN: Oh, come! Confidence for confidence. First tell me what you used to say to the ladies.

THE STATUE: I! Oh, I swore that I would be faithful to the death; that I should die if they refused me; that no woman could ever be to me what she was—

ANA: She! Who?

THE STATUE: Whoever it happened to be at the time, my dear. I

had certain things I always said. One of them was that even
when I was eighty, one white hair of the woman I loved would
make me tremble more than the thickest gold tress from the
most beautiful young head. Another was that I could not bear
the thought of anyone else being the mother of my children.

DON JUAN [*revolted*]: You old rascal!

THE STATUE [*stoutly*]: Not a bit; for I really believed it with all my
soul at the moment. I had a heart: not like you. And it was this
sincerity that made me successful.

DON JUAN: Sincerity! To be fool enough to believe a ramping,
stamping, thumping lie: that is what you call sincerity! To be
so greedy for a woman that you deceive yourself in your
eagerness to deceive her: sincerity, you call it!

THE STATUE: Oh, damn your sophistries! I was a man in love, not
a lawyer. And the women loved me for it, bless them!

Does Shaw take sides? Don Juan, advance guard for the Superman,
presumably speaks for the dramatist, but our sympathies are divided, or
perhaps not called upon at all. I hear the stance of Shelley's *Epipsychidion*
taken up in Don Juan's rhetoric, probably as a deliberate allusion on Shaw's
part. The Statue though, splendid fellow, speaks the universal rhetoric of
all ordinary men in love, and his rather dialectical "sincerity" has its own
persuasiveness. Much trickier, and a larger achievement, is Shaw's man-
agement of the fencing match between the Shavian Don Juan and that
Wildean-Paterian Aesthete, the Devil. Shaw's lifelong animus against
Pater, and his repressed anxiety caused by Wilde's genius as an Anglo-Irish
comic dramatist, emerge with authentic sharpness and turbulence as Don
Juan and the Devil face off. They are as elaborately courteous as Shaw and
Wilde always were with one another, but their mutual distaste is palpable,
as pervasive as the deep dislike of Shaw and Wilde for each other's works,
ideas, and personalities:

THE DEVIL: None, my friend. You think, because you have a purpose, Nature must have one. You might as well expect it to
have fingers and toes because you have them.

DON JUAN: But I should not have them if they served no purpose.
And I, my friend, am as much a part of Nature as my own finger is a part of me. If my finger is the organ by which I grasp
the sword and the mandoline, my brain is the organ by which
Nature strives to understand itself. My dog's brain serves only
my dog's purposes; but my own brain labors at a knowledge

which does nothing for me personally but make my body bitter to me and my decay and death a calamity. Were I not possessed with a purpose beyond my own I had better be a ploughman than a philosopher; for the ploughman lives as long as the philosopher, eats more, sleeps better, and rejoices in the wife of his bosom with less misgiving. This is because the philosopher is in the grip of the Life Force. This Life Force says to him "I have done a thousand wonderful things unconsciously by merely willing to live and following the line of least resistance: now I want to know myself and my destination, and choose my path; so I have made a special brain—a philosopher's brain—to grasp this knowledge for me as the husbandman's hand grasps the plough for me. And this" says the Life Force to the philosopher "must thou strive to do for me until thou diest, when I will make another brain and another philosopher to carry on the work."

THE DEVIL: What is the use of knowing?

DON JUAN: Why, to be able to choose the line of greatest advantage instead of yielding in the direction of the least resistance. Does a ship sail to its destination no better than a log drifts nowhither? The philosopher is Nature's pilot. And there you have our difference: to be in hell is to drift: to be in heaven is to steer.

THE DEVIL: On the rocks, most likely.

DON JUAN: Pooh! which ship goes oftenest on the rocks or to the bottom? the drifting ship or the ship with a pilot on board?

THE DEVIL: Well, well, go your way, Señor Don Juan. I prefer to be my own master and not the tool of any blundering universal force. I know that beauty is good to look at; that music is good to hear; that love is good to feel; and that they are all good to think about and talk about. I know that to be well exercised in these sensations, emotions, and studies is to be a refined and cultivated being. Whatever they may say of me in churches on earth, I know that it is universally admitted in good society that the Prince of Darkness is a gentleman; and that is enough for me. As to your Life Force, which you think irresistible, it is the most resistable thing in the world for a person of any character. But if you are naturally vulgar and credulous, as all reformers are, it will thrust you first into religion, where you will sprinkle water on babies to save their souls from me; then it will drive you from religion into science, where you will snatch the babies from the water sprinkling and inoculate them with disease to save them from catching it accidentally; then you will take to politics, where you will become the catspaw of corrupt functionaries and the henchman of ambitious humbugs; and the end will be despair and decrepitude, broken nerve and shattered hopes, vain regrets for that worst and silliest of wastes and sacrifices, the waste and sacrifice of the power of enjoyment: in a word, the punishment of the fool who pursues the better before he has secured the good.

DON JUAN: But at least I shall not be bored. The service of the Life Force has that advantage, at all events. So fare you well, Señor Satan.

THE DEVIL [*amiably*]: Fare you well, Don Juan. I shall often think of our interesting chats about things in general. I wish you every happiness: heaven, as I said before, suits some people. But if you should change your mind, do not forget that the gates are always open here to the repentant prodigal. If you feel at any time that warmth of heart, sincere unforced affection, innocent enjoyment, and warm, breathing, palpitating reality—

This is hardly fair to the Devil, whose Paterian sense of repetition is a powerful answer to the Idealism of Schopenhauer's Life Force, and whose Ecclesiastes-like vision of vanity does not exclude the holiness of the heart's affections. Don Juan regards the Devil as a sentimentalist, but the Creative Evolution preached by the Shavian Don now seems precisely the sentimentality of a lost world. By a paradox that Shaw would not have enjoyed, the Aesthetic vision of Pater and Wilde now appears to be Ruskin's abiding legacy, while Shaw's Fabian Evolutionism would seem to have been a Ruskinian dead end. *Man and Superman* is effective enough farce, and its "Don Juan in Hell" is more than that, being one of the rare efforts to turn intellectual debate into actable and readable drama. Yet *Man and Superman* survives as theater; if you want an artist-philosopher in social comedy, then you are better off returning to the sublime nonsense and Aesthetic vision of *The Importance of Being Earnest*, a play that Shaw so curiously condemned as being "heartless."

Major Barbara

Shaw initially planned to call *Major Barbara* by the rather more imposing title of *Andrew Undershaft's Profession*. The play has been so popular (deservedly so) that we cannot think of it by any other title, but the earlier notion would have emphasized Undershaft's strength and centrality. He dwarfs Cusins, and dominates Barbara, as much during her rebellion against him as in her return. And he raises the fascinating question of Shaw's own ambivalence toward the Socialist ideal, despite Shaw's lifelong labor in behalf of that ideal. Undershaft may be the archetype of the capitalist as amoral munitions-monger, but his arms establishment dangerously resembles a benign state socialism, and the drama moves finally in a direction equally available for interpretation by the extreme Left or the extreme Right.

Despite his ignorance of Freud, Shaw in *Major Barbara* (1905) wrote a drama wholly consonant with Freud's contemporary works, *The Interpretation of Dreams* and *Three Essays on the Theory of Sexuality*. Consider the first amiable confrontation of Barbara and her father Undershaft, who has not seen her since she was a baby:

> UNDERSHAFT: For me there is only one true morality; but it might not fit you, as you do not manufacture aerial battleships. There is only one true morality for every man; but every man has not the same true morality.
>
> LOMAX [*overtaxed*]: Would you mind saying that again? I didnt quite follow it.
>
> CUSINS: It's quite simple. As Euripides says, one man's meat is another man's poison morally as well as physically.
>
> UNDERSHAFT: Precisely.
>
> LOMAX: Oh, that! Yes, yes, yes. True. True.
>
> STEPHEN: In other words, some men are honest and some are scoundrels.
>
> BARBARA: Bosh! There are no scoundrels.
>
> UNDERSHAFT: Indeed? Are there any good men?
>
> BARBARA: No. Not one. There are neither good men nor scoundrels: there are just children of one Father; and the sooner they stop calling one another names the better. You neednt talk to me: I know them. Ive had scores of them through my hands: scoundrels, criminals, infidels, philanthropists, missionaries, county councillors, all sorts. Theyre all just the same sort of sinner; and theres the same salvation ready for them all.
>
> UNDERSHAFT: May I ask have you ever saved a maker of cannons?
>
> BARBARA: No. Will you let me try?
>
> UNDERSHAFT: Well, I will make a bargain with you. If I go to see

you tomorrow in your Salvation Shelter, will you come the
day after to see me in my cannon works?

BARBARA: Take care. It may end in your giving up the cannons for
the sake of the Salvation Army.

UNDERSHAFT: Are you sure it will not end in your giving up the
Salvation Army for the sake of the cannons?

BARBARA: I will take my chance of that.

UNDERSHAFT: And I will take my chance of the other. [*They shake
hands on it.*] Where is your shelter?

BARBARA: In West Ham. At the sign of the cross. Ask anybody in
Canning Town. Where are your works?

UNDERSHAFT: In Perivale St Andrews. At the sign of the sword.
Ask anybody in Europe.

LOMAX: Hadnt I better play something?

BARBARA: Yes. Give us Onward, Christian Soldiers.

LOMAX: Well, thats rather a strong order to begin with, dont you
know. Suppose I sing Thourt passing hence, my brother. It's
much the same tune.

BARBARA: It's too melancholy. You get saved, Cholly; and youll pass
hence, my brother, without making such a fuss about it.

LADY BRITOMART: Really, Barbara, you go on as if religion were a
pleasant subject. Do have some sense of propriety.

UNDERSHAFT: I do not find it an unpleasant subject, my dear. It is
the only one that capable people really care for.

Barbara, having replaced the absent Undershaft by God the Father
in his Salvation Army guise, begins by accepting her phallic father as
one more sinner to be saved. Their prophetic interchange of signs—
daughterly cross and fatherly sword—bonds them against the mother,
as each stands for a version of the only subject that the capable Shaw
really cares for: religion as the Life Force, Creative Evolution. The
daughter and the father, in mutual recognition, have commenced upon
their inevitably narcissistic dance of repressed psychosexual courtship.
Cusins shrewdly sums up the enigma in his act 2 dialogue with
Undershaft:

UNDERSHAFT: Religion is our business at present, because it is
through religion alone that we can win Barbara.

CUSINS: Have you, too, fallen in love with Barbara?

UNDERSHAFT: Yes, with a father's love.

CUSINS: A father's love for a grown-up daughter is the most

dangerous of all infatuations. I apologize for mentioning my own pale, coy, mistrustful fancy in the same breath with it.

Undershaft's love for Barbara is conversionary and therefore complex; its aim is to transform family romance into societal romance. After three quarters of a century, G.K. Chesterton remains much the best of Shaw's early critics, but he insisted upon a weak misreading of Undershaft's (and Shaw's) scheme:

> The ultimate epigram of *Major Barbara* can be put thus. People say that poverty is no crime; Shaw says that poverty is a crime; that it is a crime to endure it, a crime to be content with it, that it is the mother of all crimes of brutality, corruption, and fear. If a man says to Shaw that he is born of poor but honest parents, Shaw tells him that the very word "but" shows that his parents were probably dishonest. In short, he maintains here what he had maintained elsewhere: that what the people at this moment require is not more patriotism or more art or more religion or more morality or more sociology, but simply more money. The evil is not ignorance or decadence or sin or pessimism; the evil is poverty. The point of this particular drama is that even the noblest enthusiasm of the girl who becomes a Salvation Army officer fails under the brute money power of her father who is a modern capitalist. When I have said this it will be clear why this play, fine and full of bitter sincerity as it is, must in a manner be cleared out of the way before we come to talk of Shaw's final and serious faith. For this serious faith is in the sanctity of human will, in the divine capacity for creation and choice rising higher than environment and doom; and so far as that goes, *Major Barbara* is not only apart from his faith but against his faith. *Major Barbara* is an account of environment victorious over heroic will. There are a thousand answers to the ethic in *Major Barbara* which I should be inclined to offer. I might point out that the rich do not so much buy honesty as curtains to cover dishonesty: that they do not so much buy health as cushions to comfort disease. And I might suggest that the doctrine that poverty degrades the poor is much more likely to be used as an argument for keeping them powerless than as an argument for making them rich. But there is no need to find such answers to the materialistic pessimism of *Major Barbara*. The best answer to it is in Shaw's own best and crowning philosophy.

Is the environment of Undershaft's "spotlessly clean and beautiful hillside town" of well-cared-for munitions workers victorious over Barbara's heroic will? Has the sanctity of human will, its divine capacity for creation and choice, been violated by Undershaft playing the part of Machiavel? Who could be more Shavian than the great Life Forcer, Undershaft, who cheerfully provides the explosives with which the present can blast itself into the future, in a perhaps involuntary parody of Creative Evolution? How far is Undershaft from the Caesar of *Caesar and Cleopatra?* The questions are so self-answering as to put Chesterton, splendid as he is, out of court.

But that still gives us the problem of Barbara's conversion: to what precisely has she come? The scene of her instruction is a characteristic Shavian outrage, persuasive and absurd. Cusins.asks Undershaft the crucial question as to his munitions enterprise: "What drives the place?"

> UNDERSHAFT [*enigmatically*]: A will of which I am a part.
>
> BARBARA [*startled*]: Father! Do you know what you are saying; or are you laying a snare for my soul?
>
> CUSINS: Dont listen to his metaphysics, Barbara. The place is driven by the most rascally part of society, the money hunters, the pleasure hunters, the military promotion hunters; and he is their slave.
>
> UNDERSHAFT: Not necessarily. Remember the Armorer's Faith. I will take an order from a good man as cheerfully as from a bad one. If you good people prefer preaching and shirking to buying my weapons and fighting the rascals, dont blame me. I can make cannons: I cannot make courage and conviction. Bah! you tire me, Euripides, with your morality mongering. Ask Barbara: she understands. [*He suddenly reaches up and takes Barbara's hands, looking powerfully into her eyes.*] Tell him, my love, what power really means.
>
> BARBARA [*hypnotized*]: Before I joined the Salvation Army, I was in my own power; and the consequence was that I never knew what to do with myself. When I joined it, I had not time enough for all the things I had to do.
>
> UNDERSHAFT [*approvingly*]: Just so. And why was that, do you suppose?
>
> BARBARA: Yesterday I should have said, because I was in the power of God. [*She resumes her self-possession, withdrawing her hands from his with a power equal to his own.*] But you came and shewed me that I was in the power of Bodger and Undershaft.

Today I feel—oh! how can I put it into words? Sarah: do you remember the earthquake at Cannes, when we were little children?—how little the surprise of the first shock mattered compared to the dread and horror of waiting for the second? That is how I feel in this place today. I stood on the rock I thought eternal; and without a word of warning it reeled and crumbled under me. I was safe with an infinite wisdom watching me, an army marching to Salvation with me; and in a moment, at a stroke of your pen in a cheque book, I stood alone; and the heavens were empty. That was the first shock of the earthquake: I am waiting for the second.

There will not be a second shock, nor need there be. The dialectic of Barbara's conversion is all there in the single moment when Undershaft speaks of "a will of which I am a part" and Barbara is startled into the realization that her two fathers, Undershaft and God, are one. The realization is confirmed in the covenant of power that springs up between father and daughter as Undershaft takes Barbara's hands, while hypnotizing her through the will of which he is a part. Having been driven by one version of the Life Force, she yields now to another, but it is the same force. We somehow wish to find Shavian irony here, but there is less than we seek to find. What we discover is Shavian cruelty at Barbara's expense. Yielding her will to Undershaft sends Barbara into a massive regression, which calls into question her Christian idealism at the play's opening. A baby clutching at her mother's skirt, poor Barbara ends as the most reduced and humiliated heroine anywhere in Shaw. Why is he so harsh to so vivacious a figure, exuberant in her early idealism?

Eric Bentley observes accurately that "Barbara's final conversion has much less force than her previous disillusionment." This is useful as far as it goes, but Bentley is too fond of Shaw to see and say that her final conversion destroys her as an adult. *Major Barbara* is not a text for feminists, and if it can be construed as one for socialists, then they are very unsocial socialists indeed. Undershaft was a brilliant indication of where Shaw was heading, toward Carlyle's worship of heroes, strong men who would impose socialism because the Superman still waited to be born. Playful, wise, and charming, Undershaft nevertheless is a dangerous vision of the father-god enforcing the will of Creative Evolution. One remembers that Shaw, though knowing better, always retained a fondness for Stalin.

Nothing is got for nothing, and Shaw makes Barbara pay the price for this extravagant triumph of the religion of power. To be reconciled with the father, she becomes a child again, in a very curious parody of the

Christian second birth. Perhaps she is a Shavian self-punishment that masquerades as a Nietzschean will revenging itself against time. Her pathetic dwindling remains a dark tonality at the conclusion of one of Shaw's most enduring farces.

Pygmalion

Part of the lovely afterglow of *Pygmalion* (1913) resides in its positioning both in Shaw's career and in modern history. The First World War (1914–1918) changed Shaw's life and work, and nothing like so effective and untroubled a comedy was to be written by him again. If we seek his strong plays after *Pygmalion*, we find *Heartbreak House* (1916), *Back to Methuselah* (1921), *Saint Joan* (1923), and *Too True to be Good* (1932), none of them free of heavy doctrine, tendentious prophecy, and an unpleasant ambivalence toward human beings as they merely are. Fifty-eight and upon the heights of his comedic inventiveness, Shaw reacted to the onset of a catastrophic war with his bitter satiric pamphlet *Common Sense About the War*, which denounced both sides and called for instant peace.

British reaction, justifiably predictable, was hostile to Shaw until late 1916, when the increasing slaughter confirmed the accuracy of his prophetic views. By war's end, Shaw's public reputation was more than restored, but an impressively impersonal bitterness pervades his work from *Heartbreak House* until his death. *Pygmalion*, hardly by design, is Shaw's farewell to the Age of Ruskin, to an era when that precursor prophet, Elijah to his Elisha cried out in the wilderness to the most class-ridden of societies. Since Great Britain now, in 1986, is more than ever two nations, Shaw's loving fable of class distinctions and of a working girl's apotheosis, her rise into hard-won self-esteem, has a particular poignance that seems in no immediate danger of vanishing.

Pygmalion manifests Shaw's mythopoeic powers at their most adroit, and it is certainly Shaw himself who is still central and triumphant both in the film (which he wrote) and in the musical *My Fair Lady*. Mythmaking most affects us when it simultaneously both confirms and subverts sexual stereotypes, which is clearly Shaw's dramatic advantage over such male vitalists as D.H. Lawrence or the entire coven of literary feminists, from Doris Lessing to Margaret Atwood.

The best judgment of *Pygmalion* as drama that I have encountered is again Eric Bentley's:

> It is Shavian, not in being made up of political or philosophic discussions, but in being based on the standard conflict of vitality and

system, in working out this conflict through an inversion of romance, in bringing matters to a head in a battle of wills and words, in having an inner psychological action in counterpoint to the outer romantic action, in existing on two contrasted levels of mentality, both of which are related to the main theme, in delighting and surprising us with a constant flow of verbal music and more than verbal wit.

That is grand, but is *Pygmalion* more "an inversion of romance," more a *Galatea*, as it were, than it is a *Pygmalion*? Shaw subtitled it "A Romance in Five Acts." All romance, literary or experiential, depends upon enchantment, and enchantment depends upon power or potential rather than upon knowledge. In Bentley's reading, Eliza acquires knowledge both of her own vitality and of something lacking in Higgins, since he is incarcerated by "system," by his science of phonetics. This means, as Bentley severely and lucidly phrases it, that Higgins is suspect: "He is not really a life-giver at all." The title of the play, and its subtitle, are thus revealed as Shaw's own interpretive ironies. Higgins is not Pygmalion, and the work is not a romance.

That Eliza is more sympathetic than Higgins is palpably true, but it remains his play (and his film, though not his musical). In making that assertion, I do not dissent wholly from Bentley, since I agree that Higgins is no life-giver, no Prometheus. Shaw after all has no heroes, only heroines, partly because he is his own hero, as prophet of Creative Evolution, servant only of God, who is the Life Force. Higgins is another Shavian self-parody, since Shaw's passion for himself was nobly unbounded. The splendid Preface to *Pygmalion*, called *A Professor of Phonetics*, makes clear that Shaw considers Higgins a man of genius, a composite of Shaw himself, Henry Sweet who was Reader of Phonetics at Oxford, and the poet Robert Bridges, "to whom perhaps Higgins may owe his Miltonic sympathies," as Shaw slyly added.

Higgins, like Carlyle and Shaw, is a fierce Miltonist, an elitist who adopts toward women that great Miltonic maxim (so beloved by literary feminists): "He for God only, she for God in him," where the reference is to Adam and Eve in their relation to Milton's God. The myth of Shaw's *Pygmalion* is that of Pygmalion and Galatea, but also that of Adam and Eve, though as a Shavian couple they are never to mate (at least in Shaw's interpretation). Shaw rewrote some aspects of his *Pygmalion* in the first play, *In the Beginning*, of his *Back to Methuselah* cycle. There Adam and Eve repeat, in a sadly less comedic tone, the contrast between Higgins and Eliza:

ADAM: There is a voice in the garden that tells me things.

EVE: The garden is full of voices sometimes. They put all sorts of thoughts into my head.

ADAM: To me there is only one voice. It is very low; but it is so near that it is like a whisper from within myself. There is no mistaking it for any voice of the birds or beasts, or for your voice.

EVE: It is strange that I should hear voices from all sides and you only one from within. But I have some thoughts that come from within me and not from the voices. The thought that we must not cease to be comes from within.

Like Adam, Higgins hears the inner voice only, which is the Miltonic response to reality. Eve, like Eliza, hears the voice of the Life Force. Yet Adam, like Higgins, is no slave to "system." They serve the same God as Eve and Eliza, but they cannot accommodate themselves to change even when they have brought about change, as Higgins has worked to develop Eliza, and wrought better than, at first, he has been able to know or to accept, or ever be able to accept fully.

The famous final confrontation of Higgins and Eliza is capable of several antithetical interpretations, which is a tribute to Shaw's dialectical cunning, as he too wrought better (perhaps) than he knew, but then he truly was a Pygmalion:

HIGGINS [*wondering at her*]: You damned impudent slut, you! But it's better than snivelling; better than fetching slippers and finding spectacles, isn't it? [*Rising*] By George, Eliza, I said I'd make a woman of you; and I have. I like you like this.

LIZA: Yes: you turn round and make up to me now that I'm not afraid of you, and can do without you.

HIGGINS: Of course I do, you little fool. Five minutes ago you were like a millstone round my neck. Now youre a tower of strength: a consort battleship. You and I and Pickering will be three old bachelors instead of only two men and a silly girl.

　　Mrs Higgins returns, dressed for the wedding. Eliza instantly becomes cool and elegant.

MRS HIGGINS: The carriage is waiting, Eliza. Are you ready?

LIZA: Quite. Is the Professor coming?

MRS HIGGINS: Certainly not. He cant behave himself in church. He makes remarks out loud all the time on the clergyman's pronunciation.

LIZA: Then I shall not see you again, Professor. Goodbye. [*She goes to the door.*]

MRS HIGGINS [*coming to Higgins*]: Goodbye, dear.

HIGGINS: Goodbye, mother. [*He is about to kiss her, when he recollects something.*] Oh, by the way, Eliza, order a ham and a Stilton cheese, will you? And buy me a pair of reindeer gloves, number eights, and a tie to match that new suit of mine. You can choose the color. [*His cheerful, careless, vigorous voice shews that he is incorrigible.*]

LIZA [*disdainfully*]: Number eights are too small for you if you want them lined with lamb's wool. You have three new ties that you have forgotten in the drawer of your washstand. Colonel Pickering prefers double Gloucester to Stilton; and you dont notice the difference. I telephoned Mrs Pearce this morning not to forget the ham. What you are to do without me I cannot imagine. [*She sweeps out.*]

MRS HIGGINS: I'm afraid youve spoilt that girl, Henry. I should be uneasy about you and her if she were less fond of Colonel Pickering.

HIGGINS: Pickering! Nonsense: she's going to marry Freddy. Ha ha! Freddy! Freddy!! Ha ha ha ha ha!!!!! [*He roars with laughter as the play ends.*]

Shaw, in an epilogue to the play, married Eliza off to Freddy and maintained Higgins and Eliza in a perpetual transference, both positive and negative, in which Higgins took the place of her father, Doolittle:

That is all. That is how it has turned out. It is astonishing how much Eliza still manages to meddle in the housekeeping at Wimpole Street in spite of the shop and her own family. And it is notable that though she never nags her husband, and frankly loves the Colonel as if she were his favorite daughter, she has never got out of the habit of nagging Higgins that was established on the fatal night when she won his bet for him. She snaps his head off on the faintest provocation, or on none. He no longer dares to tease her by assuming an abysmal inferiority of Freddy's mind to his own. He storms and bullies and derides; but she stands up to him so ruthlessly that the Colonel has to ask her from time to time to be kinder to Higgins; and it is the only request of his that brings a mulish expression into her face. Nothing but some emergency or calamity great enough to break down all likes and dislikes, and throw them both back on their common humanity—and may they be spared any such trial!—will ever alter this. She knows that

Higgins does not need her, just as her father did not need her. The very scrupulousness with which he told her that day that he had become used to having her there, and dependent on her for all sorts of little services, and that he should miss her if she went away (it would never have occurred to Freddy or the Colonel to say anything of the sort) deepens her inner certainty that she is "no more to him than them slippers"; yet she has a sense, too, that his indifference is deeper than the infatuation of commoner souls. She is immensely interested in him. She has even secret mischievous moments in which she wishes she could get him alone, on a desert island, away from all ties and with nobody else in the world to consider, and just drag him off his pedestal and see him making love like any common man. We all have private imaginations of that sort. But when it comes to business, to the life that she really leads as distinguished from the life of dreams and fancies, she likes Freddy and she likes the Colonel; and she does not like Higgins and Mr Doolittle. Galatea never does quite like Pygmalion: his relation to her is too godlike to be altogether agreeable.

Shaw is clearly Pygmalion-Higgins here, and Mrs. Patrick Campbell is Galatea-Eliza. Mrs. Campbell, the actress who first played Eliza, had jilted Shaw definitively the year before *Pygmalion* opened in London, thus ending their never-consummated love affair. The price of being the prophet of Creative Evolution, in art as in experience, is that you never do get to make love to the Life Force.

Saint Joan

Saint Joan (1923) is a work written against its own literary age, the era of Proust, Joyce, Kafka, and above all others, Freud. It seems astonishing that *Saint Joan* is contemporary with Eliot's *The Waste Land* (1922). Eliot, whose own once-fashionable neo-Christianity now seems a refined superstition, rejected Shaw with his customary generosity of spirit: "The potent ju-ju of the Life Force is a gross superstition." That might be Stagumber crying out as he drags Joan out to be burned in Shaw's play, but then Eliot had become more English than the English. Luigi Pirandello, Shaw's peer as dramatist (as Eliot was not; *Murder in the Cathedral* weirdly concludes with a blatant imitation of the end of *Saint Joan*) made the inevitably accurate comment on the play, which is that it could as well have been called *Saint Bernard Shaw*:

Joan, at bottom, quite without knowing it, and still declaring herself a faithful daughter of the Church, is a Puritan, like Shaw himself—affirming her own life impulse, her unshakable, her even tyrannical will to live, by accepting death itself.

That "tyrannical will to live" is once again Shaw's revision of Schopenhauer by way of Ruskin and Lamarck—the only wealth is life, as Ruskin taught, and the will creatively modifies the evolution of life in the individual, as Shaw strongly misread Lamarck. Eric Bentley, always the brilliantly sympathetic defender of Shaw, reads *Saint Joan* as a triumphant resolution of Shaw's worn-out agon between system and vitality, between society and the individual, a resolution that is comprised of an exactly equal sympathy for the old antagonists. The sympathy cannot be denied, but the play is overwhelmingly Protestant and its rhetoric wars against its argument, and so takes the side of Joan.

What precisely is Joan's religion, which is to ask: Can we make a coherent doctrine out of the religion of Bernard Shaw—his religion as a dramatist rather than as G.B.S. the polemicist and public personality? Did he indeed believe that what he called the Evolutionary Appetite was "the only surviving member of the Trinity," the Holy Spirit? Milton, Shaw's greatest precursor as exalter of the Protestant Will and its holy right of private judgment, had invoked that Spirit as one that descended, in preference to all temples, in order to visit the pure and upright heart—of John Milton in particular. We know how prophetically serious Milton was in this declaration, and his sublime rhetoric persuades us to wrestle with his self-election. But what are we to do with Shaw, whose rhetoric perhaps can beguile us sometimes but never can persuade?

Joan, like Shaw, does very well without either God the Father or Jesus Christ His Son. Though her ghost concludes the epilogue by addressing the "God that madest this beautiful earth," she does not intend her auditor to be the Jehovah of Genesis. Her initial divine reference in the play is to "orders from my Lord," but immediately she tells us that "that is the will of God that you are to do what He has put into my mind," which means that her own will simply is the will of God. Since she is, like Shaw, an Anglo-Irish Protestant, she never once invokes Jesus or His Mother. Instead, she listens to the voices of "the blessed saints Catherine and Margaret, who speak to me every day," and who might as well be girls from her own village. Her battle cry is: "Who is for God and His Maid?" And her last words, before she is pushed off stage to the stake, make dear that she is Shaw's substitute for Jesus of Nazareth:

His ways are not your ways. He wills that I go through the fire to His bosom; for I am His child, and you are not fit that I should live among you. This is my last word to you.

In the queer but effective *The Adventures of the Black Girl in Her Search for God*, Shaw has his surrogate, whose "face was all intelligence," explain to the black girl his doctrine of work: "For we shall never be able to bear His full presence until we have fulfilled all His purposes and become gods ourselves.... If our work were done we should be of no further use: that would be the end of us." Carlyle would have winced at our becoming gods ourselves, but the gospel of labor remains essentially Carlyle's and Ruskin's. Defending *The Black Girl* in a letter to a friendly but pugnacious Abbess, Shaw associated himself with the prophet Micah and refused to take as his idea of God "the anti-vegetarian deity who, after trying to exterminate the human race by drowning it, was coaxed out of finishing the job by a gorgeous smell of roast meat." That is good enough fun, but we return to *Saint Joan* to ask a question that has nothing in common with the Anglo-Catholic Eliot's indictment of a gross superstition. Vocabulary aside, is Joan at all interested in God, any God at all? Is Shaw?

If the term "God" is to retain any crucial aspect of its Biblical range of reference, then Joan and Shaw could not care less. The Life Force has no personality, whereas Jehovah most certainly does, however uncomfortable it makes us. Is Joan anything except an embodiment of the Life Force? Has Shaw endowed her with a personality? Alas, I think not. The play holds the stage, but that will not always be true. Shaw's rhetoric is not provident or strong enough to give us the representation of a coherent psychology in Joan. The figure of the first few scenes has nothing in common with the heroine who repudiates her own surrender at the trial, or with the shade of a saint who appears to the King of France in his dream that forms the epilogue. No development or unfolding authentically links the country girl with the martyr.

Shaw's bravura as a dramatist saves the play as a performance piece, but cannot make it into enduring literature. Its humor works; its caricatures amuse us; its ironies, though too palpable, provoke analysis and argument. But Joan, though she listens to voices, cannot change by listening to her own voice speaking, which is what even the minor figures in Shakespeare never fail to do. Creative Evolution, as a literary religion, could not do for Shaw what he could not do for himself. In *Saint Joan*, he fails at representing persons, since they are more than their ideas.

Anton Chekhov

(1860–1904)

CHEKHOV'S BEST CRITICS TEND TO AGREE THAT HE IS ESSENTIALLY A
dramatist, even as a writer of short stories. Since the action of his plays is
both immensely subtle and absolutely ineluctable, the stories also are dramatic in Chekhov's utterly original way. D.S. Mirsky, in his helpful *History
of Russian Literature*, rather severely remarks upon "the complete lack of
individuality in his characters and in their way of speaking." That seems
unjust, but a critic, like myself, who reads no Russian perhaps cannot dispute Mirsky, who also indicts Chekhov's Russian:

> It is colorless and lacks individuality. He had no feeling for words.
> No Russian writer of anything like his significance used a language
> so devoid of all raciness and verve. This makes Chekhov (except
> for topical allusions, technical terms and occasional catch-words)
> so easy to translate; of all Russian writers, he has the least to fear
> from the treachery of translators.

It is difficult to believe that this helps account for the permanent popularity of Chekhov's plays in the English-speaking theater, or of his stories
with readers of English. Chekhov, as Mirsky also says, is uniquely original
and powerful at one mode of representation in particular: "No writer excels
him in conveying the mutual unsurpassable isolation of human beings and
the impossibility of understanding each other." Mirsky wrote this in 1936,
and presumably in ignorance of Kafka, before the advent of Beckett, but
they verge upon vision or phantasmagoria; Chekhov seems to represent a
simpler and more available reality, but by no means a cruder one.

The best critical observation on Chekhov that I have encountered is a
remark that Gorky made about the man rather than the stories and plays:

"It seems to me that in the presence of Anton Pavlovich, everyone felt an unconscious desire to be simpler, more truthful, more himself." That is the effect upon me of rereading "The Student" or "The Lady with Dog," or of attending a performance of *Three Sisters* or *The Cherry Orchard*. That hardly means we will be made any better by Chekhov, but on some level we will wish we could be better. That desire, however repressed, seems to me an aesthetic rather than a moral phenomenon. Chekhov, with his artist's wisdom, teaches us implicitly that literature is a form of desire and wonder and not a form of the good.

The Seagull

As a modern version of *Hamlet*, *The Seagull* surpasses Pirandello's *Henry IV* and even Beckett's *Endgame*, precisely because its *Hamlet* is so hopelessly weak. I do not mean by this that *The Seagull* is of the dramatic eminence of *Endgame*, or even of *Henry IV*; it is not, and seems to me the weakest and most contrived of Chekhov's four major plays. Its use of *Hamlet*, however, is shrewd and effective, and despite *The Seagull*'s limitations, few comedies stage better or remain as authentically funny.

Trigorin, in one of Chekhov's frightening ironies, appears to be a self-parody on Chekhov's own part. One hardly knows who is funnier, more outrageously deceptive, and ultimately self-deceived, the novelist or the actress. Trigorin begins by savoring Nina's naive but sincere offer to be ruined by him, which he, Arkadina, and we know he is going to take up anyway. That makes wholly and deliciously rancid Trigorin's deliberations: "Why do I hear so much sorrow in this cry sent by someone so pure in soul? Why does it wring so much pain in my own heart?" But even better is his address to Arkadina, beginning: "If you wanted to, you could be extraordinary." And yet better is the ferocious hilarity of the exchange after the actress has fallen upon her knees, with Arkadina assuring Trigorin that he is "Russia's one and only hope," and the submissive writer collapsing into: "Take me, carry me off, but just don't let me go one single step away from you." These beauties deserve, and will go on deserving, one another, and Chekhov has achieved the highest comedy with them, rather clearly modeling these extravagant charmers upon his own relation to various actresses.

Wherever it is pure comedy, *The Seagull* seems to me magnificent. Unfortunately, it has two aesthetic disasters, the unfortunate Konstantin, bad writer and mama's boy, who inconsiderately delays shooting himself until the very end of the play, and the aspiring actress Nina, Trigorin's eager victim, whose endless vows of high-mindedness always make me wish a director would interject a rousing chorus or two of Noel Coward's

"Don't put your daughter on the stage, Mrs. Worthington—don't put your daughter on the stage!" One sees what Chekhov meant to do with Nina, and Ibsen might have gotten away with it, but Chekhov was too good a comedian not to subvert his own presentation of Nina's idealism. That does not quite save Chekhov, and us, from having to hear Nina proclaim, "Know how to bear your cross and have faith." Subtlest of writers, Chekhov did not make that mistake again in a drama.

Uncle Vanya

Eric Bentley, in his superb essay on *Uncle Vanya*, observes that "what makes Chekhov seem most formless is precisely the means by which he achieves strict form—namely, the series of tea-drinkings, arrivals, departures, meals, dances, family gatherings, casual conversations of which his plays are made." This only apparent formlessness, as Bentley goes on to show, allows Chekhov to naturalize such unrealistic conventions as the tirade and "self-explaining soliloquies" spoken with others present but with no reference to others. "Naturalizing the unrealistic" is indeed a summary of Chekhov's dramatic art except that Chekhov's deep wisdom is always to remind us how strange "the realistic" actually is. One might venture, quite naively, that Chekhov's most indisputable power is the impression we almost invariably receive, reading his stories or attending his plays, that here at last is the truth of our existence. It is as though Chekhov's quest had been to refute Nietzsche's declaration that we possess art lest we perish from the truth.

Uncle Vanya, as it happens, is my earliest theatrical memory except for the Yiddish theater, since I saw the Old Vic production when I was a teenager. Alas, I have forgotten Laurence Olivier as Astrov, and even those three extraordinary actresses—Joyce Redman, Sybil Thorndike, Margaret Leighton—but that is because I was so permanently mesmerized by Ralph Richardson as Vanya, a performance eclipsed in my memory only by seeing Richardson, years later, as Falstaff. I have seen *Uncle Vanya* several times since, but in less splendid productions, and like *The Seagull*, it seems to survive any director. The audience discovers what Vanya and Sonya and even Astrov discover: our ordinary existence has a genuine horror in it, however we mask the recognition lest we become mad or violent. Sonya's dark, closing tirade can neither be forgotten nor accepted, and makes us reflect that *The Seagull* and *The Cherry Orchard* are subtitled as comedies in four acts, and *Three Sisters* as a drama in four acts, but *Uncle Vanya*, a play where all life must be lived vicariously, has the ironic subtitle "Scenes from Country Life in Four Acts."

Serebryakov is an effective if simplistic representation of all those qualities of obtuseness, vainglory, and ignorance that are the curse of the academic profession at all times and in all places. We are confronted again by the singular power of Chekhov's armory of ironies; it is the low intellectual and spiritual quality of Professor Serebryakov that helps reveal to Vanya and Sonya, Astrov and Yelena, their own lucid consciousnesses and ranges of significant emotion, a revelation that only serves to make a bad enough life still worse for all of them. You shall know the truth and the truth shall make you despair would be the gospel of Anton Chekhov, except that this gloomy genius insists upon being cheerful. As Bentley says, your fate is unsettled because that is how Chekhov sees the truth.

The highest tribute that can be made to *Uncle Vanya* is that the play partakes of the madness of great art; to describe it is to believe that attending it or reading it would be depressing, but the aesthetic dignity of this drama produces a very different effect, somber but strong, a dirge for the unlived life. If *Uncle Vanya* is not quite of the order of *Three Sisters* and *The Cherry Orchard*, still it surpasses *The Seagull* and is imperishable.

Three Sisters

Three Sisters seems to me, as to many other readers, Chekhov's masterpiece, outdoing even the grand epilogue to his work in *The Cherry Orchard* and such magnificent stories as "The Darling," "The Lady with Dog," and "The Bishop." But *Three Sisters* is darker even than *Uncle Vanya*, though more vitalistic in that darkness. Howard Moss, in a preternaturally Chekhovian essay on the play, began by noting that "the inability to act becomes the action of the play." That suggests to me a particular tradition in tragedy, one that includes the *Prometheus Bound* of Aeschylus and the Book of Job, and Job's inheritors in Milton's *Samson Agonistes* and Shelley's *The Cenci*. Since *Three Sisters* is not a tragedy, but deliberately only "a drama," of no genre, we are left perplexed by the play's final effect upon us, which does appear to be a Chekhovian ambiguity.

Moss's comparison to *Hamlet* applies throughout *Three Sisters* far more adequately than in *The Seagull*, though there the use of *Hamlet* is overt. Chekhov's three sisters—Olga, Masha, and Irina—together with their brother Andrew, make up a kind of fourfold parody of the prince of Denmark, rather in the way that the Karamazov—brothers Ivan, Mitya, Alyosha, and the bastard Smerdyakov—make up a sort of necessarily indeliberate parody of Blake's primordial man, Albion, by way of the Four Zoas who constitute him. Moss justly remarks that Olga is the least interesting of the three sisters, but that is only because Masha and Irina are so profoundly fascinating, and are more at home in the erotic realm than she is. Yet Olga has her own enchantments for the playgoer or reader, being both motherly and exceedingly fragile, incarnating the good, but unable to defend it, whether in herself or others.

An Ibsenite terror, much as we adore her, Masha gives everyone, on stage and in the audience, more truth than anyone can hope to bear, and she certainly is almost too much for her lover, the weak but imaginative Vershinin, who seems to be another of Chekhov's remarkably unflattering self-portraits. We do not know very much about some of the greatest writers of the past, but what we do know about some of the titans, such as Milton and Wordsworth, does not make us love them. Chekhov, of all the major writers, would appear to have been the best human being, something we could hardly know from his various self-presentations.

Masha is more intricate than Irina, but matched by her in vitality. What we remember best about Irina though is her grim metaphor in which she calls herself a locked piano to which she herself has lost the key. She is very young, but maturation will not make her able to return the passions that she so frequently provokes, and even if she reached the Moscow of her visions, her heart would not spring open there. Greatly deluded, Irina takes the erotic place of her dead mother, being her visual representative in the play, yet otherwise strangely unconnected to her. As for Andrew, he is less than his sisters, being little more than an amiable aesthete and his fierce wife's willing victim. Yet he is the artist among the four, even as Masha is the intellectual, Irina the dreamer, and Olga the benign embodiment of maternal care. All of them self-defeating, all worthy of love, all yearners for culture, kindness, and the spirit, the four Prozorovs are quite enough to break the heart of any playgoer.

Hamlet, particularly in Act 5, is beyond our love, and very nearly beyond even the most transcendental of our apprehensions. The sisters' suffering affects us so greatly because, unlike Hamlet, they are within the limits of the possible for us. Alas, they are incapable of learning to live to the full within the limits of the possible for themselves. The sisters' self-frustration remains as much a mystery as their failure to resist their rapacious sister-in-law, Natasha. Moss, again almost more Chekhovian than Chekhov was, insists that they are survivors and not losers, too alive to be quite mortal: "They may languish in life but they refuse to die in art, and with a peculiar insistence—an irony only good plays manage to achieve because it is only on the stage that the human figure is always wholly represented and representative." Chekhov would have agreed, but Tolstoy, as Moss well knows, would not. The sisters lament that they do not know enough, which Moss translates as their stasis, their inability to be elsewhere, to be different, to be in Moscow or in the world of open vision. So profound is Chekhov's play that I suspect the sisters must be right. They embody the truth but cannot know it, yet surely that is just as well. Unlike Vanya, they go on living not wholly without hope.

The Cherry Orchard is far less intricate in texture than Three Sisters, but like that greater play it is of no genre, though Chekhov insisted upon his subtitle: "A Comedy in Four Acts." Whatever Chekhov's intentions, we attend or read the drama now and are compelled to find in it the author's pastoral elegy both for himself and his world. There are strong elements of farce in The Cherry Orchard, and the merchant Lopakhin, though he has some complex elements, could be at home in a relatively pure farce. But the distinguished and doom-eager protagonist, Lyubov Andreevna Ranevsskaya, who is fated to lose the cherry orchard, is a figure of immense pathos, stylized yet intensely moving, and she prevents the play from being farce or pure comedy. The Cherry Orchard is a lyric meditation—theatrical through and through but a theater-poem, as Francis Fergusson usefully called it.

Genre hardly matters in Chekhov anyway, since like Shakespeare he excelled in the representation of change, or even impending change, and the dramatic image of a crossing or transition necessarily participates in the nature of what Emerson splendidly termed "shooting the gulf" or "darting to an aim." Chekhov is not much interested in the aim or in change as such, so I am impressed by Fergusson's complete phrase for The Cherry Orchard: "A Theater-Poem of the suffering of change." The pathos of change in this play is strangely similar to the pathos of stasis in Three Sisters, so it seems clear that Chekhov by "change" does not mean anything so vulgar or reductive as social and economic, let alone political metamorphoses. Lopakhin, before the play ends, is almost as much a figure of pathos as Lyubov. It is true that her life has been one long disaster: an alcoholic husband, dead of drink; an endless love affair with a scoundrel, who stole from her and abandoned her; the death by drowning of her little boy; the coming sale of her ancestral property. In contrast to this self-destructive and charming gentlewoman, Lopakhin is a very tough soul archetype of the self-made man. Son of a muzhik, Lopakhin has considerable cruelty in him, but his deep feeling is for Lyubov, with whom we can surmise he always will be, quite hopelessly, in love. But then, so are we, with this endlessly mobile and magnificent woman, this large-souled vision of passion on the old, grand, high scale. In his elegy for himself, the lover of women Anton Chekhov has given us his most vivid representation of an embodied Sublime in Lyubov.

Yet Lopakhin is even more interesting, and perhaps enables us to encounter a more profound pathos. The one respect in which *The Cherry Orchard* could be termed an advance over the astonishing *Three Sisters* is that in this masterpiece Chekhov had to give us Natasha as a very negative figure. I do not agree with Robert Brustein when he sees Natasha's victory as "the triumph of pure evil" and says she is "without a single redeeming trait." Unlike the sisters, whose vitality is thwarted, the uncultured Natasha is extending the life of the Prozorov family; she is peopling the house with babies, though it is unclear whether they are Prozorovs or the children of her onstage lover, one Protopopov, whose splendid name is that of a contemporary literary critic whom Chekhov despised. In any case, Lopakhin is no Natasha; he is not a villain, but a good man, though clownish and hard, and there is something curiously Shakespearean in his complex mixture of force and nostalgia, his pragmatic workmanship and his reverence for, almost awe of the glorious Lyubov.

It is almost as frustrating to attempt a description of the aesthetic effects of *The Cherry Orchard* as it is to venture an analysis of the almost absurdly rich *Three Sisters*. Chekhov, in his two finest plays, writes a theatrical poetry that relies upon perspectives unlike any achieved before him. Consider only the famous and weirdly poignant end of Act 3, Lopakhin's great moment, which calls for an extraordinary actor. Chekhov wrote it for Stanislavsky himself, who declined the part. Charles Laughton played it in London in 1933, and I always envision him as Lopakhin when I reread the play. One sees him handling that persuasive antithetical movement from Lopakhin proclaiming, "Music, start playing!" to his tenderly rough reproach to the bitterly weeping Lyubov, until he himself passes to tears, with the immense, "Oh, if only this would pass by as quickly as possible, if only we could hurry and change our life somehow, this unhappy, helterskelter way we live." The change he wants he cannot have—to be married to Lyubov, eternally too high above him—and his clownish exit ("I can pay for everything!") reverberates darkly as we listen to Anya's ineffectual and self-deceiving but sincere and loving consolation of her mother. We see why Chekhov, in his letters, described Lopakhin as a gentle and honest person, and as a man who did not shout. Chekhov, confronting change, humanized it, and goes on humanizing us.

Luigi Pirandello

(1867–1936)

RHETORIC, IN ITS ORIGINS, WAS A SICILIAN ART, AND IT IS FITTING THAT THE most rhetorical of modern dramatists, Luigi Pirandello, was also a Sicilian. The founder of rhetoric was the Sicilian shaman Empedocles, who preceded Plato in attempting to transform language from *doxa* (opinion) to truth, from the image-thinking of poetry to the concept-thinking of philosophy. Yet rhetoric stubbornly remained poetic, the instrument of a will-to-identity rather than a knower/known dualism. Gorgias, the Sicilian sophist who followed Empedocles, used rhetoric as Pirandello did, to enchant the audience into a realization of the antithetical nature of all truth. Plato, opposing this relativism, brought psychology and rhetoric overtly closer, but in essence they seem to me always one, with ancient and Renaissance cosmology making a third. In Pirandello, the Sicilian identity of rhetoric, psychology, and cosmology is confirmed. Though I agree with Eric Bently, Pirandello's canonical critic, that the dramatist of *Henry IV* and *Six Characters in Search of an Author* is an Ibsenite, I find Pirandello closest to Gorgias. Pirandello is the playwright-as-sophist, leading us to the relativity of all truth, through an antithetical style.

An opportunistic perspectivism, *kairos*, is the occasion for the Pirandello drama as it was for the Gorgias oration. Bently acutely notes the rhetoricity of Pirandello, which masks as an antirhetoric but is a stormy counter-rhetoric.

His strongest weapon is his prose. Its torrential eloquence and pungent force are unique in the whole range of modern drama, and recall the Elizabethans (in contrast to our verse playwrights who imitate the Elizabethans and do not in the least recall them). He gets effects that one would not have thought possible to colloquial prose, thus compelling us to reopen the discussion of poetry and drama, in which it has always been assumed that prose was a limitation.

Bentley quotes Pirandello on his own achievement, in a passage that carries us back to ancient Sicily and Gorgias's insistence upon *kairos*, the opportune word for the opportune moment, here in Pirandello "the word that will be the action ... the living word ... the immediate expression." One wonders if there is an element in Sicilian culture, repressive and sublimely explosive, that guarantees this continuity with ancient rhetoric even as Pirandello expounds his idea of dramatic composition:

> So that the characters may leap from the written pages alive and self-propelled, the playwright needs to find the word that will be the action itself spoken, the living word that moves, the immediate expression, having the same nature as the act itself, the unique expression that cannot but be this—that is, appropriate to this given character in this given situation; words, expressions, which are not invented but are born, where the author has identified himself with his creature to the point of feeling as it feels itself, wishing it as it wishes itself.

An art this rhetorical carries us back to Jacobean drama, the closest modern equivalent of which I would locate in Pirandello's extraordinary *Henry IV* (1922), though Beckett's *Endgame* comes to mind as an even darker rival. If Pirandello's *Henry IV*, generally regarded as a tragical farce, is also to be granted the status of tragedy, of a modern *Hamlet*, it can only be if the representation of the nameless nobleman, Pirandello's protagonist, possesses the aesthetic dignity appropriate to tragic art. That dignity turns upon his rhetorical persuasiveness, since the nameless one *wants* to be a tragic hero. Bentley, with great shrewdness, notes that Pirandello is not persuaded by his own creature:

> The protagonist insists on tragedy; the author does not. The protagonist is a character in search of the tragic poet: such is Pirandello's subject, which therefore comes out absurd, grotesque, tragicomic.

Dialectically, Bentley is accurate, and I think he interprets the play as Pirandello wished it to be interpreted. But strong rhetoric resists our will-to-power when we seek to interpret it, and the nameless one is a powerful rhetorician. Bentley thinks him essentially mad and regards his final stabbing of Belcredi as a crime. Belcredi is a skeptic and a jokester; in the world of *Henry IV* that marks him for death. Against such a view, Bentley argues that "this is not a tragedy, a heroic genre, but post-Dostoevski psychological drama showing the decline and fall of a man through mental sickness to crime." Time sustains Bentley, but then tragedy is no longer a heroic genre for us. It still is for the nameless one who has played at being Henry IV, and I am on his side as against Bentley and Pirandello, whose cruel joke it is that this character has found the wrong author at the wrong time.

That still leaves us with the puzzle of aesthetic dignity in *Henry IV*. The nameless one surely is in search of Kleist to serve as his author, or if he cannot and Idealist protagonist fir his Materialist play, and I suspect that the nameless one stabs Belcredi as a substitute for Pirandello himself, for having failed to let himself become a Kleist or a Schiller. If the nameless one is our Hamlet, then Pirandello is our Claudius in this clash of mighty opposites. *Henry IV* becomes its protagonist's revenge upon Pirandello for refusing to write a tragedy rather than a farce. And yet the grand rhetoric of this Sicilian descendant of Empedocles and Gorgias takes a subtler and more beautiful revenge. Few moments in modern drama have the poignance of the vision Pirandello grants us of the nameless one and his inadequate retainers sitting together in the lamplight, with the marvelous antithesis of the actors, acting the part of acting Henry IV and his retainers, set against the rhetoric, at once ironic and opportunistic, of the nameless Idealist:

HENRY IV: Ah, a little light! Sit there around the table, no, not like that; in an easy, elegant manner! ...
(*To Harold.*) Yes, you, like that!
(*Poses him.*)
(*Then to Berthold.*) You, so! ... and I, here!
(*Sits opposite them.*) We could do with a little decorative moonlight. It's very useful for us, the moonlight. I feel a real necessity for it, and pass a lot of time looking up at the moon from my window. Who would think, to look at her that she knows that eight hundred years have passed, and that I, seated at the window, cannot really be Henry IV gazing at the moon like any poor devil? But, look, look! See what a magnificent might scene we have here: the emperor surrounded by his faithful counselors! ... How do you like it?

How do we like it? Despite the overt irony, it seems too tragic for farce, but perhaps only for this single moment. Pirandello, in his counter-rhetoric, does remain an ancient Sicilian rhetorician and charms us into relativity by the incantation of his antitheses. His influence upon other dramatists came through his innovations as a counter-illusionist, but his continued influence upon us is rhetorical as well as dramatic.

John Millington Synge

(1871–1909)

Playboy of the Western World

EIGHTY YEARS AFTER ITS RIOT-PROVOKING FIRST PERFORMANCE (1907), Synge's *Playboy of the Western World* retains an extraordinary freshness. Whether or not it was or is an accurate representation of peasant life in the impoverished rural west of Ireland seems rather unimportant. What matters is the play's aesthetic originality and power as a kind of phantasmagoric farce, vitalistic in its ideology, anticlerical in its parodistic drive, and exalting the persuasiveness of rhetoric over the reductive world of the reality principle.

Synge's *Playboy*, as a stage comedy, has important debts to Shakespeare, Ben Jonson, and Molière, and a closer relationship to the exuberant vitalism of that savage visionary, Yeats, but its originality is the most salient quality that a rereading establishes. A reader is likelier to think of Sean O'Casey, Synge's successor, than of Synge's own precursors. In *Playboy*, Synge triumphantly made it new, partly by an art of perspectivism learned from Molière and partly by an almost Chaucerian and Shakespearean genius for representing the change of a character who changes precisely by listening to his own language. Christy Mahon is transformed by overhearing himself, and his extraordinary metamorphosis in act 3 is one of the glories of modern drama.

Allegorizations of Synge's *Playboy* generally fail, not because they venture too much, but because they tend to be timid and mechanical. Christy Mahon does not seem to me a parody either of Christ or of Oedipus, though his parodistic relationship to Cuchulain, hero of Ireland and of Yeats, is clear enough. But so original is Synge's mode of visionary farce that parody becomes phantasmagoric reality, and the spirit of Cuchulain inhabits Christy throughout act 3. Cervantes hovers near, and Synge himself invoked Don Quixote as relevant to Christy Mahon. Celtic chivalry, brutal in its rhetoric and in its myths, returns from the repressed in *The Playboy of the Western World*, a drama never likely to be popular with Irish Catholic audiences, whether in Eire or America.

One paradox of the Irish dramatic tradition is that it is Protestant; another is that it celebrates not only Protestant individuality but Romantic vitalism, even when it at last reaches the abyss, in *Waiting for Godot*, *Endgame*, and *Krapp's Last Tape*. From the title until its extraordinary final lament, the *Playboy* is one of the most extravagant ironies ever to be played upon the stage. The "Western World" turns out to be northwest Mayo, hardly in 1907 a breeding ground for playboys. When, at drama's end, Pegeen Mike pulls her shawl over her head, we hear a somewhat surprising lamentation: "Oh my grief, I've lost him surely. I've lost the only Playboy of the Western World." The surprise is that the charming young Pegeen, only a few moments before, has blown up the fire with a bellows, so as to lift up a lighted sod in order to scorch the Playboy's leg, while he is pinned down on the floor by her companions. One doubts that the Dublin and American riots against the *Playboy* really were caused by Christy's celebrated image of "a drift of chosen females, standing in their shifts itself, maybe, from this place to the Eastern World." Synge's image of west Ireland is joyous in its presentation, but what it reflects is barbaric squalor, credulity, brutal cupidity—a world of drunken louts and their hopelessly desperate women.

The only exception is Christy Mahon himself, one of the most curious heroes that even modern drama has engendered. For two acts he is scarcely an improvement over those he has come among, and at first we do not like him any better when he enters, dressed as a jockey, after his offstage triumphs in act 3. His courtship of Pegeen is then conducted in the rhetoric of a lowlife Tamburlaine, and he is as piteous as ever when his perpetually resurrected father, the old Mahon, rushes in upon him. Synge's finest moment is the epiphany of Christy's transformation after Pegeen turns against him, for reasons just as bad as first moved her towards him:

> CHRISTY (*to Mahon, very sharply*): Leave me go!
> CROWD: That's it. Now Christy. If them two set fighting, it will
>   lick the world.
> MAHON (*making a grab at Christy*): Come here to me.
> CHRISTY (*more threateningly*): Leave me go, I'm saying.
> MAHON: I will maybe, when your legs is limping, and your back is
>   blue.

CROWD: Keep it up, the two of you. I'll back the old one. Now the playboy.

CHRISTY (*in low and intense voice*): Shut your yelling, for if you're after making a mighty man of me this day by the power of a lie, you're setting me now to think if it's a poor thing to be lonesome, it's worse maybe to go mixing with the fools of earth.

(*Mahon makes a movement towards him.*)

CHRISTY (*almost shouting*): Keep off ... lest I do show a blow unto the lot of you would set the guardian angels winking in the clouds above.

(*He swings round with a sudden rapid movement and picks up a loy.*)

CROWD (*half frightened, half amused*): He's going mad! Mind your-selves! Run from the idiot!

CHRISTY: If I am an idiot, I'm after hearing my voice this day say-ing words would raise the topknot on a poet in a merchant's town. I've won your racing, and your lepping, and ...

MAHON: Shut your gullet and come on with me.

CHRISTY: I'm going, but I'll stretch you first.

(*He runs at old Mahon with the loy, chases him out of the door, followed by crowd and Widow Quin. There is a great noise outside, then a yell, and dead silence for a moment. Christy comes in, half dazed, and goes to fire.*)

WIDOW QUIN (*coming in, hurriedly, and going to him*): They're turn-ing again you. Come on, or you'll be hanged, indeed.

CHRISTY: I'm thinking, from this out, Pegeen'll be giving me praises the same as in the hours gone by.

That low and intense voice in which Christy celebrates the power of a lie marks the incarnation of a new self in him, a self that might even be called (as it was in the eighteenth century) the Poetical Character. When Christy comes in, half dazed, it is with the repeated, mistaken belief that *this time* he indeed has murdered his father. He proceeds to continue his absurdly Romantic quest for Pegeen until he Suffers the horror of her fall from imagination:

CHRISTY: What ails you?

SHAWN (*triumphantly, as they pull the rope tight on his arms*): Come on to the peelers, till they stretch you now.

CHRISTY: Me!

MICHAEL: If we took pity on you, the Lord God would, maybe,

bring us ruin from the law to-day, so you'd best come easy, for
hanging is an easy and a speedy end.

CHRISTY: I'll not stir. (*To Pegeen.*) And what is it you'll say to me,
and I after doing it this time in the face of all?

PEGEEN: I'll say, a strange man is a marvel, with his mighty talk;
but what's a squabble in your backyard, and the blow of a loy,
have taught me that there's a great gap between a gallous story
and a dirty deed. (*To Men.*) Take him on from this, or the lot
of us will be likely put on trial for his deed to-day.

CHRISTY (*with horror in his voice*): And it's yourself will send me off,
to have a horny-fingered hangman hitching his bloody slip-
knots at the butt of my ear.

MEN (*pulling rope*): Come on, will you?

(*He is pulled down on the floor.*)

CHRISTY (*twisting his legs round the table*): Cut the rope, Pegeen,
and I'll quit the lot of you, and live from this out, like the
madmen of Keel, eating muck and green weeds, on the faces
of the cliffs.

From playboy to mad outcast is the rhetorical gesture, but the psychic
reality is that the nastily pragmatic Pegeen has just stimulated Christy into
falling out of love, which Iris Murdoch splendidly reminds us is one of the
great human experiences, causing us to see the world again with awakened
eyes. After battling bravely and almost gaily against the whole pack of
Mayo men and suffering Pegeen's judicious efforts with the hot sod,
Christy greets Old Mahon with a marvelous humor: "Are you coming to
be killed a third time, or what ails you now?" Soon enough, resurrected
father and newly born son are reconciled, with their former authority relationship reversed, and Christy bestows a final blessing upon the louts and
dionysiac women he leaves behind him:

CHRISTY: Ten thousand blessings upon all that's here, for you've
turned me a likely gaffer in the end of all, the way I'll go
romancing through a romping life time from this hour to the
dawning of the judgment day.

(*He goes out.*)

MICHAEL: By the will of God, we'll have peace now for our drinks.
Will you draw the porter, Pegeen?

SHAWN (*going up to her*): It's a miracle Father Reilly can wed us in
the end of all, and we'll have none to trouble us when his
vicious bite is healed.

PEGEEN (*hitting him a box on the ear*): Quit my sight. (*Putting her shawl over her head and breaking out into wild lamentations.*) Oh my grief, I've lost him surely. I've lost the only Playboy of the Western World.

He goes out, and the spirit of romance goes with him, leaving the unhappy Pegeen with her cowardly betrothed and with the Western World of Father Reilly. To call Synge sardonic is weak and inadequate, if only because the apotheosis of Christy from timid brat to roaring boy has a Marlovian persuasiveness about it. Synge took the large dramatic risk of linking the imagination to familial violence in a purely comic context. *The Playboy of the Western World*, his masterwork, places Synge securely between Wilde and Shaw, just before him, and O'Casey and Beckett, coming after. To have written a comedy as original as *The Importance of Being Earnest* or *Pygmalion*, and as dark in its nihilistic implications as *Juno and the Paycock* or *Endgame*, is an astonishingly integrated achievement.

Sean O'Casey

(1884-1964)

SEAN O'CASEY, BY CIRCUMSTANCES NOT BY BIRTH AN AUTHENTIC WORKING-class writer, was a crucial figure in that Irish Protestant tradition of play-wrights who constitute very nearly all of the British drama that matters after Shakespeare: Congreve, Goldsmith, Sheridan, Wilde, Shaw, Synge, Yeats, O'Casey, Beckett. As the secretary of the Irish Citizen Army, the paramilitary wing of Jim Larkin's Irish Transport and General Workers Union, O'Casey helped prepare the way for the Easter Rising of 1916, but fortunately for literature he did not fight in it, because he had quarreled with James Connolly, who had succeeded Larkin as the leader of the Irish Labor movement. Connolly was executed for leading the Rising, together with the poets Pearse and MacDonagh, and the military man MacBride, who had married Yeats's Beatrice, the Nationalist agitator Maud Gonne. O'Casey survived to write one good play, *The Shadow of a Gunman*, and two great plays, *Juno and the Paycock* and *The Plough and the Stars*.

A nationalist riot against *The Plough and the Stars* at the Abbey Theatre in Dublin, on February 11, 1926, led by the formidable Mrs. Sheehy-Skeffington, widow of one of the hero-martyrs of the Easter Rising, helped create a climate of hostility that impelled O'Casey to take up permanent residence in England. This exile proved to be as unfortunate for O'Casey's art as his not joining the Rising was fortunate and became another sad instance of Emerson's iron law of Compensation: "Nothing is got for noth-ing." The plays that O'Casey wrote in London and Devon were all a waste of his genius; literature remembers him for his three grand Dublin plays, in which the shadow of revolutionary violence falls across the Hogarthian exuberance of the working-class tenements. All three plays were called tragedies by O'Casey, and critics call them tragicomedies, but their genre is pragmatically indescribable. They are, to use Ben Jonson's great phrase, rammed with life; they have Shakespearean verve, though alas nothing like Shakespearean powers of representation or of language.

The Easter Rebellion of 1916 is the context of *The Plough and the Stars*, while the Anglo-Irish War of 1919–21 between the Nationalists and the British is the setting of *The Shadow of a Gunman*. *Juno and the Paycock*, O'Casey's masterwork, takes the very different background of the Irish Civil War of 1922–23. O'Casey, essentially a Communist, believed only in class war and therefore regarded the Easter Rising, the Anglo-Irish War, and the Irish Civil War as betrayals of the Dublin working class, or at best irrelevant to its interests. It is crucial to reading or attending O'Casey's Dublin plays that we start with the realization of the dramatist's disaffection from all the Irish patriotic myths and glorifications of national troubles.

Donal Danoren, the poet who is the rueful hero of *The Shadow of a Gunman*, identifies himself with Shelley, and even more with Shelley's Prometheus, tortured by Jupiter. O'Casey, more truly a Shelleyan than a Marxist, always identified the Irish working class with the figure of Prometheus. The satiric intensities of the Dublin plays mask, but only barely, O'Casey's angry love for the Dublin poor. It is the curious triumph of O'Casey that his two most important plays convert his compassion and identification into an aesthetic quality. St. John Ervine, writing on *The Plough and the Stars* in 1927, made the best comment I have seen upon this:

> I have more than once described Mr. O'Casey as an Irish Chekhov, and I abide by that description, but I might more aptly describe him as a sentimental Hogarth, a Hogarth without any savagery in him. Mr. O'Casey, who must have found himself in congenial company the other night when he sat by the side of Mr. Augustus John, paints his pictures with the same veracity that Hogarth painted his, but he has not Hogarth's insane detachment from his subjects. If anything is manifest in [the plays] it is the immense pity and love which Mr. O'Casey feels for the people in the tenements. They are offered to us without any middle-class palliation or contempt—a fact which no doubt accounts for the hysterical wrath of the refined ladies who kicked up a hullabaloo in the Abbey—and are neither condemned nor exalted. There they are, as they are and for what they are, creatures full of vanity and windy emotions, child-like, superstitious, sentimental, kindly, greedy, full of ferocity and fear, capable of courage, play-acting, and a sour sort of romance; and with it all, pitiable. They have their strutting vanity, and their mouths are full of wrecked words,

lost in Ireland when the Elizabethan tradition foundered in the appalling mess of industrialism in England; but they have, too, a comic dignity and glory which raises them above their sordid circumstances and relates them to the age of romance and the swaggering grace of men who still possess rights in their own minds. That is why these people, as they are offered to us by Mr. O'Casey, steal into our affections, even while we are informing each other that they are hopeless and can never be regenerate.

"A sentimental Hogarth" ought to be an impossibility; I would prefer "a Shelleyan Hogarth," which is even more uncanny. O'Casey's power as a dramatist in his two strong plays is that he does fuse incompatibles, perhaps not Shelley and Hogarth, but certainly a strain of militant idealism and a current of comic realism, so that a noble exuberance, original and heartening, momentarily comes to birth.

Juno and the Paycock

The Victorian authors who most influenced O'Casey were Ruskin and Dickens. Ruskin, who made so many thinking men and women into socialists, certainly contributed more than Marx or Lenin to O'Casey's Communism. Dickens shares with Shakespeare and the Protestant Bible the role of the crucial influence upon *Juno and the Paycock*, which merits the honor of being called a Dickensian play. "Captain" Jack Boyle has a superficial resemblance to the great Falstaff, but to bring Boyle and Falstaff into juxtaposition is to destroy Boyle, who is no monarch of wit. Poor Boyle needs defense, even against his creator, O'Casey, who somewhat maligned his creature in an afterthought of 1955:

> It is a tragedy of vanity, and of subservience to vanity. There is a touch of Boyle in all of us. We strut along thinking that our shadows shine. There's a touch of Joxer in a lot of us: saying yes where we ought to say no. And I hope there is some Mrs. Boyle in all of us. To be brave even at the eleventh hour.

If Boyle were vanity alone, a peacock strutting before his Juno, then even his flamboyance could not sustain the play. But he is sublimely comic, not mastering reality with wit, as Falstaff can, but ignoring reality as a grand charlatan must. He goes back through Dickens to the Ben Jonson of *The Alchemist*, partly because he is on the border between self-deception and a phantasmagoria that is a kind of near-madness. In an odd sense, the

O'Casey of the Dublin plays was an Elizabethan throwback, an impression strengthened by the surviving traces of Elizabethan diction and rhetoric in the extravagant speech of Boyle, Joxer, and others. A lovely sequence in act 1 of *Juno and the Paycock* weaves together the chant of a coal vendor with Boyle's bluster and Joxer's supporting refrain:

> *The voice of a coal-block vendor is heard chanting in the street.*
> VOICE OF COAL VENDOR: Blocks ... coal-blocks! Blocks ... coal-blocks!
> JOXER: God be with the young days when you were steppin' the deck of a manly ship, with the win' blowin' a hurricane through the masts, an' the only sound you'd hear was, "Port your helm!" an' the only answer, "Port it is, sir!"
> BOYLE: Them was days, Joxer, them was days. Nothin' was too hot or too heavy for me then. Sailin' from the Gulf o' Mexico to the Antanartic Ocean. I seen things, I seen things, Joxer, that no mortal man should speak about that knows his Catechism. Ofen, an' ofen, when I was fixed to the wheel with a marlin-spike, an' the win's blowin' fierce an' the waves lashin' an' lashin', till you'd think every minute was goin' to be your last, an' it blowed, an' blowed—blew is the right word, Joxer, but blowed is what the sailors use....
> JOXER: Aw, it's a darlin' word, a daarlin' word.
> BOYLE: An', as it blowed an' blowed, I ofen looked up at the sky an' assed meself the question—what is the stars, what is the stars?
> VOICE OF COAL VENDOR: Any blocks, coal-blocks; blocks, coal-blocks!
> JOXER: Ah, that's the question, that's the question—what is the stars?
> BOYLE: An' then, I'd have another look, an' I'd ass meself—what is the moon?
> JOXER: Ah, that's the question—what is the moon, what is the moon?
> *Rapid steps are heard coming towards the door.* Boyle *makes desperate efforts to hide everything;* Joxer *rushes to the window in a frantic effort to get out;* Boyle *begins to innocently lilt "Oh, me darlin' Jennie, I will be thrue to thee," when the door is opened, and the black face of the* Coal Vendor *appears.*
> THE COAL VENDOR: D'yez want any blocks?
> BOYLE (*with a roar*): No, we don't want any blocks!

JOXER (*coming back with a sigh of relief*): That's afther puttin' the heart across me—I could ha' sworn it was Juno. I'd betther be goin', Captain; you couldn't tell the minute Juno'd hop in on us.

BOYLE: Let her hop in; we may as well have it out first as at last. I've made up me mind—I'm not goin' to do only what she damn well likes.

JOXER: Them sentiments does you credit, Captain; I don't like to say anything as between man an' wife, but I say as a butty, as a butty, Captain, that you've stuck it too long, an' that it's about time you showed a little spunk.

How can a man die betther than facin' fearful odds,
For th' ashes of his fathers an' the temples of his gods?

BOYLE: She has her rights—there's no one denyin' it, but haven't I me rights too?

JOXER: Of course you have—the sacred rights o' man!

BOYLE: Today, Joxer, there's goin' to be issued a proclamation be me, establishin' an independent Republic, an' Juno'll have to take an oath of allegiance.

JOXER: Be firm, be firm, Captain; the first few minutes'll be the worst: if you gently touch a nettle it'll sting you for your pains; grasp it like a lad of mettle, an' as soft as silk remains!

VOICE OF JUNO OUTSIDE: Can't stop, Mrs. Madigan—I haven't a minute!

JOXER (*flying out of the window*): Holy God, here she is!

BOYLE (*packing the things away with a rush in the press*): I knew that fella ud stop till she was in on top of us!

Joxer parodies Hotspur on the nettle of danger and the flower of safety, but the humor here is necessarily more Jonsonian than Shakespearean. The voice of the coal vendor breaks like reality across the delicious absurdities of Boyle and Joxer, and there is a fine contrast between the sublimely silly "what is the moon?" and the sudden apparition of the not very moonlike coal-black face of the vendor.

The final scene of the play, though still exquisitely comic, has a rancid intensity that is one of O'Casey's salient qualities. We watch Boyle and Joxer stagger in drunk and we are vastly amused, but we do not forget that Boyle's son has been dragged off to be executed by the Nationalists, and that Boyle's pregnant daughter, twice-jilted, has departed with the indomitable Juno, her mother. Boyle has been cast out by Juno, who will never return, but will devote herself to her daughter and grandchild. The last we hear from Juno, just before Boyle and Joxer stagger in, is a fierce prayer directed against the Irish Civil War:

> Sacred Heart o' Jesus, take away our hearts o' stone, and give us hearts o' flesh! Take away this murdherin' hate, an' give us Thine own eternal love!

Against that reverberation, the antics of Boyle and Joxer are partly hollowed out and yet remain a representation that gives us great pleasure:

> *There is a pause; then a sound of shuffling steps on the stairs outside. The door opens and* Boyle *and* Joxer, *both of them very drunk, enter.*
>
> BOYLE: I'm able to go no farther.... Two polis, ey ... what were they doin' here, I wondher? ... Up to no good, anyhow ... an' Juno an' that lovely daughter o' mine with them. (*Taking a sixpence from his pocket and looking at it*) Wan single, solitary tanner left out of all I borreyed.... (*He lets it fall.*) The last o' the Mohicans.... The blinds is down, Joxer, the blinds is down!
>
> JOXER (*walking unsteadily across the room, and anchoring at the bed*): Put all ... your throubles ... in your oul' kit-bag ... an' smile ... smile ... smile!
>
> BOYLE: The counthry'll have to steady itself ... it's goin' ... to hell ... Where'r all ... the chairs ... gone to ... steady itself, Joxer ... Chairs'll ... have to ... steady themselves ... No matther ... what any one may ... say ... Irelan' sober ... is Irelan' ... free.
>
> JOXER (*stretching himself on the bed*): Chains ... an' ... slaveree ... that's a darlin' motto ... a daaarlin' ... motto!
>
> BOYLE: If th' worst comes ... to th' worse ... I can join a ... flyin' ... column.... I done ... me bit ... in Easther Week ... had no business ... to ... be ... there ... but Captain Boyle's Captain Boyle!
>
> JOXER: Breathes there a, man with soul ... so ... de ... ad ... this ... me ... o ... wn, me nat ... ive l ... an'!
>
> BOYLE (*subsiding into a sitting posture on the floor*): Commandant Kelly died ... in them... arms ... Joxer.... Tell me Volunteer Butties ... says he ... that ... I died for ... Irelan'!
>
> JOXER: D'jever rade Willie ... Reilly ... an' his own ... Colleen ... Bawn? It's a darlin' story, a daarlin' story!
>
> BOYLE: I'm telling you ... Joxer ... th' whole words ... in a terr ... ible state o' ... chassis!
>
> CURTAIN

I cannot imagine a more splendid conclusion to *Juno and the Paycock* than the double truth: "Irelan' sober ... is Irelan' ... free," and "th' whole words ... in a terr ... ible state o' ... chassis!" We remember O'Casey, at his best, as we remember Dickens (who also revered Ben Jonson). To be the modern dramatist who returns us to the worlds of *The Alchemist* and of the *Pickwick Papers* is no mean distinction. O'Casey became the friend and admirer of Eugene O'Neill, who returned the admiration and sincerely cried out that he wished he could write like O'Casey. There is a sublime, even a tragic grandeur in *The Iceman Cometh* and *A Long Day's Journey into Night* that the exuberant O'Casey lacked to some degree. But one does indeed wish that O'Neill could have written with the humor and "beautiful, laughing speech" (Yeats on Blake) of O'Casey. I think sometimes that—despite the splendor of Synge—the Irish playwright we lack in our time would have combined O'Neill and O'Casey in a single body, as it were. And in any case, with the common playgoer and the common reader, I find myself happily in agreement; *Juno and the Paycock* is one of the permanent dramas of our time. William Hazlitt, best of drama critics, would have adored it, for it has what he demanded of art: gusto.

The Plough and the Stars

Though it lacks the ebullience of *Juno and the Paycock*, *The Plough and the Stars* is an equally satisfying drama. Yeats, furious and eloquent as he confronted the rioters at the Abbey, recalled a similar confrontation fifteen years before when riots broke out against Synge's *Playboy of the Western World*:

> You have disgraced yourselves again. Is this to be an ever recurring celebration of the arrival of Irish genius? Synge first and then O'Casey. The news of the happening of the last few minutes will go from country to country. Dublin has rocked the cradle of genius. From such a scene in this theatre went forth the fame of Synge. Equally the fame of O'Casey is born here tonight. This is his apotheosis.

There is a story that O'Casey left the Abbey at this point in order to get home to look up the word "apotheosis." He had achieved an apotheosis in any case, and hardly because of Mrs. Sheehy-Skeffington and her fellow rioters. *The Plough and the Stars* has no central figures as memorable as Juno, Boyle, and Joxer, yet O'Casey's strength at characterization is powerful, manifested by the colorful subsidiary persons: The Covey, Fluther

Good, Mrs. Gogan, the splendid Bessie Burgess, and the anonymous orator, the Figure in the Window, who is clearly Padraic Pearse, poet and revolutionary, the soul of the Easter Rising. Despite these vivid portrayals, I
would locate the power of *The Plough and the Stars* elsewhere, in its savage
representation of how an historical event like the Easter Rising, later
mythologized, actually intersects with individual human lives.

Raymond Williams, the most severe of O'Casey's critics, has emphasized how inadequately *The Plough and the Stars* handles the political and
social realities of the Easter Rising. I do not think that any critic can win
over O'Casey on that matter, because O'Casey's point, in life and in his
drama, is that he had no use for the Rising, which he saw as one more
betrayal of the Dublin working class. *The Plough and the Stars* indeed treats
the Easter Rebellion as an absurd and inhumane theatrical event, a monument to male vanity and to Padraic Pearse's sadomasochistic frenzy for
Irish self-immolation. Hurt as O'Casey was by the Abbey Theatre riot, one
feels that it was inevitable, so thoroughly are the martyrs discredited by
O'Casey's tragic farce.

O'Casey, modifying the text of actual speeches by Pearse, gives us an
orator who cries out that "bloodshed is a cleansing and sanctifying thing,"
and then delivers this peroration:

> Comrade soldiers of the Irish Volunteers and of the Citizen Army,
> we rejoice in this terrible war. The old heart of the earth needed
> to be warmed with the red wine of the battlefields.... Such august
> homage was never offered to God as this: the homage of millions
> of lives given gladly for love of country. And we must be ready to
> pour out the same red wine in the same glorious sacrifice, for
> without shedding of blood there is no redemption!

Too shrewd to ridicule Pearse's rhetoric, O'Casey juxtaposes it with his
vigorous pub scenes, which have a clear relation to the Falstaffian tavern
scenes of the *Henry IV* plays. James Agate, reviewing the play's first
London production in 1926, overstated the relation yet certainly caught
O'Casey's allusive intention:

> Mr. O'Casey has done what Balzac and Dickens did—he has cre-
> ated an entirely new gallery of living men and women.... You may
> be appalled, but you do not blame; these people are alive, and you
> refrain from judging them.... [The play] moves to its tragic close
> through scenes of high humour and rich, racy fooling, about
> which there is something of Elizabethan gusto. Young Covey

roars his gospel of economic regeneration with the emphasis of Pistol; there is a Falstaffian ring about Fluther, mercurial excitability taking the place of the lethargic sweep; old Flynn is Shallow all over again; and Rose is pure Doll.

That is to give O'Casey the best of it, rather too generously, but one cannot begrudge the comparison, since what other modern dramatist except Brecht could merit it, and Brecht has the vigor without the authentic high spirits of O'Casey. As in *Juno and the Paycock*, O'Casey has his eye on Falstaff and his companions, but actually gives us a touch of Ben Jonson's fierce comedy and humors rather than Shakespeare's. At his best, as in the final moment of *The Plough and the Stars*, O'Casey offers us an authentic originality. Poor Bessie Burgess, tough and capable, has been shot dead by British troops, under the delusion that she was a sniper. Bessie, a Protestant and a supporter of the British Crown, feebly sings a hymn, and then dies. With marvelous audacity, O'Casey gives us this as his final vision:

> *She ceases singing, and lies stretched out, still and very rigid. A pause.*
> *Then* Mrs. Gogan *runs hastily in.*
> MRS. GOGAN (*quivering with fright*): Blessed be God, what's after happenin'? (To Nora) What's wrong, child, what's wrong? (*She sees* Bessie, *runs to her and heeds over the body*) Bessie, Bessie! (*She shakes the body*) Mrs. Burgess, Mrs. Burgess! (*She feels* Bessie's *forehead*) My God, she's as cold as death. They're after murderin' th' poor inoffensive woman! (Sergeant Tinley *and* Corporal Stoddart *enter agitatedly, their rifles at the ready.*)
> SERGEANT TINLEY (*excitedly*): This is the 'ouse. That's the window!
> NORA (*pressing back against the wall*): Hide it, hide it; cover it up, cover it up!
> SERGEANT TINLEY (*going over to the body*): 'Ere, what's this? Who's this? (*Looking at* Bessie) Oh Gawd, we've plugged one of the women of the 'ouse.
> CORPORAL STODDART: Whoy the 'ell did she gow to the window? Is she dead?
> SERGEANT TINLEY: Oh, dead as bedamned. Well, we couldn't afford to toike any chawnces.
> NORA (*screaming*): Hide it, hide it; don't let me see it! Take me away, take me away, Mrs. Gogan!
> Mrs. Gogan *runs into room, Left, and runs out again with a sheet which she spreads over the body of Bessie.*

MRS. GOGAN (*as she spreads the sheet*): Oh, God help her, th' poor woman, she's stiffenin' out as hard as she can! Her face has written on it th' shock o' sudden agony, an' her hands is whitenin' into th' smooth shininess of wax.

NORA (*whimperingly*): Take me away, take me away; don't leave me here to be lookin' an' lookin' at it!

MRS. GOGAN (*going over to* Nora *and putting her arm around her*): Come on with me, dear, an' you can doss in poor Mollser's bed, till we gather some neighbours to come an' give th' last friendly touches to Bessie in th' lonely layin' of her out. [Mrs. Gogan *and* Nora *go slowly out.*]

CORPORAL STODDART (*who has been looking around*, to Sergeant Tinley): Tea here, Sergeant. Wot abaht a cup of scald?

SERGEANT TINLEY: Pour it aht, Stoddart, pour it aht. I could scoff hanything just now.

Corporal Stoddart *pours out two cups of tea, and the two soldiers begin to drink. In the distance is heard a bitter burst of rifle and machine gun fire, interspersed with the boom, boom of artillery. The glare in the sky seen through the window flares into a fuller and a deeper red.*

SERGEANT TINLEY: There gows the general attack on the Powst Office.

VOICES IN A DISTANT STREET: Ambu ... lance, Ambu ... lance! Red Cro ... ss, Red Cro ... ss!

The voices of soldiers at a barricade outside the house are heard singing:

They were summoned from the 'illside,
They were called in from the glen,
And the country found 'em ready
At the stirring call for men.
Let not tears add to their 'ardship,
As the soldiers pass along,
And although our 'eart is breaking,
Make it sing this cheery song.

SERGEANT TINLEY *and* CORPORAL STODDART (*joining in the chorus, as they sip the tea*):

Keep the 'owme fires burning,
While your 'earts are yearning;
Though your lads are far away
They dream of 'owme;

There's a silver loining
Through the dark cloud shoining,
Turn the dark cloud inside out,
Till the boys come 'owme!

We receive the shock and mourning of the women, and then we close on the Tommies singing as they drink their tea, with Bessie shrouded under the sheet nearby and the window illuminated by the red glare of a burning Dublin as the British machine guns and artillery open up on Pearse, Connolly, and their diehards barricaded in the General Post Office. O'Casey has no politics in his ultimate vision, and no feeling against the Tommies. Pearse has made the tenements of Dublin into a bonfire, and O'Casey is not exactly grateful to the murderous idealist, but we have to infer that reaction throughout the play. Raymond Williams must have understood, implicitly, that O'Casey, who died a good Communist and perpetual admirer of Stalin, nevertheless was, like G.B. Shaw, a Ruskinian rather than a Marxist. The final burden of *The Plough and the Stars* is that the proper answer to the blood-intoxicated Pearse is Ruskin's great apothegm from *Unto This Last*: "The only wealth is life." Fluther and his companions are O'Casey's sense of Irish life: drunken, ranting, vain, but vital, vital to the end.

Eugene O'Neill

(1888-1953)

IT IS AN INEVITABLE ODDITY THAT THE PRINCIPAL AMERICAN DRAMATIST TO date should have no American precursors. Eugene O'Neill's art as a playwright owes most to Strindberg's, and something crucial, though rather less, to Ibsen's. Intellectually, O'Neill's ancestry also has little to do with American tradition, with Emerson or William James or any other of our cultural speculators. Schopenhauer, Nietzsche, and Freud formed O'Neill's sense of what little was possible for any of us. Even where American literary tradition was strongest, in the novel and poetry, it did not much affect O'Neill. His novelists were Zola and Conrad; his poets were Dante Gabriel Rossetti and Swinburne. Overwhelmingly an Irish-American, with his Jansenist Catholicism transformed into anger at God, he had little active interest in the greatest American writer, Whitman, though his spiritual darkness has a curious, antithetical relation to Whitman's overt analysis of our national character.

Yet O'Neill, despite his many limitations, is the most American of our handful of dramatists who matter most: Williams, Miller, Wilder, Albee, perhaps Mamet and Shepard. A national quality that is literary, yet has no clear relation to our domestic literary traditions, is nearly always present in O'Neill's strongest works. We can recognize Hawthorne in Henry James, and Whitman (however repressed) in T.S. Eliot, while the relation of Hemingway and Faulkner to Mark Twain is just as evident as their debt to Conrad. Besides the question of his genre (since there was no vital American drama before O'Neill), there would seem to be some hidden factor that governed O'Neill's ambiguous relation to our literary past. It was certainly not the lack of critical discernment on O'Neill's part. His admiration for Hart Crane's poetry, at its most difficult, was solely responsible for the publication of Crane's first volume, *White Buildings*, for which O'Neill initially offered to write the introduction, withdrawing in favor of Allen

Tate when the impossibility of his writing a critical essay on Crane's complexities became clear to O'Neill. But to have recognized Hart Crane's genius, so early and so helpfully, testifies to O'Neill's profound insights into the American literary imagination at its strongest.

The dramatist whose masterpieces are *The Iceman Cometh* and *Long Day's Journey into Night*, and, in a class just short of those, *A Moon for the Misbegotten* and *A Touch of the Poet*, is not exactly to be regarded as a celebrator of the possibilities of American life. The central strain in our literature remains Emersonian, from Whitman to our contemporaries like Saul Bellow and John Ashbery. Even the tradition that reacted against Emerson—from Poe, Hawthorne, and Melville through Gnostics of the abyss like Nathanael West and Thomas Pynchon—remains always alert to transcendental and extraordinary American possibilities. Our most distinguished living writer, Robert Penn Warren, must be the most overtly anti-Emersonian partisan in our history, yet even Warren seeks an American Sublime in his still-ongoing poetry. O'Neill would appear to be the most non-Emersonian author of any eminence in our literature. Irish-American through and through, with an heroic resentment of the New England Yankee tradition, O'Neill from the start seemed to know that his spiritual quest was to undermine Emerson's American religion of self-reliance.

O'Neill's own Irish Jansenism is curiously akin to the New England Puritanism he opposed, but that only increased the rancor of his powerful polemic in *Desire under the Elms*, *Mourning Becomes Electra*, and *More Stately Mansions*. *The Will to Live* is set against New England Puritanism in what O'Neill himself once called "the battle of moral forces in the New England scene" to which he said he felt closest as an artist. But since this is Schopenhauer's rapacious Will to Live, and not Bernard Shaw's genial revision of that Will into the Life Force of a benign Creative Evolution, O'Neill is in the terrible position of opposing one death-drive with another. Only the inescapable Strindberg comes to mind as a visionary quite as negative as O'Neill, so that *The Iceman Cometh* might as well have been called *The Dance of Death*, and *Long Day's Journey into Night* could be retitled *The Ghost Sonata*. O'Neill's most powerful self-representations—as Edmund in *Long Day's Journey* and Larry Slade in *Iceman*—are astonishingly negative identifications, particularly in an American context.

Edmund and Slade do not long for death in the mode of Whitman and his descendants—Wallace Stevens, T.S. Eliot, Hart Crane, and Theodore Roethke—all of whom tend to incorporate the image of a desired death into the great, triple trope of night, the mother, and the sea. Edmund Tyrone and Larry Slade long to die because life without transcendence is impossible, and yet transcendence is totally unavailable. O'Neill's true polemic against his country and its spiritual tradition is not, as he insisted, that "its main idea is that everlasting game of trying to possess your own soul by the possession of something outside it." Though uttered in 1946, in remarks before the first performance of *The Iceman Cometh*, such a reflection is banal and represents a weak misreading of *The Iceman Cometh*. The play's true argument is that your own soul cannot be possessed, whether by possessing something or someone outside it, or by joining yourself to a transcendental possibility, to whatever version of an Emersonian Oversoul that you might prefer. The United States, in O'Neill's dark view, was uniquely the country that had refused to learn the truths of the spirit, which are that good and the means of good, love and the means of love, are irreconcilable.

Such a formulation is Shelleyan, and reminds one of O'Neill's High Romantic inheritance, which reached him through pre-Raphaelite poetry and literary speculation. O'Neill seems a strange instance of the Aestheticism of Rossetti and Pater, but his metaphysical nihilism, desperate faith in art, and phantasmagoric naturalism stem directly from them. When Jamie Tyrone quotes from Rossetti's "Willowwood" sonnets, he gives the epigraph not only to *Long Day's Journey* but to all of O'Neill: "Look into my face. My name is Might-Have-Been; / I am also called No More, Too Late, Farewell." In O'Neill's deepest polemic, the lines are quoted by, and for, all Americans of imagination whatsoever.

Long Day's Journey into Night

By common consent, *Long Day's Journey into Night* is Eugene O'Neill's masterpiece. The Yale paperback in which I have just reread the play lists itself as the fifty-sixth printing in the thirty years since publication. Since O'Neill, rather than Williams or Miller, Wilder or Albee, is recognized as our leading dramatist, *Long Day's Journey* must be the best play in our more than two centuries as a nation. One rereads it therefore with awe and a certain apprehension, but with considerable puzzlement also. Strong work it certainly is, and twice I have been moved by watching it well directed and well performed. Yet how can this be the best stage play that an exuberantly dramatic people has produced? Is it equal to the best of our imaginative literature? Can we read it in the company of *The Scarlet Letter* and *Moby-Dick*, *Adventures of Huckleberry Finn* and *The Portrait of a Lady*, *As I Lay Dying Lay Dying* and *Gravity's Rainbow*? Does it have the aesthetic distinction of our greatest poets, of Whitman, Dickinson, Frost, Stevens, Eliot, Hart Crane, Elizabeth Bishop, and John Ashbery? Can it stand intellectually with the crucial essays of Emerson and of William James?

These questions, alas, are self-answering. O'Neill's limitations are obvious and need not be surveyed intensively. Perhaps no major dramatist has ever been so lacking in rhetorical exuberance, in what Yeats once praised Blake for having: "beautiful, laughing speech." O'Neill's convictions were deeply held, but were in no way remarkable, except for their incessant sullenness. It is embarrassing when O'Neill's exegetes attempt to expound his ideas, whether about his country, his own work, or the human condition. When one of them speaks of "two kinds of nonverbal, tangential poetry in *Long Day's Journey into Night*" as the characters' longing "for a mystical union of sorts," and the influence of the setting, I am compelled to reflect that insofar as O'Neill's art is nonverbal it must also be nonexistent.

My reflection however is inaccurate, and O'Neill's dramatic art is considerable, though it does make us revise our notions of just how strictly literary an art drama necessarily has to be. Sophocles, Shakespeare, and Molière are masters alike of language and of a mimetic force that works through gestures that supplement language, but O'Neill is mastered by language and relies instead upon a drive-towards-staging that he appears to have learned from Strindberg. Consider the close of *Long Day's Journey*. How much of the power here comes from what Tyrone and Mary say, and how much from the extraordinarily effective stage directions?

> TYRONE (*trying to shake off his hopeless stupor*): Oh, we're fools to pay any attention. It's the damned poison. But I've never known her to drown herself in it as deep as this. (*Gruffly.*) Pass me that bottle, Jamie. And stop reciting that damned morbid poetry. I won't have it in my house! (*Jamie pushes the bottle toward him. He pours a drink without disarranging the wedding gown he holds carefully over his other arm and on his lap, and shoves the bottle back. Jamie pours his and passes the bottle to Edmund, who, in turn, pours one. Tyrone lifts his glass and his sons follow suit mechanically, but before they can drink Mary speaks and they slowly lower their drinks to the table, forgetting them.*)
>
> MARY (*staring dreamily before her. Her face looks extraordinarily youthful and innocent. The shyly eager, trusting smile is on her lips as she talks aloud to herself*): I had a talk with Mother Elizabeth. She is so sweet and good. A saint on earth. I love her dearly. It may be sinful of me but I love her better than my own mother. Because she always understands, even before you say a word. Her kind blue eyes look right into your heart. You can't keep any secrets from her. You couldn't deceive her, even if you

were mean enough to want to. (*She gives a little rebellious toss of her head—with girlish pique.*) All the same, I don't think she was so understanding this time. I told her I wanted to be a nun. I explained how sure I was of my vocation, that I had prayed to the Blessed Virgin to make me sure, and to find me worthy. I told Mother I had had a true vision when I was praying in the shrine of Our Lady of Lourdes, on the little island in the lake. I said I knew, as surely as I knew I was kneeling there, that the Blessed Virgin had smiled and blessed me with her consent. But Mother Elizabeth told me I must be more sure than that, even, that I must prove it wasn't simply my imagination. She said, if I was so sure, then I wouldn't mind putting myself to a test by going home after I graduated, and living as other girls lived, going out to parties and dances and enjoying myself; and then if after a year or two I still felt sure, I could come back to see her and we would talk it over again. (*She tosses her head—indignantly.*) I never dreamed Holy Mother would give me such advice! I was really shocked. I said, of course, I would do anything she suggested, but I knew it was simply a waste of time. After I left her, I felt all mixed up, so I went to the shrine and prayed to the Blessed Virgin and found peace again because I knew she heard my prayer and would always love me and see no harm ever came to me so long as I never lost my faith in her. (*She pauses and a look of growing uneasiness comes over her face. She passes a hand over her forehead as if brushing cobwebs from her brain—vaguely.*) That was in the winter of senior year. Then in the spring something happened to me. Yes, I remember. I fell in love with James Tyrone and was so happy for a time. (*She stares before her in a sad dream. Tyrone stirs in his chair. Edmund and Jamie remain motionless.*)
CURTAIN

Critics have remarked on how fine it is that the three alcoholic Tyrone males slowly lower their drinks to the table, forgetting them, as the morphine-laden wife and mother begins to speak. One can go further; her banal if moving address to herself, and Tyrone's petulant outbursts, are considerably less eloquent than the stage directions. I had not remembered anything that was spoken, returning to the text after a decade, but I had held on to that grim family tableau of the three Tyrones slowly lowering their glasses. Again, I had remembered nothing actually said between

Edmund and his mother at the end of act one, but the gestures and glances between them always abide with me, and Mary's reactions when she is left alone compel in me the Nietzschean realization that the truly memorable is always associated with what is most painful.

> (*She puts her arms around him and hugs him with a frightened, protective tenderness.*)
>
> EDMUND (*soothingly*): That's foolishness. You know it's only a bad cold.
>
> MARY: Yes, of course, I know that!
>
> EDMUND: But listen, Mama. I want you to promise me that even if it should turn out to be something worse, you'll know I'll soon be all right again, anyway, and you won't worry yourself sick, and you'll keep on taking care of yourself—
>
> MARY (*frightenedly*): I won't listen when you're so silly! There's absolutely no reason to talk as if you expected something dreadful! Of course, I promise you. I give you my sacred word of honor! (*Then with a sad bitterness.*) But I suppose you're remembering I've promised before on my word of honor.
>
> EDMUND: No!
>
> MARY (*her bitterness receding into a resigned helplessness*): I'm not blaming you, dear. How can you help it? How can any one of us forget? (*Strangely.*) That's what makes it so hard—for all of us. We can't forget.
>
> EDMUND (*grabs her shoulder*): Mama! Stop it!
>
> MARY (*forcing a smile*): All right, dear. I didn't mean to be so gloomy. Don't mind me. Here. Let me feel your head. Why, it's nice and cool. You certainly haven't any fever now.
>
> EDMUND: Forget! It's you—
>
> MARY: But I'm quite all right, dear. (*With a quick, strange, calculating, almost sly glance at him.*) Except I naturally feel tired and nervous this morning, after such a bad night. I really ought to go upstairs and lie down until lunch time and take a nap. (*He gives her an instinctive look of suspicion—then, ashamed of himself, looks quickly away. She hurries on nervously.*) What are you going to do? Read here? It would be much better for you to go out in the fresh air and sunshine. But don't get overheated, remember. Be sure and wear a hat. (*She stops, looking straight at him now. He avoids her eyes. There is a tense pause. Then she speaks jeeringly.*) Or are you afraid to trust me alone?
>
> EDMUND (*tormentedly*): No! Can't you stop talking like that! I

think you ought to take a nap. (*He goes to the screen door—forcing a joking tone.*) I'll go down and help Jamie bear up. I love to lie in the shade and watch him work. (*He forces a laugh in which she makes herself join. Then he goes out on the porch and disappears down the steps. Her first reaction is one of relief. She appears to relax. She sinks down in one of the wicker armchairs at rear of table and leans her head back, closing her eyes. But suddenly she grows terribly tense again. Her eyes open and she strains forward, seized by a fit of nervous panic. She begins a desperate battle with herself. Her long fingers, warped and knotted by rheumatism, drum on the arms of the chair, driven by an insistent life of their own, without her consent.*)
CURTAIN

That grim ballet of looks between mother and son, followed by the terrible, compulsive drumming of her long fingers, has a lyric force that only the verse quotations from Baudelaire, Swinburne, and others in O'Neill's text are able to match. Certainly a singular dramatic genius is always at work in O'Neill's stage directions, and can be felt also, most fortunately, in the repressed intensities of inarticulateness in all of the Tyrones.

It seems to me a marvel that this can suffice, and in itself probably it could not. But there is also O'Neill's greatest gift, more strongly present in *Long Day's Journey* than it is even in *The Iceman Cometh*. Lionel Trilling, subtly and less equivocally than it seemed, once famously praised Theodore Dreiser for his mixed but imposing representation of "reality in America," in his best novels, *Sister Carrie* and *An American Tragedy*. One cannot deny the power of the mimetic art of *Long Day's Journey into Night*. No dramatist to this day, among us, has matched O'Neill in depicting the nightmare realities that can afflict American family life, indeed family life in the twentieth-century Western world. And yet that is the authentic subject of our dramatists who matter most after O'Neill: Williams, Miller, Albee, with the genial Thornton Wilder as the grand exception. It is a terrifying distinction that O'Neill earns, and more decisively in *Long Day's Journey into Night* than anywhere else. He is the elegist of the Freudian "family romance," of the domestic tragedy of which we all die daily, a little bit at a time. The helplessness of family love to sustain, let alone heal, the wounds of marriage, of parenthood, and of sonship, have never been so remorselessly and so pathetically portrayed, and with a force of gesture too painful ever to be forgotten by any of us.

The Iceman Cometh

Like its great precursor play, Strindberg's *The Dance of Death*, O'Neill's *The Iceman Cometh* must be one of the most remorseless of what purport to be tragic dramas since the Greeks and the Jacobeans. Whatever tragedy meant to the incredibly harsh Strindberg, to O'Neill it had to possess a "transfiguring nobility," presumably that of the artist like O'Neill himself in his relation to his time and his country, of which he observed that "we are tragedy, the most appalling yet written or unwritten." O'Neill's strength was never conceptual, and so we are not likely to render his stances into a single coherent view of tragedy.

Whitman could say that: "these States are themselves the greatest poem," and we know what he meant, but I do not know how to read O'Neill's "we are tragedy." When I suffer through *The New York Times* every morning, am I reading tragedy? Does *The Iceman Cometh* manifest a "transfiguring nobility?" How could it? Are Larry Slade in *Iceman* or Edmund Tyrone in *Long Day's Journey into Night*, both clearly O'Neill's surrogates, either of them tragic in relation to their time and country? Or to ask all this in a single question: are the crippling sorrows of what Freud called "family romances" tragic or are they not primarily instances of strong pathos, reductive processes that cannot, by definition, manifest an authentic "transfiguring nobility?"

I think that we need to ignore O'Neill on tragedy if we are to learn to watch and read *The Iceman Cometh* for the dramatic values it certainly possesses. Its principal limitation, I suspect, stems from its tendentious assumption that "we are tragedy," that "these States" have become the "most appalling" of tragedies. Had O'Neill survived into our Age of Reagan, and observed our Yuppies on the march, doubtless he would have been even more appalled. But societies are not dramas, and O'Neill was not Jeremiah the prophet. His strength was neither in stance nor style, but in the dramatic representation of illusions and despairs, in the persuasive imitation of human personality, particularly in its self-destructive weaknesses.

Critics have rightly emphasized how important O'Neill's lapsed Irish Catholicism was to him and to his plays. But "importance" is a perplexing notion in this context. Certainly the absence of the Roman Catholic faith is the given condition of *The Iceman Cometh*. Yet we would do O'Neill's play wrong if we retitled it *Waiting for the Iceman*, and tried to assimilate it to the Gnostic cosmos of Samuel Beckett, just as we would destroy *Long Day's Journey into Night* if we retitled it *Endgame in New London*. All that O'Neill and Beckett have in common is Schopenhauer, with whom they share a Gnostic sense that our world is a great emptiness, the *kenoma*, as the Gnostics of the second century of the common era called it. But Beckett's post-Protestant cosmos could not be redeemed by the descent of the alien god. O'Neill's post-Catholic world longs for the suffering Christ and is angry at him for not returning. Such a longing is by no means in itself dramatic, unlike Beckett's ironically emptied-out cosmos.

A comparison of O'Neill to Beckett is hardly fair, since Beckett is infinitely the better artist, subtler mind, and finer stylist. Beckett writes apocalyptic farce, or tragicomedy raised to its greatest eminence. O'Neill doggedly tells his one story and one story only, and his story turns out to be himself. *The Iceman Cometh*, being O'Neill at his most characteristic, raises the vexed question of whether and just how dramatic value can survive a paucity of eloquence, too much commonplace religiosity, and a thorough lack of understanding of the perverse complexities of human nature. Plainly *Iceman* does survive, and so does *Long Day's Journey*. They stage remarkably, and hold me in the audience, though they give neither aesthetic pleasure nor spiritually memorable pain when I reread them in the study.

For sheer bad writing, O'Neill's only rival among significant American authors is Theodore Dreiser, whose *Sister Carrie* and *An American Tragedy* demonstrate a similar ability to evade the consequences of rhetorical failure. Dreiser has some dramatic effectiveness, but his peculiar strength appears' to be mythic. O'Neill, unquestionably a dramatist of genius, fails also on the mythic level; his anger against God, or the absence of God, remains petulant and personal, and his attempt to universalize that anger by turning it against his country's failure to achieve spiritual reality is simply misguided. No country, by definition, achieves anything spiritual anyway. We live and die, in the spirit, in solitude, and the true strength of *Iceman* is its intense dramatic exemplification of that somber reality.

Whether the confessional impulse in O'Neill's later plays ensued from Catholic *praxis* is beyond my surmise, though John Henry Raleigh and other critics have urged this view. I suspect that here too the influence of the non-Catholic Strindberg was decisive. A harsh expressionism dominates *Iceman* and *Long Day's Journey*, where the terrible confessions are not made to priestly surrogates but to fellow sinners, and with no hopes of absolution. Confession becomes another station on the way to death, whether by suicide, or by alcohol, or by other modes of slow decay.

Iceman's strength is in three of its figures, Hickman (Hickey), Slade, and Parritt, of whom only Slade is due to survive, though in a minimal sense. Hickey, who preaches nihilism, is a desperate self-deceiver and so a deceiver of others, in his self-appointed role as evangelist of the abyss.

Slade, evasive and solipsistic, works his way to a more authentic nihilism than Hickey's. Poor Parritt, young and self-haunted, cannot achieve the sense of nothingness that would save him from Puritanical self-condemnation.

Life, in *Iceman*, is what it is in Schopenhauer: illusion. Hickey, once a great sustainer of illusions, arrives in the company of "the Iceman of Death," hardly the "sane and sacred death" of Whitman, but insane and impious death, our death. One feels the refracted influence of Ibsen in Hickey's twisted deidealizings, but Hickey is an Ibsen protagonist in the last ditch. He does not destroy others in his quest to destroy illusions, but only himself. His judgments of Harry Hope's patrons are intended not to liberate them but to teach his old friends to accept and live with failure. Yet Hickey, though pragmatically wrong, means only to have done good. In an understanding strangely akin to Wordsworth's in the sublime *Tale of Margaret* (*The Ruined Cottage*), Hickey sees that we are destroyed by vain hope more inexorably than by the anguish of total despair. And that is where I would locate the authentic mode of tragedy in *Iceman*. It is Hickey's tragedy, rather than Slade's (O'Neill's), because Hickey is slain between right and right, as in the Hegelian theory of tragedy. To deprive the derelicts of hope is right, and to sustain them in their illusory "pipe dreams" is right also.

Caught between right and right, Hickey passes into phantasmagoria, and in that compulsive condition he makes the ghastly confession that he murdered his unhappy, dreadfully saintly wife. His motive, he asserts perversely, was love, but here too he is caught between antitheses, and we are not able to interpret with certainty whether he was more moved by love or hatred:

> HICKEY: (*Simply*) So I killed her. (*There is a moment of dead silence. Even the detectives are caught in it and stand motionless.*)
> PARRITT: (*Suddenly gives up and relaxes limply in his chair—in a low voice in which there is a strange exhausted relief.*) I may as well confess, Larry. There's no use lying any more. You know, anyway. I didn't give a damn about the money. It was because I hated her.
> HICKEY: (*Obliviously*) And then I saw I'd always known that was the only possible way to give her peace and free her from the misery of loving me. I saw it meant peace for me, too, knowing she was at peace. I felt as though a ton of guilt was lifted off my mind. I remember I stood by the bed and suddenly I had to laugh. I couldn't help it, and I knew Evelyn would forgive

> me. I remember I heard myself speaking to her, as if it was
> something I'd always wanted to say: "Well, you know what
> you can do with your pipe dream now, you damned bitch!"
> (*He stops with a horrified start, as if shocked out of a nightmare, as
> if he couldn't believe he heard what he had just said. He stammers*)
> No! I never—!
>
> PARRITT: (*To LARRY sneeringly*) Yes, that's it! Her and the damned
> old Movement pipe dream! Eh, Larry?
>
> HICKEY: (*Bursts into frantic denial*) No! That's a lie! I never said—!
> Good God, I couldn't have said that! If I did, I'd gone insane!
> Why, I loved Evelyn better than anything in life! (*He appeals
> brokenly to the crowd*) Boys, you're all my old pals! You've
> known old Hickey for years! You know I'd never—(*His eyes fix
> on HOPE*) You've known me longer than anyone, Harry. You
> know I must have been insane, don't you, Governor?

Rather than a demystifier, whether of self or others, Hickey is revealed
as a tragic enigma, who cannot sell himself a coherent account of the horror he has accomplished. Did he slay Evelyn because of a hope hers or
his—or because of a mutual despair? He does not know, nor does O'Neill,
nor do we. Nor does anyone know why Parritt betrayed his mother, the
anarchist activist, and her comrades and his. Slade condemns Parritt to a
suicide's death, but without persuading us that he has uncovered the
motive for so hideous a betrayal. Caught in a moral dialectic of guilt and
suffering, Parritt appears to be entirely a figure of pathos, without the
weird idealism that makes Hickey an interesting instance of High
Romantic tragedy.

Parritt at least provokes analysis; the drama's failure is Larry Slade,
much against O'Neill's palpable intentions, which were to move his surrogate from contemplation to action. Slade ought to end poised on the
threshold of a religious meditation on the vanity of life in a world from
which God is absent. But his final speech, expressing a reaction to Parritt's
suicide, is the weakest in the play:

> LARRY. (*In a whisper of horrified pity*) Poor devil! (*A long-forgotten
> faith returns to him for a moment and he mumbles*) God rest his
> soul in peace. (*He opens his eyes—with a bitter self-derision*) Ah,
> the damned pity—the wrong kind, as Hickey said! Be God,
> there's no hope! I'll never be a success in the grandstand—or
> anywhere else! Life is too much for me! I'll be a weak fool
> looking with pity at the two sides of everything till the day I

die! (*With an intense bitter sincerity*) May that day come soon! (*He pauses startledly, surprised at himself—then with a sardonic grin*) Be God, I'm the only real convert to death Hickey made here. From the bottom of my coward's heart I mean that now!

The momentary return of Catholicism is at variance with the despair of the death-drive here, and Slade does not understand that he has not been converted to any sense of death, at all. His only strength would be in emulating Hickey's tragic awareness between right and right, but of course without following Hickey into violence: "I'll be a weak fool looking with pity at the two sides of everything till the day I die!" That vision of the two sides, with compassion, is the only hope worthy of the dignity of any kind of tragic conception. O'Neill ended by exemplifying Yeats's great apothegm: he could embody the truth, but he could not know it.

T.S. Eliot

(1888-1965)

Murder in the Cathedral

T.S. ELIOT, FOR WHOM THE ESSAYS OF EMERSON WERE "ALREADY AN encumbrance," to cite his own testimony, was haunted by transcendence, very much in the mode of his Emersonian ancestors, rather than in the more severe and traditional mode, Anglo-Catholic and Counter-Reformation, towards which he aspired. Michael Goldman argues that the fear of being haunted by transcendence is the central design of Eliot's dramas, including *Murder in the Cathedral*. Since *Murder in the Cathedral* was composed for the Canterbury Festival of june 1935, the play assumes that its audience will be at least ostensibly Christian. Francis Fergusson aptly applied to Eliot's Canterbury drama Pascal's analysis of the three discontinuous orders—nature, mind, charity—which Eliot had commended to "the modern world" in his introduction to the *Pensées*. On this reading, the Chorus are in the order of nature; Tempters, Knights and Priests belong to the order of mind; Thomas alone is in the transcendent order of charity.

Representing the order of divine love is, as all would agree, a rather difficult task, particularly upon a stage. Dante is the inevitable master here but no one would think of mounting a production of the *Paradiso*. *Sweeney Agonistes*, in my humble judgment, is by far Eliot's finest dramatic work, easily surpassing *Murder in the Cathedral* and its successors. Dame Helen Gardner, who admired both Eliot's poetry and his dogmatic convictions, admitted that the Canterbury drama lacked action and had an unconvincing hero, but found it "intensely moving and at times exciting when performed." I have attended only one presentation of the play, somewhat reluctantly, but my reactions are to be distrusted, even by me, since I am not precisely the audience Eliot had in mind. Eliot remarked, in his

"Thoughts after Lambeth," that there could be no such thing as "a civilized non-Christian mentality." I wonder always at a view of civilization and its discomforts that excludes Freud as the representative instance of a civilized mentality in our era, but then Eliot's literary survival does not depend upon his ideological tractates.

How authentic a literary achievement is *Murder in the Cathedral*? Both Francis Fergusson and Stephen Spender have compared it to Wagner's operatic texts, and Eliot, who shared little else with Bernard Shaw, was as Wagnerian as Shaw. In some sense, *Murder in the Cathedral* mixes Wagner and Shaw, creating an amalgam of *Parsifal* and *Saint Joan*, an unlikely composite. Since Baudelaire, Milton, and Sophocles are echoed also, sometimes gratuitously, one sometimes wonders why Eliot ransacks the tradition as he does in *Murder in the Cathedral*. He may have felt that he needed all the help he could get, since his multiple allusions give the effect of baroque elaboration, rather than that of fulfilling or transcending dramatic and literary tradition.

If Eliot's purpose had been essentially liturgical, then the triumph of *Murder in the Cathedral* would be unquestioned, since the drama, as doctrine, would have constituted a preaching to the supposedly converted. A saint's play is a hard matter in our time, and Shaw managed it, barely, by joining his Joan to the mode of Bunyan. Eliot commends *Everyman* as the unique play within the limits of art, but *Murder in the Cathedral* hardly sustains comparison to *Everyman*. Well, an admirer of Eliot might reply, *Saint Joan* is not exactly of the eminence of *The Pilgrim's Progress*, but then Bunyan's great narrative is not a stage drama. How well does Eliot do in the dramatic representation of Archbishop Thomas Becket? All that I ever can remember of what Eliot's Becket says is the first part of his climactic speech, after the Chorus implores him to save himself so that they too can survive, and just before he preaches his Christmas Morning sermon, which ends part 1 of the play. The Women of Canterbury fear the coming change, whether it be transcendence or the withdrawal of transcendence. Thomas ignores them, since he is interested only in the final Tempter, who offers what he desires, and appears to be his true self. Does he reject that true self, or Fourth Tempter?

> Now is my way clear, now is the meaning plain:
> Temptation shall not come in this kind again.
> The last temptation is the greatest treason:
> To do the right deed for the wrong reason.
> The natural vigour in the venial sin
> Is the way in which our lives begin.

Thirty years ago, I searched all the ways
That lead to pleasure, advancement and praise.
Delight in sense, in learning and in thought,
Music; and philosophy, curiosity,
The purple bullfinch in the lilac tree,
The tilt-yard skill, the strategy of chess,
Love in the garden, singing to the instrument,
Were all things equally desirable.
Ambition comes when early force is spent
And when we find no longer all things possible.
Ambition comes behind and unobservable.

But how can you represent, dramatically, a potential saint's refusal to yield to his own lust for martyrdom? Eliot did not know how to solve that dilemma, and evaded it, with some skill. There is epigrammatic force in Thomas's crucial couplet, but is there dramatic insight as well?

The last temptation is the greatest treason;
To do the right deed for the wrong reason.

Let us, wickedly, experiment with altering that neat couplet:

The last temptation is the greatest treason:
To write a Christian play for the wrong reason.

It is no accident that Thomas's speech takes its pathos from Eliot's literary and intellectual career, the movement from searching all the ways available to an authentic contemporary poetry, on to the spiritual ambition that came when early force was spent. It is also no accident that the imagery of the Chorus of the Women of Canterbury grows increasingly violent, until the poor ladies seem to have become victims of their own pathological fantasies:

I have smelt them, the death-bringers; now is too late
For action, too soon for contrition.
Nothing is possible but the shamed swoon
Of those consenting to the last humiliation.
I have consented, Lord Archbishop; have consented.
Am torn away, subdued, violated,
United to the spiritual flesh of nature,
Mastered by the animal powers of spirit,

Dominated by the lust of self-demolition,
By the final utter uttermost death of spirit,
By the final ecstasy of waste and shame,
    O Lord Archbishop, O Thomas Archbishop, forgive us,
        forgive us, pray for us that we may pray for you,
        out of our shame.

There is an oxymoronic rapture in that chorus that amounts to having the right rape performed upon one for the wrong reason. Thomas replies by assuring the women that: "This is one moment, / But know that another / Shall pierce you with a sudden painful joy." Presumably he prophesies his own martyrdom, which they are bound to misapprehend. His rather odd attempt at consoling them ends with one of the most famous of Eliotic lines: "Human kind cannot bear very much reality." Freud says much the same, but by "reality" he meant the authentic consciousness of one's own mortality. Eliot meant the breaking in upon us of the order of charity. Between the Chorus of the Women of Canterbury and the sanctified Thomas, every reader and playgoer chooses the Chorus, who save Eliot's drama from having to bear too much of a transcendent reality that evades dramatic representation.

Thornton Wilder

(1897–1975)

REREADING *OUR TOWN* AND *THE MATCHMAKER* IN 2002 PROVIDES A VERY mixed literary experience. One sees the past glories, but does not feel them. It is rather like—for me anyway—reseeing Fellini movies I had enjoyed immensely several decades ago. Time's revenges are inexorable, and all debates about canonical survival are resolved pragmatically by the grim process in which popular works become Period Pieces.

Aside from a few of his shorter plays, Wilder's only prospect for survival is *The Skin of Our Teeth*, again in my wavering judgment. I remember participating in occasional seminars on *Finnegans Wake* led by Wilder when I was a graduate student at Yale in the early Fifties. Genial and well-informed, Wilder particularly moved one by his clear love for Joyce's great, always-to-be-neglected Book of the Night. Rereading *The Skin of Our Teeth*, the charm of those seminars returns to me. Wilder emphasized Joyce's skill in rendering different eras of time simultaneously, which is his principal debt in the Antrobus family saga to Joyce.

It is not that the play can hold up when read too closely against the impacted mosaic of *Finnegans Wake*, but then what could? The Earwickers are obviously larger and more multivalent than the Antrobuses: they are also more Shakespearean, because of Joyce's deliberate *agon* with "the Englishman." Great "Shapesphere" puns his way through the *Wake*, where the generational struggles and family romances overtly remake *Hamlet*. One might wish that Wilder had taken even more from *Finnegans Wake*: an overtone of *Hamlet* might help to relieve the banality of the Antrobus children or the eternally unfailing goodness of Mrs. Antrobus, who would be enlivened by a touch of that sexual magnet, Queen Gertrude.

Doubtless *The Skin of Our Teeth* still stages better than it reads, but I fear that its simplifications are not intensifications but reductions.

Theatrically, we are now in the Age of Sam Shepard and Tony Kushner. *Their* intensifications yet may prove to lack permanence: our theater is still Artaud's, with his angry motto: "No more masterpieces."

Bertolt Brecht

(1898-1956)

"BERTOLT BRECHT," AS WE CONTINUE TO LEARN, WAS A BRAND NAME, applied by Bert Brecht, a survivor, to the writing of some of the women he made love to and exploited: Elisabeth Hauptmann, Margarete Steffin, and Ruth Berlau. Brecht himself was remarkably reluctant to write plays, poems, or stories entirely on his own. Of the five plays studied in this volume, Hauptmann composed most of *The Threepenny Opera* (80 to 90 percent) and Steffin the larger part of *Mother Courage and Her Children, Galileo, The Good Woman of Sezuan,* and *The Caucasian Chalk Circle.* Berlau wrote part of *The Good Woman of Sezuan,* so this book actually should be called *Bloom's Dramatists: Elisabeth Hauptmann, Margarete Steffin, Ruth Berlau, and Bert Brecht,* but a brand name is a brand name, as I cheerfully acknowledge.

Marxist anti-individualism, served with French sauces, is now nearly dominant in the university, and affects the media and entertainment industries. Doubtless, Brecht was acting on his principles, though one can wince at his sermons on "goodness," while enjoying his famous maxims: "First comes eating, then comes morality" and "For this life no person is bad enough." His early poem, "Concerning Poor B.B.," has a delicious passage where he reclines, amidst a pair of women, whom he assures: "In me you behold a man upon whom absolutely you can't rely." Whether Hauptmann wrote some, or even all, of *this* poem is a nice question.

At what point does anti-individualism become plain theft? As a lifelong anti-Nazi, Brecht had his heroic aspect. Unfortunately, he defended Stalin endlessly, slyly blind even to the disappearance of old friends into the gulag. The truth appears to be that Marxism had nothing to do with Brecht's lifelong exploitation of his many women. He was a timeless womanizer and cad, greatly gifted in the mysteries by which women of genius are caught and held.

All this is merely preamble to the rest of this Introduction, where the brand name "Brecht" is employed, even though the dramatist's name ought to be Hauptmann, or Steffin, or Steffin and Berlau. As research more fully establishes actual authorship, Hauptmann and Steffin, in particular, will replace Brecht, and will be seen as major dramatists in the German language. But it is awkward to keep putting "Brecht" into quotation marks, so I will just say Brecht, while urging the reader to keep in mind that Brecht was not Brecht.

Since Brecht may have composed no more than a tenth of *The Threepenny Opera*, perhaps we ought to start calling it Hauptmann/Brecht/ Weill anyway. Even that is inaccurate, since Brecht usurped Karl Kammer's translations of poems by François Villon, without changing a word, and of course without acknowledgment, so we actually have *The Threepenny Opera* (1928) by Hauptmann/Brecht/Weill/Kammer. John Gay and Villon mix well, Brecht cleverly saw. As a poet, Brecht owed something to Heine, a touch to Villon and Rimbaud, but most to Elisabeth Hauptmann, and then to Margarete Steffin, after her.

The Threepenny Opera has taken the place of *The Beggar's Opera*, its archetype, though I still prefer John Gay's work, whether as reading or in performance. "The Ballad of Mac the Knife," as sung and trumpeted by Louis Armstrong, remains the largest intrusion of Brecht and Company into popular American consciousness.

Tony Kushner, a generous and gifted Marxist idealizer, tells us that: "The smallest divisible human unit is two people, not one; one is a fiction." Alas, the experience of a lifetime teaches me otherwise: two is a fiction. Bert Brecht, whatever he said he believed, pragmatically demonstrated that, except for Bert, everyone else was a staged fiction.

The plays, when well directed and performed, are more impressive than they are on the page. Reading Brecht and Company is, for me, a mixed aesthetic experience, because much of the cynicism is dated, the ideology is glaring, and the theories of alienation and of epic theater are all too relevant to the plays. Are there any personalities involved, let along characters? The flight from pathos is brilliantly complete: why should we care? Didactic literature, Christian or Marxist, is moralism, not literature. Eloquence abides in Brecht and Company, and there are a wealth of dramatic effects, but to compare *Galileo* to *Hamlet* is an absurdity.

Eric Bentley, a dramatic critic to whom I defer, maintains his long devotion to Brecht and Company, and so I have to assume that, as a critic, I am insensitive to parable as a dramatic form. Still, there are questions to put to the Brechtians. If *Hamlet* were the political drama that Brecht turned it into, could it be of perpetual relevance, so universal, free of all restrictions of time and place? I attended the *Life of Galileo* that Charles Laughton brought to Broadway in December 1947, and recall being stunned by Laughton's vehement presence, his extraordinary pathos, which seemed incongruous in the context of the more-or-less Brechtian play, which was so uneasy with its own Shakespeareanism that I emerged from the theater totally confused. Reading the play's various texts since, in German, does not enlighten me, more than a half-century later. Even *Coriolanus* defeated Brecht's attempt to empty it of pathos, but the *Hamlet*-haunted *Galileo* attempts to hollow out what is much larger than itself. The land that does not need a hero is yet to be found. Brecht and Company was a brave and original venture, but a final aesthetic judgment upon it would still be premature.

Samuel Beckett

(1906-1989)

JONATHAN SWIFT, SO MUCH THE STRONGEST IRONIST IN THE LANGUAGE AS to have no rivals, wrote the prose masterpiece of the language in *A Tale of a Tub*. Samuel Beckett, as much the legitimate descendant of Swift as he is of his friend James Joyce, has written the prose masterpieces of the language in this century, sometimes as translations from his own French originals. Such an assertion does not discount the baroque splendors of *Ulysses* and *Finnegans Wake*, but prefers to them the purity of *Murphy* and *Watt*, and of Beckett's renderings into English of *Malone Dies, The Unnamable*, and *How It Is*. Unlike Swift and Joyce, Beckett is only secondarily an ironist and, despite his brilliance at tragicomedy, is something other than a comic writer. His Cartesian dualism seems to me less fundamental than his profoundly Schopenhauerian vision. Perhaps Swift, had he read and tolerated Schopenhauer, might have turned into Beckett.

A remarkable number of the greatest novelists have found Schopenhauer more than congenial: one thinks of Turgenev, Tolstoy, Zola, Hardy, Conrad, Thomas Mann, even of Proust. As those seven novelists have in common only the activity of writing novels, we may suspect that Schopenhauer's really horrifying system helps a novelist to do his work. This is not to discount the intellectual and spiritual persuasiveness of Schopenhauer. A philosopher who so deeply affected Wagner, Nietzsche, Wittgenstein, and (despite his denials) Freud, hardly can be regarded only as a convenient aid to storytellers and storytelling. Nevertheless, Schopenhauer evidently stimulated the arts of fiction, but why? Certain it is that we cannot read *The World as Will and Representation* as a work of fiction. Who could bear it as fiction? Supplementing his book, Schopenhauer characterizes the Will to Live:

Here also life presents itself by no means as a gift for enjoyment, but as a task, a drudgery to be performed; and in accordance with this we see, in great and small, universal need, ceaseless cares, constant pressure, endless strife, compulsory activity, with extreme exertion of all the powers of body and mind.... All strive, some planning, others acting; the tumult is indescribable. But the ultimate aim of it all, what is it? To sustain ephemeral and tormented individuals through a short span of time in the most fortunate case with endurable want and comparative freedom from pain, which, however, is at once attended with ennui; then the reproduction of this race and its striving. In this evident disproportion between the trouble and the reward, the will to live appears to us from this point of view, if taken objectively, as a fool, or subjectively, as a delusion, seized by which everything living works with the utmost exertion of its strength for something that is of no value. But when we consider it more closely, we shall find here also that it is rather a blind pressure, a tendency entirely without ground or motive.

Hugh Kenner suggests that Beckett reads Descartes as fiction. Beckett's fiction suggests that Beckett reads Schopenhauer as truth. Descartes as a precursor is safely distant; Joyce was much too close, and *Murphy* and even *Watt* are Joycean books. Doubtless, Beckett turned to French in *Molloy* so as to exorcise Joyce, and certainly, from *Malone Dies* on, the prose when translated back into English has ceased to be Joycean. Joyce is to Beckett as Milton was to Wordsworth. *Finnegans Wake*, like *Paradise Lost*, is a triumph demanding study; Beckett's trilogy, like *The Prelude*, internalizes the triumph by way of the compensatory imagination, in which experience and loss become one. Study does little to unriddle Beckett or Wordsworth. The Old Cumberland Beggar, Michael, Margaret of *The Ruined Cottage*; these resist analysis as do Molloy, Malone, and the Unnamable. Place my namesake, the sublime Poldy, in *Murphy* and he might fit, though he would explode the book. Place him in *Watt*? It cannot be done, and Poldy (or even Earwicker) in the trilogy would be like Milton (or Satan) perambulating about in *The Prelude*.

The fashion (largely derived from French misreaders of German thought) of denying a fixed, stable ego is a shibboleth of current criticism. But such a denial is precisely like each literary generation's assertion that it truly writes the common language rather than a poetic diction. Both stances define modernism, and modernism is as old as Hellenistic Alexandria. Callimachus is as modernist as Joyce, and Aristarchus, like

Hugh Kenner, is an antiquarian modernist or modernist antiquarian. Schopenhauer dismissed the ego as an illusion, life as torment, and the universe as nothing, and he rightly credited these insights to that great modernist, the Buddha. Beckett too is as modernist as the Buddha, or as Schopenhauer, who disputes with Hume the position of the best writer among philosophers since Plato. I laugh sometimes in reading Schopenhauer, but the laughter is defensive. Beckett provokes laughter, as Falstaff does, or in the mode of Shakespeare's clowns.

II

In his early monograph, *Proust*, Beckett cites Schopenhauer's definition of the artistic procedure as "the contemplation of the world independently of the principle of reason." Such more-than-rational contemplation gives Proust those Ruskinian or Paterian privileged moments that are "epiphanies" in Joyce but which Beckett mordantly calls "fetishes" in Proust. Transcendental bursts of radiance necessarily are no part of Beckett's cosmos, which resembles, if anything at all, the Demiurge's creation in ancient Gnosticism. Basilides or Valentinus, Alexandrian heresiarchs, would have recognized instantly the world of the trilogy and of the major plays: *Waiting for Godot, Endgame, Krapp's Last Tape*. It is the world ruled by the Archons, the kenoma, non-place of emptiness. Beckett's enigmatic spirituality quests, though sporadically, for a void that is a fullness, the Abyss or *pleroma* that the Gnostics called both forefather and foremother. Call this a natural rather than a revealed Gnosticism in Beckett's case, but Gnosticism it is nevertheless. Schopenhauer's quietism is at last not Beckett's, which is to say that for Beckett, as for Blake and for the Gnostics, the Creation and the Fall were the same event.

The young Beckett, bitterly reviewing a translation of Rilke into English, memorably rejected Rilke's transcendental self-deceptions, where the poet mistook his own tropes as spiritual evidences:

> Such a turmoil of self-deception and naif discontent gains nothing in dignity from that prime article of the Rilkean faith, which provides for the interchangeability of Rilke and God.... He has the fidgets, a disorder which may very well give rise, as it did with Rilke on occasion, to poetry of a high order. But why call the fidgets God, Ego, Orpheus and the rest?

In 1938, the year that *Murphy* was belatedly published, Beckett declared his double impatience with the language of transcendence and with the transcendence of language, while intimating also the imminence of the swerve away from Joyce in the composition of *Watt* (1942–44):

> At first it can only be a matter of somehow finding a method by which we can represent this mocking attitude towards the word, through words. In this dissonance between the means and their use it will perhaps become possible to feel a whisper of that final music or that silence that underlies All.
>
> With such a program, in my opinion, the latest work of Joyce has nothing whatever to do. There it seems rather to be a matter of an apotheosis of the word. Unless perhaps Ascension to Heaven and Descent to Hell are somehow one and the same.

As a Gnostic imagination, Beckett's way is Descent, in what cannot be called a hope to liberate the sparks imprisoned in words. Hope is alien to Beckett's mature fiction, so that we can say its images are Gnostic but not its program, since it lacks all program. A Gnosticism without potential transcendence is the most negative of all possible negative stances, and doubtless accounts for the sympathetic reader's sense that every crucial work by Beckett necessarily must be his last. Yet the grand paradox is that lessness never ends in Beckett.

III

"Nothing is got for nothing." That is the later version of Emerson's law of Compensation, in the essay "Power" of *The Conduct of Life*. Nothing is got for nothing even in Beckett, this greatest master of nothing. In the progression from *Murphy* through *Watt* and the trilogy onto *How It Is* and the briefer fictions of recent years, there is loss for the reader as well as gain. The same is true of the movement from *Godot*, *Endgame*, and *Krapp's Last Tape* down to the short plays of Beckett's current and perhaps final phase. A wild humor abandons Beckett, or is transformed into a comedy for which we seem not to be ready. Even an uncommon reader can long for those marvelous Pythagoreans, Wylie and Neary, who are the delight of *Murphy*, or for the sense of the picturesque that makes a last stand in *Molloy*. Though the mode was Joyce's, the music of Wylie and Neary is Beckett's alone:

> "These are dark sayings," said Wylie.
> Neary turned his cup upside down.
> "Needle," he said, "as it is with the love of the body, so with

the friendship of the mind, the full is only reached by admittance to the most retired places. Here are the pudenda of my psyche."

"Cathleen," cried Wylie.

"But betray me," said Neary, "and you go the way of Hippasos."

"The Adkousmatic, I presume," said Wylie. "His retribution slips my mind."

"Drowned in a puddle," said Neary, "for having divulged the incommensurability of side and diagonal."

"So perish all babblers," said Wylie....

"Do not quibble," said Neary harshly. "You saved my life. Now palliate it."

"I greatly fear," said Wylie, "that the syndrome known as life is too diffuse to admit of palliation. For every symptom that is eased, another is made worse. The horse leech's daughter is a closed system. Her quantum of wantum cannot vary."

"Very prettily put," said Neary.

One can be forgiven for missing this, even as one surrenders these easier pleasures for the more difficult pleasures of *How It Is*:

my life above what I did in my life above a little of everything tried everything then gave up no worse always a hole a ruin always a crust never any good at anything not made for that farrago too complicated crawl about in corners and sleep all I wanted I got it nothing left but go to heaven.

The Sublime mode, according to a great theorist, Angus Fletcher, has "the direct and serious function of destroying the slavery of pleasure." Beckett is certainly the strongest Western author living in the year 1987, the last survivor of the sequence that includes Proust, Kafka, and Joyce. It seems odd to name Beckett, most astonishing of minimalists, as a representative of the Sublime mode, but the isolation and terror of the High Sublime return in the catastrophe creations of Beckett, in that vision Fletcher calls "catastrophe as a gradual grinding down and slowing to a dead stop." A Sublime that moves towards silence necessarily relies upon a rhetoric of waning lyricism, in which the entire scale of effects is transformed, as John Hollander notes:

Sentences, phrases, images even, are the veritable arias in the plays and the later fiction. The magnificent rising of the kite at the end of *Murphy* occurs in a guarded but positive surge of ceremonial song, to which he will never return.

Kafka's Hunter Gracchus, who had been glad to live and was glad to die, tells us that "I slipped into my winding sheet like a girl into her marriage dress. I lay and waited. Then came the mishap." The mishap, a moment's error on the part of the death-ship's pilot, moves Gracchus from the heroic world of romance to the world of Kafka and of Beckett, where one is neither alive nor dead. It is Beckett's peculiar triumph that he disputes with Kafka the dark eminence of being the Dante of that world. Only Kafka, or Beckett, could have written the sentence in which Gracchus sums up the dreadfulness of his condition: "The thought of helping me is an illness that has to be cured by taking to one's bed." Murphy might have said that; Malone is beyond saying anything so merely expressionistic. The "beyond" is where Beckett's later fictions and plays reside. Call it the silence, or the abyss, or the reality beyond the pleasure principle, or the metaphysical or spiritual reality of our existence at last exposed, beyond further illusion. Beckett cannot or will not name it, but he has worked through to the art of representing it more persuasively than anyone else.

Endgame

Trying to understand *Endgame*, Theodor W. Adorno attained to a most somber conclusion:

> Consciousness begins to look its own demise in the eye, as if it wanted to survive the demise, as these two want to survive the destruction of their world. Proust, about whom the young Beckett wrote an essay, is said to have attempted to keep protocol on his own struggle with death.... *Endgame* carries out this intention like a mandate from a testament.

Hugh Kenner, a very different ideologue than Adorno, was less somber: "The despair in which he traffics is a conviction, not a philosophy." A reader and playgoer who, like myself, enjoys *Endgame* more than any other stage drama of this century, may wish to dissent from both Adorno and Kenner. Neither the struggle with death nor the conviction of despair seems to me central in the play. An extraordinary gusto informs *Endgame*, surpassing even Brecht, Pirandello, and Ionesco in that quality. It is a gusto quite indistinguishable from an acute anxiety attack, but anxiety and anxious expectations need not be confused with despair (or hope)

or with a struggle against death. *Endgame* contrives to be both biblical and
Shakespearean, despite its customary Schopenhauerian and Gnostic
assumptions. Anxiety, Freud noted, is the reaction to the danger of object
loss, and Hamm fears losing Clov. Or, as Freud ironically also observes,
anxiety after all is only a perception—of possibilities of anxiety.

Hamm, a bad chess player, faces his endgame with a compulsive intensity, so that he is formidable though a blunderer. His name necessarily suggests Ham, who saw the nakedness of his father Noah, and whose son
Canaan was cursed into servitude for it. That would make Nagg and Nell
into Mr. and Mrs. Noah, which seems not inappropriate, but is sufficient
without being altogether necessary, as it were. There is enough of a ruined
Hamlet in Hamm to work against the story of Noah's flood, and overtly
("our revels now are ended") a touch of a ruined Prospero also. I tend to
vote for Beckett's deepest orientations again. Take away from Schopenhauer
his aesthetic Sublime, and from ancient Gnosticism its transcendent if alien
god, and you are very close to the cosmos of Beckett's *Endgame*.

As in *Waiting for Godot*, we are back in the *kenoma*, or sensible emptiness, a kind of vast yet dry flood. A bungler in Hamm's own image, doubtless the Demiurge, has created this *kenoma*, written this play, except that
Hamm himself may be the Demiurge, the artisan or bad hammer responsible for driving in Clov, Nagg, Nell, and all the other nails (to follow
Kenner, but with a Gnostic difference). The drama might be titled
Endgame of the Demiurge or even *Hamlet's Revenge upon Himself*. Kenner
and other exegetes have centered upon a single moment in *Hamlet*, where
the prince tells Rosencrantz and Guildenstern what they are not capable of
knowing, even after they are told:

HAMLET: Denmark's a prison.
ROSENCRANTZ: Then is the world one.
HAMLET: A goodly one, in which there are many confines, wards,
    and dungeons, Denmark being one o' th' worst.
ROSENCRANTZ: We think not so, my lord.
HAMLET: Why then 'tis none to you; for there is nothing either
    good or bad, but thinking makes it so. To me it is a prison.
ROSENCRANTZ: Why then your ambition makes it one. 'Tis too
    narrow for your mind.
HAMLET: O God, I could be bounded in a nutshell, and count
    myself a king of infinite space—were it not that I have bad
    dreams.
    (ll. 243–56)

Hamm's world has become a prison, with a single confine, ward, and dungeon, a nutshell reduced from infinite space by the Demiurge's bad dreams. *Endgame* is hardly Hamm's bad dream, but a Kafkan Hamlet could be Hamm, Nagg an amalgam of the ghost and Claudius, Nell a plausible Gertrude, and poor Clov a ruined Horatio. Contaminate Hamlet with Kafka's "The Hunter Gracchus," and you might get *Endgame*. Schopenhauer's dreadful Will to Live goes on ravening in Hamm, Clov, Nagg, and Nell, as it must in any dramatic representation, since there can be no mimesis without appetite. Where the Will to Live is unchecked, there are anxious expectations, and anxiety or Hamm is king, but a king on a board swept nearly bare. Kenner thinks Clov a knight and Hamm's parents pawns, but they seem to me out of the game, or taken already. But that raises the authentic aesthetic puzzle of *Endgame*. is there another, an opposing side, with a rival king, or is there only Hamm, a perfect solipsist where even Hamlet was an imperfect one?

I do not think that Hamm lacks an opponent, since his solipsism is not perfect, hence his anxiety as to losing Clov. The Demiurge, like every bad actor, finds his opponent in the audience, which comes to be beguiled but stays to criticize. Kafka, with high deliberation, wrote so as to make interpretation impossible, but that only displaces what needs interpretation into the question of Kafka's evasiveness. Beckett does not evade; *Endgame* is his masterpiece, and being so inward it is also his most difficult work, with every allusion endstopped, despite the reverberations. There is no play in *Endgame*; it is all Hamlet's *Mousetrap*, or Hamm's. We have only a play-within-a-play, which gives us the difficulty of asking and answering: what then is the play that contains *Endgame*? If the audience is the opponent, and Hamm is bound to lose the endgame, then the enclosing play is the larger entity that can contain the chess game between Hamm and ourselves. That is not quite the play of the world, yet it remains a larger play than any other dramatist has given us in this century.

Waiting for Godot

Hugh Kenner wisely observes that, in *Waiting for Godot*, bowler hats "are removed for thinking but replaced for speaking." Such accurate observation is truly Beckettian, even as was Lyndon Johnson's reflection that Gerald Ford was the one person in Washington who could not walk and chew gum at the same time. Beckett's tramps, like President Ford, keep to one activity at a time. Entropy is all around them and within them, since they inhabit, they are, that cosmological emptiness the Gnostics named as the *kenoma*.

Of the name *Godot*, Beckett remarked, "and besides, there is a rue
Godot, a cycling racer named Godot, so you see, the possibilities are rather
endless." Actually, Beckett seems to have meant Godet, the director of the
Tour de France, but even the mistake is Beckettian, and reminds us of a
grand precursor text, Alfred Jarry's "The Passion Considered as an Uphill
Bicycle Race," with its superb start: "Barabbas, slated to race, was
scratched."

Nobody is scratched in *Waiting for Godot*, but nobody gets started
either. I take it that "Godot" is an emblem for "recognition," and I thereby accept Deirdre Bair's tentative suggestion that the play was written
while Beckett waited for recognition, for his novels to be received and
appreciated, within the canon. A man waiting for recognition is more likely than ever to be obsessed that his feet should hurt continually, and perhaps to be provoked also to the memory that his own father invariably
wore a bowler hat and a black coat.

A play that moves from "Nothing to be done" (referring to a recalcitrant boot) on to "Yes, let's go," after which they do not move, charmingly does not progress at all. Time, the enemy above all others for the
Gnostics, is the adversary in *Waiting for Godot*, as it was in Beckett's *Proust*.
That would be a minor truism, if the play were not set in the world made
not by Plato's Demiurge but by the Demiurge of Valentinus, for whom
time is hardly the moving image of eternity:

> When the Demiurge further wanted to imitate also the boundless,
> eternal, infinite, and timeless nature of the Abyss, but could not
> express its immutable eternity, being as he was a fruit of defect, he
> embodied their eternity in times, epochs, and great numbers of
> years, under the delusion that by the quantity of times he could
> represent their infinity. Thus truth escaped him and he followed
> the lie.

Blake's way of saying this was to remind us that in equivocal worlds up
and down were equivocal. Estragon's way is: "Who am I to tell my private
nightmares to if I can't tell them to you?" Lucky's way is the most Gnostic,
since how could the *kenoma* be described any better than this?

> the earth in the great cold the great dark the air and the earth
> abode of stones in the great cold alas alas in the year of their Lord
> six hundred and something the air the earth the sea the earth
> abode of stones in the great deeps the great cold on sea on land
> and in the air I resume for reasons unknown in spite of the tennis

the facts are there but time will tell I resume alas alas on on in short in fine on on abode of stones who can doubt it I resume but not so fast I resume the skull fading fading fading and concurrently simultaneously what is more for reasons unknown.

Description that is also lament—that is the only lyricism possible for the Gnostic, ancient or modern, Valentinus or Schopenhauer, Beckett or Shelley:

> Art thou pale for weariness
> Of climbing heaven and gazing on the earth,
>   Wandering companionless
> Among the stars that have a different birth—
> And ever changing, like a joyless eye
> That finds no object worth its constancy?

Shelley's fragment carefully assigns the stars to a different birth, shared with our imaginations, a birth that precedes the Creation–Fall that gave us the cosmos of *Waiting for Godot*. When the moon rises, Estragon contemplates it in a Shelleyan mode: "Pale for weariness ... of climbing heaven and gazing on the likes of us." This negative epiphany, closing act 1, is answered by another extraordinary Shelleyan allusion, soon after the start of act 2:

VLADIMIR: We have that excuse.
ESTRAGON: It's so we won't hear.
VLADIMIR: We have our reasons.
ESTRAGON: All the dead voices.
VLADIMIR: They make a noise like wings.
ESTRAGON: Like leaves.
VLADIMIR: Like sand.
ESTRAGON: Like leaves.
    Silence.
VLADIMIR: They all speak at once.
ESTRAGON: Each one to itself.
    Silence.
VLADIMIR: Rather they whisper.
ESTRAGON: They rustle.
VLADIMIR: They murmur.
ESTRAGON: They rustle.
    Silence.

VLADIMIR: What do they say?

ESTRAGON: They talk about their lives.

VLADIMIR: To have lived is not enough for them.

ESTRAGON: They have to talk about it.

VLADIMIR: To be dead is not enough for them.

ESTRAGON: It is not sufficient.

   Silence.

VLADIMIR: They make a noise like feathers.

ESTRAGON: Like leaves.

VLADIMIR: Like ashes.

ESTRAGON: Like leaves.

   Long silence.

VLADIMIR: Say something!

It is the ultimate, dark transumption of Shelley's fiction of the leaves in the apocalyptic "Ode to the West Wind." Involuntary Gnostics, Estragon and Vladimir are beyond apocalypse, beyond any hope for this world. A tree may bud overnight, but this is not so much like an early miracle (as Kenner says) as it is "another of your nightmares" (as Estragon says). The reentry of the blinded Pozzo, now reduced to crying "Help!" is the drama's most poignant moment, even as its most dreadful negation is shouted by blind Pozzo in his fury, after Vladimir asks a temporal question once too often:

POZZO: (*suddenly furious*). Have you not done tormenting me with your accursed time! It's abominable! When! When! One day, is that not enough for you, one day he went dumb, one day I went blind, one day we'll go deaf, one day we were born, one day we shall die, the same day, the same second, is that not enough for you? (*Calmer.*) They give birth astride of a grave, the light gleams an instant, then it's night once more.

Pozzo, originally enough of a brute to be a Demiurge himself, is now another wanderer in the darkness of the *kenoma*. Estragon's dreadful question, as to whether Pozzo may not have been Godot, is answered negatively by Vladimir, but with something less than perfect confidence. Despite the boy's later testimony, I suspect that the tragicomedy centers precisely there: in the possible identity of Godot and Pozzo, in the unhappy intimation that the Demiurge is not only the god of this world, the spirit of Schopenhauer's Will to Live, but the only god that can be uncovered anywhere, even anywhere out of this world.

Tennessee Williams

(1911–1983)

IT IS A SAD AND INEXPLICABLE TRUTH THAT THE UNITED STATES, A DRAMATIC nation, continues to have so limited a literary achievement in the drama. American literature, from Emerson to the present moment, is a distinguished tradition. The poetry of Whitman, Dickinson, Frost, Stevens, Eliot, W.C. Williams, Hart Crane, R.P. Warren, Elizabeth Bishop down through the generation of my own contemporaries—John Ashbery, James Merrill, A.R. Ammons, and others—has an unquestionable eminence, and takes a vital place in Western literature. Prose fiction from Hawthorne and Melville on through Mark Twain and Henry James to Cather and Dreiser, Faulkner, Hemingway, Fitzgerald, Nathanael West, and Pynchon, has almost a parallel importance. The line of essayists and critics from Emerson and Thoreau to Kenneth Burke and beyond constitutes another crucial strand of our national letters. But where is the American drama in comparison to all this, and in relation to the long cavalcade of western drama from Aeschylus to Beckett?

The American theater, by the common estimate of its most eminent critics, touches an initial strength with Eugene O'Neill, and then proceeds to the more varied excellences of Thornton Wilder, Tennessee Williams, Arthur Miller, Edward Albee, and Sam Shepard. That sequence is clearly problematical, and becomes even more worrisome when we move from playwrights to plays. Which are our dramatic works that matter most? *Long Day's Journey Into Night*, certainly; perhaps *The Iceman Cometh*; evidently *A Streetcar Named Desire* and *Death of a Salesman*; perhaps again *The Skin of Our Teeth* and *The Zoo Story*—it is not God's plenty. And I will venture the speculation that our drama palpably is not yet literary enough. By this I do not just mean that O'Neill writes very badly, or Miller very baldly; they do, but so did Dreiser, and *Sister Carrie* and *An American Tragedy* prevail nevertheless. Nor do I wish to be an American Matthew Arnold (whom I loathe above all other critics) and proclaim that our dramatists simply have not known enough. They know more than enough, and that is part of the trouble.

Literary tradition, as I have come to understand it, masks the agon between past and present as a benign relationship, whether personal or societal. The actual transferences between the force of the literary past and the potential of writing in the present tend to be darker, even if they do not always or altogether follow the defensive patterns of what Sigmund Freud called "family romances." Whether or not an ambivalence, however repressed, towards the past's force is felt by the new writer and is manifested in his work seems to depend entirely upon the ambition and power of the oncoming artist. If he aspires after strength, and can attain it, then he must struggle with both a positive and a negative transference, false connections because necessarily imagined ones, between a composite precursor and himself. His principal resource in that agon will be his own native gift for interpretation, or as I am inclined to call it, strong misreading. Revising his precursor, he will create himself, make himself into a kind of changeling, and so he will become, in an illusory but highly pragmatic way, his own father.

The most literary of our major dramatists, and clearly I mean "literary" in a precisely descriptive sense, neither pejorative nor eulogistic, was Tennessee Williams. Wilder, with his intimate connections to *Finnegans Wake* and Gertrude Stein, might seem to dispute this placement, and Wilder was certainly more literate than Williams. But Wilder had a benign relation to his crucial precursor, Joyce, and did not aspire after a destructive strength. Williams did, and suffered the fate he prophesied and desired; the strength destroyed his later work, and his later life, and thus joined itself to the American tradition of self-destructive genius. Williams truly had one precursor only: Hart Crane, the greatest of our lyrical poets, after Whitman and Dickinson, and the most self-destructive figure in our national literature, surpassing all others in this, as in so many regards.

Williams asserted he had other precursors also: D.H. Lawrence, and Chekhov in the drama. These were outward influences, and benefited Williams well enough, but they were essentially formal, and so not the personal and societal family romance of authentic poetic influence. Hart Crane made Williams into more of a dramatic lyrist, though writing in prose, than the lyrical dramatist that Williams is supposed to have been. Though this influence—perhaps more nearly an identification—helped form *The Glass Menagerie* and (less overtly) *A Streetcar Named Desire*, and in a lesser mode *Summer and Smoke* and *Suddenly Last Summer*, it also led

to such disasters of misplaced lyricism as the dreadful *Camino Real* and the
dreary *The Night of the Iguana*. (*Cat on a Hot Tin Roof*, one of Williams's best
plays, does not seem to me to show any influence of Crane.) Williams's
long aesthetic decline covered thirty years, from 1953 to 1983, and reflect-
ed the sorrows of a seer who, by his early forties, had outlived his own
vision. Hart Crane, self-slain at thirty-two, had set for Williams a High
Romantic paradigm that helped cause Williams, his heart as dry as summer
dust, to burn to the socket.

Cat on a Hot Tin Roof

It is difficult to argue for the aesthetic achievement of Tennessee
Williams's long, final phase as a dramatist. Rereading persuades me that his
major plays remain *The Glass Menagerie*, *A Streetcar Named Desire*, *Suddenly
Last Summer*, and the somewhat undervalued *Summer and Smoke*. *Cat on a
Hot Tin Roof* was a popular and critical success, on stage and as a film. I
have just reread it in the definitive *Library of America* edition, which prints
both versions of Act III, the original, which Williams greatly preferred,
and the Broadway revision, made to accommodate the director Elia Kazan.
Here is the ambiguous original conclusion, followed by the revision:

> MARGARET: And so tonight we're going to make the lie true, and
> when that's done, I'll bring the liquor back here and we'll get
> drunk together, here, tonight, in this place that death has
> come into ... —What do you say?
> BRICK: I don't say anything. I guess there's nothing to say.
> MARGARET: Oh, you weak people, you weak, beautiful people!—
> who give up.—What you want is someone to—
> (*She turns out the rose-silk lamp.*)
> —take hold of you.—Gently, gently, with love! And—
> (*The curtain begins to fall slowly.*)
> I *do* love you, Brick, I *do*!
> BRICK: (*smiling with charming sadness*): Wouldn't it be funny if that
> was true?
>
> ***
>
> MARGARET: And you lost your driver's license! I'd phone ahead and
> have you stopped on the highway before you got halfway to
> Ruby Lightfoot's gin mill. I told a lie to Big Daddy, but we can
> make that lie come true. And then I'll bring you liquor, and
> we'll get drunk together, here, tonight, in this place that death
> has come into! What do you say? What do you say, baby?

BRICK: (*X to L side bed*)
> I admire you, Maggie.

(*Brick sits on edge of bed. He looks up at the overhead light, then at Margaret. She reaches for the light, turns it out; then she kneels quickly beside Brick at foot of bed.*)

MARGARET: Oh, you weak, beautiful people who give up with such grace. What you need is someone to take hold of you—gently, with love, and hand your life back to you, like something gold you let go of—and I can! I'm determined to do it—and nothing's more determined than a cat on a tin roof—is there? Is there, baby?

(*She touches his cheek, gently.*)

As Williams noted, his Maggie augments in charm between the two versions; his Brick modulates subtly, and is a touch more receptive to her. Shakespeare demonstrates how difficult it is to resist vitality in a stage role, by creating Sir John Falstaff with a vivacity and wit that carries all before him. There is nothing Shakespearean about Williams: he sketches archetypes, caricatures, grotesques, and cannot represent inwardness. And yet, with all his limitations, he writes well, unlike Eugene O'Neill, who is leaden, and Arthur Miller, who is drab. Thornton Wilder, Edward Albee, and Tony Kushner also have their eloquences, but Williams remains the most articulate and adequate of American dramatists up to this moment.

Yet his inability to dramatize inwardness is a considerable limitation. What is Brick's spiritual malady? His homoeroticism is palpably less a burden than is his homophobia: he will not accept Big Daddy's earlier bisexuality, anymore than he could yield to love for Skipper (or to Maggie). Brick's Narcissism is central to the play, but even more crucial would be his nihilism, if only Williams could tell us something about it. As a Hamlet, Brick does not work at all; he hasn't enough mind to express what most deeply torments him, and I fear that Williams shares this lack. What deprives *Cat on a Hot Tin Roof* of any authentic aesthetic eminence is its obscurantism, which may be indeliberate, unlike Joseph Conrad's in *Heart of Darkness*. It is as though both Williams and Brick were saying: "The horror! The horror!" without ever quite knowing what they were trying to talk about.

The ultimately benign and loving Big Daddy and the adoring Big Mama are *not* the cause of Brick's despair. Were it not for his nihilistic malaise, it seems likely that Brick eventually would turn into his dying father, and would become pragmatically bisexual or pansexual. Brick's attachment to Maggie is ambivalent, but so was his affection for Skipper. As a pure narcissist, Brick is autoerotic, in the manner of Walt Whitman.

The play's epigraph, from Dylan Thomas's "Do not go Gentle into that Good Night," is a gesture of tribute to Big Daddy, who, with Maggie the Cat, saves the play. Brick, without them, would freeze the audience, particularly now, when homosexuality is no longer an issue for an audience not dominated by Fundamentalists, Reagan Republicans, and assorted other mossbacks. Read side by side with the wistful *Summer and Smoke, Cat on a Hot Tin Roof* seems more a film script than an achieved drama.

The Glass Menagerie

In Hart Crane's last great Pindaric ode, "The Broken Tower," the poet cries aloud, in a lament that is also a high celebration, the destruction of his battered self by his overwhelming creative gift:

> The bells, I say, the bells break down their tower;
> And swing I know not where. Their tongues engrave
> Membrane through marrow, my long-scattered score
> Of broken intervals ... And I, their sexton slave!

This Shelleyan and Whitmanian catastrophe creation, or death by inspiration, was cited once by Williams as an omen of Crane's self-immolation. "By the bells breaking down their tower," in Williams's interpretation, Crane meant "the romantic and lyric intensity of his vocation." Gilbert Debusscher has traced the intensity of Crane's effect upon Williams's Romantic and lyric vocation, with particular reference to Tom Wingfield's emergent vocation in *The Glass Menagerie*. More than forty years after its first publication, the play provides an absorbing yet partly disappointing experience of rereading.

A professed "memory play," *The Glass Menagerie* seems to derive its continued if wavering force from its partly repressed representation of the quasi-incestuous and doomed love between Tom Wingfield and his crippled, "exquisitely fragile," ultimately schizophrenic sister Laura. Incest, subtly termed the most poetical of circumstances by Shelley, is the dynamic of the erotic drive throughout Williams's more vital writings. Powerfully displaced, it is the secret dynamic of what is surely Williams's masterwork, *A Streetcar Named Desire*.

The Glass Menagerie scarcely bothers at such a displacement, and the transparency of the incest motif is at once the play's lyrical strength and, alas, its dramatic weakness. Consider the moment when Williams chooses to end the play, which times Tom's closing speech with Laura's gesture of blowing out the candles:

TOM: I didn't go to the moon, I went much further—for time is the longest distance between two places. Not long after that I was fired for writing a poem on the lid of a shoebox. I left St. Louis. I descended the steps of this fire escape for a last time and followed, from then on, in my father's footsteps, attempting to find in motion what was lost in space. I traveled around a great deal. The cities swept about me like dead leaves, leaves that were brightly colored but torn away from the branches. I would have stopped, but I was pursued by something. It always came upon me unawares, taking me altogether by surprise. Perhaps it was a familiar bit of music. Perhaps it was only a piece of transparent glass. Perhaps I am walking along a street at night, in some strange city, before I have found companions. I pass the lighted window of a shop where perfume is sold. The window is filled with pieces of colored glass, tiny transparent bottles in delicate colors, like bits of a shattered rainbow. Then all at once my sister touches my shoulder. I rum around and look into her eyes. Oh, Laura, Laura, I tried to leave you behind me, but I am more faithful than I intended to be! I reach for a cigarette, I cross the street, I run into the movies or a bar, I buy a drink, I speak to the nearest stranger—anything that can blow your candles out!

[*Laura bends over the candles.*]

For nowadays the world is lit by lightning! Blow out your candles, Laura—and so goodbye....

[*She blows the candles out.*]

The many parallels between the lives and careers of Williams and Crane stand behind this poignant passage, though it is fascinating that the actual allusions and echoes here are to Shelley's poetry, but then Shelley increasingly appears to be Crane's heroic archetype, and one remembers Robert Lowell's poem where Crane speaks and identifies himself as the Shelley of his age. The cities of aesthetic exile sweep about Wingfield/Williams like the dead, brightly colored leaves of the "Ode to the West Wind," dead leaves that are at once the words of the poet and lost human souls, like the beloved sister Laura.

What pursues Tom is what pursues the Shelleyan Poet of *Alastor*, an avenging daimon or shadow of rejected, sisterly eros that manifests itself in a further Shelleyan metaphor, the shattered, colored transparencies of Shelley's dome of many-colored glass in *Adonais*, the sublime, lyrical elegy for Keats. That dome, Shelley says, is a similitude for life, and its many colors stain the white radiance of Eternity until death tramples the dome into fragments. Williams beautifully revises Shelley's magnificent trope. For Williams, life itself, through memory as its agent, shatters itself and scatters the colored transparencies of the rainbow, which ought to be, but is not, a covenant of hope.

As lyrical prose, this closing speech has its glory, but whether the dramatic effect is legitimate seems questionable. The key sentence, dramatically, is: "Oh, Laura, Laura, I tried to leave you behind me, but I am more faithful than I intended to be!" In his descriptive list of the characters, Williams says of his surrogate, Wingfield: "His nature is not remorseless, but to escape from a trap he has to act without pity." What would pity have been? And in what sense is Wingfield more faithful, after all, than he attempted to be?

Williams chooses to end the play as though its dramatic center had been Laura, but every reader and every playgoer knows that every dramatic element in the play emanates out from the mother, Amanda. Dream and its repressions, guilt and desire, have remarkably little to do with the representation of Amanda in the play, and everything to do with her children. The split between dramatist and lyrist in Williams is manifested in the play as a generative divide. Williams's true subject, like Crane's, is the absolute identity between his artistic vocation and his homosexuality. What is lacking in *The Glass Menagerie* is that Williams could not have said of Amanda, what, Flaubert-like, he did say of the heroine of *Streetcar*: "I am Blanche DuBois." There, and there only, Williams could fuse Chekhov and Hart Crane into one.

A Streetcar Named Desire

The epigraph to *A Streetcar Named Desire* is a quatrain from Hart Crane's "*The Broken Tower*," the poet's elegy for his gift, his vocation, his life, and so Crane's precise equivalent of Shelley's *Triumph of Life*, Keats's *Fall of Hyperion*, and Whitman's "*When Lilacs Last in the Dooryard Bloom'd*." Tennessee Williams, in his long thirty years of decline after composing *A Streetcar Named Desire*, had no highly designed, powerfully executed elegy for his own poetic self. Unlike Crane, his American Romantic precursor and aesthetic paradigm, Williams had to live out the slow degradation of the waning of his potential, and so endured the triumph of life over his imagination.

Streetcar sustains a first rereading, after thirty years away from it, more strongly than I had expected. It is, inevitably, more remarkable on the stage than in the study, but the fusion of Williams's lyrical and dramatic talents in it has prevailed over time, at least so far. The play's flaws, in performance, ensue from its implicit tendency to sensationalize its characters, Blanche DuBois in particular. Directors and actresses have made such sensationalizing altogether explicit, with the sad result prophesied by Kenneth Tynan twenty-five years ago. The playgoer forgets that Blanche's only strengths are "nostalgia and hope," that she is "the desperate exceptional woman," and that her fall is a parable, rather than an isolated squalor:

> When, finally, she is removed to the mental home, we should feel that a part of civilization is going with her. Where ancient drama teaches us to reach nobility by contemplation of what is noble, modern American drama conjures us to contemplate what might have been noble, but is now humiliated, ignoble in the sight of all but the compassionate.

Tynan, though accurate enough, still might have modified the image of Blanche taking a part of civilization away with her into madness. Though Blanche yearns for the values of the aesthetic, she scarcely embodies them, being in this failure a masochistic self-parody on the part of Williams himself. His *Memoirs* portray Williams incessantly in the role of Blanche, studying the nostalgias, and inching along the wavering line between hope and paranoia. Williams, rather than Blanche, sustains Tynan's analysis of the lost nobility, now humiliated, that American drama conjures us to contemplate.

The fall of Blanche is a parable, not of American civilization's lost nobility, but of the failure of the American literary imagination to rise above its recent myths of recurrent defeat. Emerson admonished us, his descendants, to go beyond the Great Defeat of the Crucifixion and to demand Victory instead, a victory of the senses as well as of the soul. Walt Whitman, taking up Emerson's challenge directly, set the heroic pattern so desperately emulated by Hart Crane, and which is then repeated in a coarser tone in Williams's life and work.

It must seem curious, at first, to regard Blanche DuBois as a failed Whitmanian, but essentially that is her aesthetic identity. Confronted by the revelation of her young husband's preference for an older man over herself, Blanche falls downwards and outwards into nymphomania, phantasmagoric hopes, pseudo-imaginative collages of memory and desire. Her Orphic, psychic rending by the amiably brutal Stanley Kowalski, a rough but effective version of D.H. Lawrence's vitalistic vision of male force, is pathetic rather than tragic, not because Stanley necessarily is mindless, but because she unnecessarily has made herself mindless, by failing the pragmatic test of experience.

Williams's most effective blend of lyrical vision and dramatic irony in the play comes in the agony of Blanche's cry against Stanley to Stella, his wife and her sister:

> He acts like an animal, has an animal's habits! Eats like one, moves like one, talks like one! There's even something—subhuman—something not quite to the stage of humanity yet! Yes, something—ape-like about him, like one of those pictures I've seen in—anthropological studies! Thousands and thousands of years have passed him right by, and there he is—Stanley Kowalski—survivor of the stone age! Bearing the raw meat home from the kill in the jungle! And you—*you* here—*waiting* for him! Maybe he'll strike you or maybe grunt and kiss you! That is, if kisses have been discovered yet! Night falls and the other apes gather! There in the front of the cave, all grunting like him, and swilling and gnawing and hulking! His poker night!—you call it—this party of apes! Somebody growls—some creature snatches at something—the fight is on! *God!* Maybe we are a long way from being made in God's image, but Stella—my sister—there has been *some* progress since then! Such things as art—as poetry and music—such kinds of new light have come into the world since then! In some kinds of people some tenderer feelings have had some little beginning! That we have got to make *grow!* And *cling* to, and hold as our flag! In this dark march toward whatever it is we're approaching.... *Don't—don't hang back with the brutes!*

The lyricism here takes its strength from the ambivalence of what at once attracts and dismays both Blanche and Williams. Dramatic irony, terrible in its antithetical pathos, results here from Blanche's involuntary self-condemnation, since she herself has hung back with the brutes while merely blinking at the new light of the aesthetic. Stanley, being what he is, is clearly less to blame than Blanche, who was capable of more but failed in will.

Williams, in his *Memoirs*, haunted as always by Hart Crane, refers to his precursor as "a tremendous and yet fragile artist," and then associates both himself and Blanche with the fate of Crane, a suicide by drowning in the Caribbean:

> I am as much of an hysteric as ... Blanche; a codicil to my will provides for the disposition of my body in this way. "Sewn up in a clean white sack and dropped over board, twelve hours north of

Havana, so that my bones may rest not too far from those of Hart
Crane ..."

At the conclusion of *Memoirs*, Williams again associated Crane both
with his own vocation and his own limitations, following Crane even in an
identification with the young Rimbaud:

> A poet such as the young Rimbaud is the only writer of whom I
> can think, at this moment, who could escape from words into the
> sensations of being, through his youth, turbulent with revolution,
> permitted articulation by nights of absinthe. And of course there
> is Hart Crane. Both of these poets touched fire that burned them
> alive. And perhaps it is only through self-immolation of such a
> nature that we living beings can offer to you the entire truth of
> ourselves within the reasonable boundaries of a book.

It is the limitation of *Memoirs*, and in some sense even of *A Streetcar
Named Desire*, that we cannot accept either Williams or poor Blanche as a
Rimbaud or a Hart Crane. Blanche cannot be said to have touched fire that
burned her alive. Yet Williams earns the relevance of the play's great epigraph to Blanche's terrible fate:

> And so it was I entered the broken world
> To trace the visionary company of love, its voice
> An instant in the wind (I know not whither hurled)
> But not for long to hold each desperate choice.

Eugène Ionesco

(1912-1994)

THE LESSON, IN MY EXPERIENCE, PLAYS BETTER THAN IT READS. PROPERLY directed and acted, it manifests a rising rhythm of sexual hysteria and violence profoundly disturbing to the audience. When the Maid tells us, after the murder, that the Professor has just dispatched his fortieth victim of the day, we are not immediately incredulous. Reading her assertion provokes more than skepticism: why not sixty, we might inquire? Ionesco's ferocious theater parable defies literalization, on a stage where philology is parodied as vampiric slaughter.

If *The Lesson* still works in the theater, after half a century, the credit goes less to politics, sexual or social, than to Ionesco's primordial sense of some of the foundations of drama. We watch a ritual sacrifice, though the ritual is a farce. Our Sexual Harassment Committees, so charming a feature of the current American academic scene, should attend compulsory performances of *The Lesson*, on a regular basis.

Rhinoceros also plays more strongly than even an acute reading could suggest. Anyone who saw Zero Mostel mug his metamorphosis into a rhinoceros is unlikely to forget it. At Yale, I have watched faculty members change into rhinoceroses steadily since the academic year 1969–70. To be sure, Political Correctness produces relatively amiable rhinoceroses, but a rhinoceros is a rhinoceros nevertheless. In honor of Ionesco, I have taken to calling one of our deans "Rataxes," the king of the rhinoceroses in the *Babar* books, which I used to read to my sons, when they were little.

Poor Bérenger is certainly a flawed hero: weak, confused, fearful, alcoholic. Yet he will not yield. No one can win the war against our rhinoceroses, and Bérenger doubtless will be gored, but he will die human.

Arthur Miller

(1915–2000)

"A MAN CAN GET ANYWHERE IN THIS COUNTRY ON THE BASIS OF BEING liked." Arthur Miller's remark, made in an interview, has a peculiar force in the context of American political and social history. One reflects upon Ronald Reagan, a President impossible (for me) either to admire or to dislike. Miller, despite his palpable literary and dramatic limitations, has a shrewd understanding of our country. *Death of Salesman* is now half a century old, and retains its apparently perpetual relevance. The American ethos is sufficiently caught up by the play so that Miller's masterwork is clearly not just a period piece, unlike *All My Sons* and *The Crucible*, popular as the latter continues to be.

Arthur Miller is an Ibsenite dramatist, though his Ibsen is mostly a social realist, and not the visionary of the great plays: *Peer Gynt*, *Brand*, *Hedda Gabler*, and *When We Dead Awaken*. That Ibsen is himself something of a troll: obsessed and daemonic. Imaginative energy of that order is not present in Miller, though *Death of a Salesman* has an energy of pathos very much its own, the entropic catastrophe that Freud (with some irony) called "Family Romances."

Family romances almost invariably are melodramatic; to convert them to tragedy, you need to be the Shakespeare of *King Lear*, or at least of *Coriolanus*. Miller has a fondness for comparing *Death of a Salesman* to *King Lear*, a contrast that itself is catastrophic for Miller's play. Ibsen, at his strongest, can sustain some limited comparison to aspects of Shakespeare, but Miller cannot. Like Lear, Willy Loman needs and wants more familial love than anyone can receive, but there the likeness ends.

Does Miller, like Eugene O'Neill, write the plays of our moral climate, or have we deceived ourselves into overestimating both of these dramatists? American novelists and American poets have vastly surpassed American playwrights: there is no dramatic William Faulkner or Wallace Stevens to be acclaimed among us. It may be that day-to-day reality in the United States is so violent that stage drama scarcely can compete with the drama of common events and uncommon persons. A wilderness of pathos may be more fecund matter for storyteller and lyricists than it can be for those who would compose tragedies.

Perhaps that is why we value *Death of a Salesman* more highly than its actual achievement warrants. Even half a century back, an universal image of American fatherhood was very difficult to attain. Willy Loman moves us because he dies the death of a father, not of a salesman. Whether Miller's critique of the values of a capitalistic society is trenchant enough to be persuasive, I continue to doubt. But Loman's yearning for love remains poignant, if only because it destroys him. Miller's true gift is for rendering anguish, and his protagonist's anguish authentically touches upon the universal sorrow of failed fatherhood.

The Crucible

Forty years ago, in his introduction to his *Collected Plays*, Arthur Miller meditated upon *The Crucible*, staged four years before, in 1953. A year after that first production, Miller was refused a passport, and in 1956–57 he endured the active persecution of the American witch-hunt for suspected Communists. The terror created in some of his former friends and associates by the possibility of being branded as warlocks and witches "underlies every word in *The Crucible*," according to Miller. "Every word" necessarily is hyperbolical, since *The Crucible* attempts to be a personal tragedy as well as a social drama. Miller, Ibsen's disciple, nevertheless suffers an anxiety of influence in *The Crucible* not so much in regard to Ibsen's *An Enemy of the People* but in relation to George Bernard Shaw's *Saint Joan*. The frequent echoes of *Saint Joan* seem involuntary, and are distracting, and perhaps fatal to the aesthetic value of *The Crucible*. For all its moral earnestness, *Saint Joan* is enhanced by the Shawian ironic wit, a literary quality totally absent from Miller, here and elsewhere. Though a very well-made play, *The Crucible* rarely escapes a certain dreariness in performance, and does not gain by rereading.

This is not to deny the humane purpose nor the theatrical effectiveness of *The Crucible*, but only to indicate a general limitation, here and elsewhere, in Miller's dramatic art. Eric Bentley has argued shrewdly that "one never knows what a Miller play is about: politics or sex." Is *The Crucible* a personal tragedy, founded upon Proctor's sexual infidelity, or is it a play of social protest and warning? There is no reason it should not be both, except for Miller's inability to fuse the genres. Here he falls short of his master, Ibsen, who concealed Shakespearean tragic purposes within frameworks of social issues, yet invariably unified the two modes. Still, one can be grateful that Miller has not revised *The Crucible* on the basis of his own afterthoughts, which have emphasized the absolute evil of the Salem powers, Danforth and Hathorne. These worthies already are mere facades, opaque to Miller's understanding and our own. Whatever their religious sensibility may or may not have been, Miller has no imaginative understanding of it, and we therefore confront them only as puppets. Had Miller made them even more malevolent, our bafflement would have been even greater. I am aware that I tend to be an uncompromising aesthete, and I cannot dissent from the proven theatrical effectiveness of *The Crucible*. Its social benignity is also beyond my questioning; American society continues to benefit by this play. We would have to mature beyond our national tendency to moral and religious self-righteousness for *The Crucible* to dwindle into another period-piece, and that maturation is nowhere in sight.

Death of a Salesman

Rather like Eugene O'Neill before him, Arthur Miller raises, at least for me, the difficult critical question as to whether there is not an element in drama that is other than literary, even contrary in value (supposed or real) to literary values, perhaps even to aesthetic values. O'Neill, a very nearly great dramatist, particularly in *The Iceman Cometh* and *Long Day's Journey into Night*, is not a good writer, except perhaps in his stage directions. Miller is by no means a bad writer, but he is scarcely an eloquent master of the language. I have just reread *All My Sons, Death of a Salesman*, and *The Crucible*, and am compelled to reflect how poorly they reread, though all of them, properly staged, are very effective dramas, and *Death of a Salesman* is considerably more than that. It ranks with *Iceman, Long Day's Journey*, Williams's *A Streetcar Named Desire*, Wilder's *The Skin of Our Teeth*, and Albee's *The Zoo Story* as one of the half-dozen crucial American plays. Yet its literary status seems to me somewhat questionable, which returns me to the issue of what there is in drama that can survive indifferent or even poor writing.

Defending *Death of a Salesman*, despite what he admits is a sentimental glibness in its prose, Kenneth Tynan memorably observed: "But the theater is an impure craft, and *Death of a Salesman* organizes its impurities with an emotional effect unrivalled in postwar drama." The observation still seems true, a quarter-century after Tynan made it, yet how unlikely a similar statement would seem if ventured about Ibsen, Miller's prime pre-cursor. Do we speak of *Hedda Gabler* organizing its impurities with an unri-valled emotional effect? Why is the American drama, except for Thornton Wilder (its one great sport), addicted to an organization of impurities, a critical phrase perhaps applicable only to Theodore Dreiser, among the major American novelists? Why is it that we have brought forth *The Scarlet Letter*, *Moby-Dick*, *Adventures of Huckleberry Finn*, *The Portrait of a Lady*, *The Sun Also Rises*, *The Great Gatsby*, *As I Lay Dying*, *Miss Lonelyhearts*, *The Crying of Lot 49*, but no comparable dramas? A nation whose poets include Whitman, Dickinson, Frost, Stevens, Eliot, Hart Crane, Elizabeth Bishop, James Merrill and John Ashbery, among so many others of the highest aes-thetic dignity—how can it offer us only O'Neill, Miller, and Williams as its strongest playwrights?

Drama at its most eminent tends not to appear either too early or too late in any national literature. The United States may be the great excep-tion, since before O'Neill we had little better than Clyde Fitch, and our major dramas (it is to be hoped) have not yet manifested themselves. I have seen little speculation upon this matter, with the grand exception of Alvin B. Kernan, the magisterial scholarly critic of Shakespeare and of Elizabethan dramatic literature. Meditating upon American plays, in 1967, Kernan tuned his initially somber notes to hopeful ones:

> Thus with all our efforts, money, and good intentions, we have not yet achieved a theater; and we have not, I believe, because we do not see life in historic and dramatic terms. Even our greatest novelists and poets, sensitive and subtle though they are, do not think dramatically, and should not be asked to, for they express themselves and us in other forms more suited to their visions (and ours). But we have come very close at moments to having great plays, if not a great theatrical tradition. When the Tyrone family stands in its parlor looking at the mad mother holding her wed-ding dress and knowing that all the good will in the world cannot undo what the past has done to them; when Willy Loman, the salesman, plunges again and again into the past to search for the point where it all went irremediably wrong and cannot find any one fatal turning point; when the Antrobus family, to end on a more cheerful note, drafts stage hands from backstage to take the place of sick actors, gathers its feeble and ever-disappointed hopes, puts its miserable home together again after another in a series of unending disasters stretching from the ice age to the present; then we are very close to accepting our entanglement in

the historical process and our status as actors, which may in time produce a true theater.

That time has not yet come, twenty years later, but I think that Kernan was more right even than he knew. Our greatest novelists and poets continue not to see life in historic and dramatic terms, precisely because our literary tradition remains incurably Emersonian, and Emerson shrewdly dismissed both history and drama as European rather than American. An overtly anti-Emersonian poet-novelist like Robert Penn Warren does see life in historic and dramatic terms, and yet has done his best work away from the stage, despite his effort to write *All the King's Men* as a play. Our foremost novelist, Henry James, failed as a dramatist, precisely because he was more Emersonian than he knew, and turned too far inward in nuanced vision for a play to be his proper mode of representation. One hardly sees Faulkner or Frost, Hemingway or Stevens as dramatists, though they all made their attempts. Nor would a comparison of *The Waste Land* and *The Family Reunion* be kind to Eliot's dramatic ambitions. The American literary mode, whether narrative or lyric, tends towards romance and rumination, or fantastic vision, rather than drama. Emerson, genius of the shores of America, directed us away from history, and distrusted drama as a revel. Nothing is got for nothing; Faulkner and Wallace Stevens, aesthetic light-years beyond O'Neill and Tennessee Williams, seem to mark the limits of the literary imagination in our American century It is unfair to *All My Sons* and *Death of a Salesman* to read them with the high expectations we rightly bring to *As I Lay Dying* and *Notes toward a Supreme Fiction*. Miller, a social dramatist, keenly aware of history, fills an authentic American need, certainly for his own time.

II

The strength of *Death of a Salesman* may be puzzling, and yet is beyond dispute; the continued vitality of the play cannot be questioned. Whether it has the aesthetic dignity of tragedy is not clear, but no other American play is worthier of the term, so far. I myself resist the drama each time I reread it, because it seems that its language will not hold me, and then I see it played on stage, most recently by Dustin Hoffman, and I yield to it. Miller has caught an American kind of suffering that is also a universal mode of pain, quite possibly because his hidden paradigm for his American tragedy is an ancient Jewish one. Willy Loman is hardly a biblical figure, and he is not supposed to be Jewish, yet something crucial in him is Jewish, and the play does belong to that undefined entity we can call Jewish literature, just as Pinter's *The Caretaker* rather surprisingly does. The only meaning of Willy Loman is the pain he suffers, and the pain his fate causes us to suffer. His tragedy makes sense only in the Freudian world of repression, which happens also to be the world of normative Jewish memory. It is a world in which everything has already happened, in which there never can be anything new again, because there is total sense or meaningfulness in everything, which is to say, in which everything hurts.

That cosmos informed by Jewish memory is the secret strength or permanent coherence of *Death of a Salesman*, and accounts for its ability to withstand the shrewd critique of Eric Bentley, who found that the genres of tragedy and of social drama destroyed one another here. Miller's passionate insistence upon tragedy is partly justified by Willy's perpetual sense of being in exile. Commenting on his play, Miller wrote that: "The truly valueless man, a man without ideals, is always perfectly at home anywhere." But Willy, in his own small but valid way, has his own version of the Nietzschean "desire to be elsewhere, the desire to be different," and it does reduce to a Jewish version. Doubtless, as Mary McCarthy first noted, Willy "could not be Jewish because he had to be American." Nearly forty years later, that distinction is pragmatically blurred, and we can wonder if the play might be stronger if Willy were more overtly Jewish.

We first hear Willy say: "It's all right. I came back." His last utterance is the mere repetition of the desperately hushing syllable: "Shhh!" just before he rushes out to destroy himself. A survivor who no longer desires to survive is something other than a tragic figure. Willy, hardly a figure of capable imagination, nevertheless is a representation of terrible pathos. Can we define precisely what that pathos is?

Probably the most famous speech in *Death of a Salesman* is Linda's preelegy for her husband, of whom she is soon to remark: "A small man can be just as exhausted as a great man." The plangency of Linda's lament has a universal poignance, even if we wince at its naked design upon us:

> Willy Loman never made a lot of money. His name was never in the paper. He's not the finest character that ever lived. But he's a human being, and a terrible thing is happening to him. So attention must be paid. He's not to be allowed to fall into his grave like an old dog. Attention, attention must be finally paid to such a person.

Behind this is Miller's belated insistence "that everyone knew Willy Loman," which is a flawed emphasis on Miller's part, since he first thought of calling the play *The Inside of His Head*, and Willy already lives in a phantasmagoria when the drama opens. You cannot know a man half lost in the American dream, a man who is unable to tell past from present. Perhaps the play should have been called *The Dying of a Salesman*, because Willy is dying throughout. That is the pathos of Linda's passionate injunction that attention must be finally paid to such a person, a human being to whom a terrible thing is happening. Nothing finds Willy anymore; everything loses him. He is a man upon whom the sun has gone down, to appropriate a great phrase from Ezra Pound.But have we defined as yet what is particular about his pathos?

I think not. Miller, a passionate moralist, all but rabbinical in his ethical vision, insists upon giving us Willy's, and his sons', sexual infidelities as synecdoches of the failure of Willy's vision of reality. Presumably, Willy's sense of failure, his belief that he has no right to his wife, despite Linda's love for him, is what motivates Willy's deceptions, and those of his sons after him. Yet Willy is not destroyed by his sense of failure. Miller may be a better interpreter of Miller than he is a dramatist. I find it wholly persuasive that Willy is destroyed by love, by his sudden awareness that his son Biff truly loves him. Miller beautifully comments that Willy resolves to die when "he is given his existence ... his fatherhood, for which he has always striven and which until now he could not achieve." That evidently is the precise and terrible pathos of Willy's character and of his fate. He is a good man, who wants only to earn and to deserve the love of his wife and of his sons. He is self-slain, not by the salesman's dream of America, but by the universal desire to be loved by one's own, and to be loved beyond what one believes one deserves. Miller is not one of the masters of metaphor, but in *Death of a Salesman* he memorably achieves a pathos that none of us would be wise to dismiss.

All My Sons

All My Sons (1947), Miller's first success, retains the flavor of post–World War II America, though it is indubitably something beyond a period piece. Perhaps all of Miller's work could be titled *The Guilt of the Fathers*, which is a dark matter for a Jewish playwright, brought up to believe in the normative tradition, with its emphasis upon the virtues of the fathers. Though it is a truism to note that *All My Sons* is an Ibsenite play, the influence relation to Ibsen remains authentic, and is part of the play's meaning, in the sense that Ibsen too is one of the fathers, and shares in their guilt. Ibsen's peculiar guilt in *All My Sons* is to have appropriated most of Miller's available stock of dramatic language. The result is that this drama is admirably constructed yet not adequately expressed. It is not just that eloquence is lacking; sometimes the characters seem unable to say what they need to say if we are to be with them as we should.

Joe Keller ought to be the hero-villain of *All My Sons*, since pragmatically he certainly is a villain. But Miller is enormously fond of Joe, and so are we; he is not a good man, and yet he lives like one, in regard to family, friends, neighbors. I do not think that Miller ever is interested in Hannah Arendt's curious notion of the banality of evil. Joe is banal, and he is not evil though his business has led him into what must be called moral idiocy, in regard to his partner and to any world that transcends his own immediate family. Poor Joe is just not very intelligent, and it is Miller's curious gift that he can render such a man dramatically interesting. An ordinary man who wants to have a moderately good time, who wants his family never to suffer, and who lacks any imagination beyond the immediate: what is this except an authentic American Everyman? The wretched Joe simply is someone who does not know enough, indeed who scarcely knows anything at all. Nor can he learn anything. What I find]east convincing in the play is Joe's moment of breaking through to a moral awareness, and a new kind of knowledge:

> MOTHER: Why are you going? You'll sleep, why are you going?
> KELLER: I can't sleep here. I'll feel better if I go.
> MOTHER: You're so foolish. Larry was your son too, wasn't he? You know he'd never tell you to do this.
> KELLER (*looking at letter in his hand*): Then what is this if it isn't telling me? Sure, he was my son. But I think to him they were all my sons. And I guess they were, I guess they were. I'll be right down.
> (Exits into *house*.)
> MOTHER (*to Chris, with determination*): You're not going to take him!
> CHRIS: I'm taking him.
> MOTHER: It's up to you, if you tell him to stay he'll stay. Go and tell him!
> CHRIS: Nobody could stop him now.
> MOTHER: You'll stop him! How long will he live in prison? Are you trying to kill him?

Nothing in Joe is spiritually capable of seeing and saying: "They were all my sons. And I guess they were, I guess they were." That does not reverberate any more persuasively than Chris crying out: "There's a universe of people outside and you're responsible to it." Drama fails Miller there, or perhaps he fails drama. Joe Keller was too remote from a felt sense of reality for Miller to represent the estrangement properly, except in regard to the blindness Joe manifested towards his two sons. Miller crossed over into his one permanent achievement when he swerved from Ibsen into the marginal world of *Death of a Salesman*, where the pain is the meaning, and the meaning has a repressed but vital relationship to the normative vision that informs Jewish memory.

Neil Simon

(1927–)

AT HIS BEST, NEIL SIMON MOVES TOWARDS A CHEKHOVIAN CONTROLLED pathos, but only rarely does he approach close to it. His comedy essentially is situational, though the overtones of Jewish traditional folk humor sometimes allow him to suggest a darker strain. He is a popular playmaker of enormous skill, and certainly persuades more easily on the stage and the screen than he does in print. If all aesthetic criteria were indeed societal, as our debased academies now tell us, then Simon would be more than an eminent hand. His plays are honorable period pieces, and will have the fate of Pinero and Odets, dramatists of their moment. And yet, there is a normative quality in his work that is heartening, and that always promises a touch more than he needs to give.

Writing what is essentially Jewish comedy after the Holocaust is not exactly an unmixed enterprise, and there is a deft quickness in Simon's rhetoric that is admirably sustained, doubtless reflecting his training as a television gag-writer. Though *Lost in Yonkers* is his sharpest and most mature play, it is marred by a forced, relatively happy ending, which has the effect of rendering the entire drama rather questionable.

The Odd Couple has entered popular consciousness, but is perhaps too overtly psychological to endure beyond our era. *Plaza Suite* can cause one to wince, in tribute to its truth-telling, but its fundamental slightness is too apparent. It is *The Sunshine Boys*, for all its sentimentality, that may last longest. Willie Clark and Al Lewis are nowhere as funny as Joe Smith and Charlie Dale, probably the greatest Jewish vaudevillians, but their ambivalent relationship is rendered as precisely representative of the complex feelings evoked by Yiddish popular culture as it transformed into the entertainment industry of American Jewry.

Neil Simon is the most popular contemporary American playwright, with a larger audience than Arthur Miller, Edward Albee, August Wilson, Tony Kushner and other real talents. It would be difficult to compare him favorably to any of them, because his range is narrow, and his mode is so deliberately restrictive. He fades away absolutely if we invoke *Death of A Salesman*, *The Zoo Story*, *Joe Turner's Come and Gone*, or *Angels in America*. And yet he is a grand entertainer, and at least in *The Sunshine Boys*, something more than that. Yiddish theater, on which I was raised, goes on more absolutely in Kushner and in David Mamet, but it finds a nostalgic echo, ebbing but sometimes poignant, in Neil Simon's comedies.

Edward Albee

(1928-)

EDWARD ALBEE IS THE CRUCIAL AMERICAN DRAMATIST OF HIS GENERATION, standing as the decisive link between our principal older dramatists— Eugene O'Neill, Thornton Wilder, Tennessee Williams, Arthur Miller— and the best of the younger ones—Sam Shepard and David Mamet, among others. Though Albee's best work came at his beginnings, with *The Zoo Story*, *The American Dream*, and *Who's Afraid of Virginia Woolf?*, he is hard-ly, at fifty-eight, to be counted out. A way into his aesthetic dilemmas is provided by the one-scene play *Fam and Yam: An Imaginary Interview*, writ-ten and staged in 1960, the year of *The American Dream*. Fam, a Famous American Playwright, is called upon by Yam, a Young American Playwright, in what is clearly an encounter between a precursor, say Tennessee Williams, and a rising latecomer, say Edward Albee. Yam is the author of an off-Broadway play, *Dilemma, Dereliction and Death*, which sounds rather like a three-word summary of *The Zoo Story*. The outer, sin-gle joke of *Fam and Yam* is that the Famous American Playwright is tricked into an interview by the Young American Playwright, but the meaning of the skit, uneasily riding its surface, is a dramatic version of the anxiety of influence (to coin a phrase).

Haunted by Williams, Albee was compelled to swerve from the master into a lyrical drama even more vehemently phantasmagoric than *The Glass Menagerie* and even more incongruously fusing realism and visionary illu-sion than *A Streetcar Named Desire*. The force of Albee's initial swerve was undeniable; *The Zoo Story*, his first play (1958), still seems to me his best, and his most ambitious and famous drama remains *Who's Afraid of Virginia Woolf?* (1961–62). After *Tiny Alice* (1964), Albee's inspiration was pretty well spent, and more than twenty years later, he still matters for his intense flowering between the ages of thirty and thirty-six. The shadow of

Williams, once held off by topological cunning and by rhetorical gusto, lengthened throughout all of Albee's plays of the 1970s. Hart Crane, Williams's prime precursor, can give the motto for Albee's relationship to Williams:

> Have you not heard, have you not seen that corps
> Of shadows in the tower, whose shoulders sway
> Antiphonal carillons launched before
> The stars are caught and hived in the sun's ray?

The Zoo Story

Any grouping of the strongest American dramas would have to include *The Iceman Cometh* and *Long Day's Journey into Night*, *Death of a Salesman* and *The Skin of Our Teeth*, *A Streetcar Named Desire* and *The Zoo Story*. A play in one scene, *The Zoo Story* remains a marvel of economy. The highest tribute one can make to it is to say that it is worthy of its stage history. I saw it during its first American production, in early 1960, when it shared a double bill, off Broadway, with Beckett's extraordinary *Krapp's Last Tape*. The Gnostic sublimity of Beckett's most powerful stage work (except for *Endgame*) ought to have destroyed any companion of the evening, but Albee's mordant lyrical encounter not only survived but took on an added lustre through the association.

I am not certain that *The Zoo Story* has any peers among the shorter works of O'Neill, Wilder, and Williams. Albee's first play, after more than a quarter-century, remains a shot out of Hell, worthy of such authentic American visions of the abyss as West's *Miss Lonelyhearts* and Pynchon's *The Crying of Lot 49*. Both Peter and Jerry are triumphs of representation; rereading the play is to renew one's surprise as to how vivid they both remain, particularly Peter, so apparently pale and stale compared to the demonic and indeed psychotic Jerry. Yet Peter retains an intense aesthetic dignity, without which the play could neither be staged—nor read. Essentially Peter represents us, the audience, rather in the way that Horatio represents us. Jerry is a New York City Hamlet—mad in all directions, even when the wind blows from the south, and manifestly he is a kind of Christ also. Peter is therefore Peter the denier as well as Horatio, the institutional rock upon which the church of the commonplace must be built.

The psychosexual relationship between Jerry and Peter necessarily is the center of *The Zoo Story*, since the zoo story is, as Jerry desperately observes, that indeed we all are animals, dying animals, in Yeats's phrase:

JERRY: Now I'll let you in on what happened at the zoo; but first, I should tell you why I went to the zoo. I went to the zoo to find out more about the way people exist with animals, and the way animals exist with each other, and with people too. It probably wasn't a fair test, what with everyone separated by bars from everyone else, the animals for the most part from each other, and always the people from the animals. But, if it's a zoo, that's the way it is. (*He pokes* PETER *on the arm*) Move over.

PETER (*Friendly*): I'm sorry, haven't you enough room? (*He shifts a little*)

JERRY (*Smiling slightly*): Well, all the animals are there, and all the people are there, and it's Sunday and all the children are there. (*He pokes* PETER *again*) Move over.

PETER (*Patiently, still friendly*): All right.

(*He moves some more, and* JERRY *has all the room he might need*)

JERRY: And it's a hot day, so all the stench is there, too, and all the balloon sellers, and all the ice cream sellers, and all the seals are barking, and all the birds are screaming. (*Pokes* PETER *harder*) Move over!

PETER (*Beginning to be annoyed*): Look here, you have more than enough room! (*But he moves more, and is now fairly cramped at one end of the bench*)

JERRY: And I am there, and it's feeding time at the lions' house, and the lion keeper comes into the lion cage, one of the lion cages, to feed one of the lions. (*Punches* PETER *on the arm, hard*) MOVE OVER!

PETER (*Very annoyed*): I can't move over any more, and stop hitting me. What's the matter with you?

Jerry begins with a cruel parody of Walt Whitman's *Song of Myself*, section 32, where the American bard idealizes the supposed difference between animals and ourselves:

I think I could turn and live with animals,
     they are so placid and self-contain'd,
I stand and look at them long and long.

They do not sweat and whine about their condition,
They do not lie awake in the dark and weep for their sins.
They do not make me sick discussing their duty to God.

The mounting hysteria of Jerry demystifies Whitman, and is answered by a rising terror in Peter. Only the catastrophic impaling of Jerry allows Jerry's zoo story to be finished:

PETER (*Breaks away, enraged*): It's a matter of genetics, not man-hood, you ... you monster.
(*He darts down, picks up the knife and backs off a little; he is breathing heavily*)
I'll give you one last chance; get out of here and leave me alone!
(*He holds the knife with a firm arm, but far in front of him, not to attack, but to defend*)

JERRY (*Sighs heavily*): So be it!
(*With a rush he charges* PETER *and impales himself on the knife. Tableau: For just a moment, complete silence,* JERRY *impaled on the knife at the end of* PETER'S *still firm arm. Then* PETER *screams, pulls away, leaving the knife in* JERRY. JERRY *is motionless, on point. Then he, too, screams, and it must be the sound of an infuriated and fatally wounded animal. With the knife in him, he stumbles back to the bench that* PETER *had vacated. He crumbles there, sitting, facing* PETER, *his eyes wide in agony, his mouth open*)

PETER (*Whispering*): Oh my God, oh my God, oh my God. (*He repeats these words many times, very rapidly*)

JERRY (JERRY *is dying; but now his expression seems to change. His features relax, and while his voice varies, sometimes wrenched with pain, for the most part he seems removed from his dying. He smiles*): Thank you, Peter. I mean that, now; thank you very much.
(PETER'S *mouth drops open. He cannot move; he is transfixed*) Oh, Peter, I was so afraid I'd drive you away. (*He laughs as best he can*) You don't know how afraid I was you'd go away and leave me. And now I'll tell you what happened at the zoo. I think ... I think this is what happened at the zoo ... I think. I think that while I was at the zoo I decided that I would walk north ... northerly, rather ... until I found you ... or somebody ... and I decided that I would talk to you ... I would tell you things ... and things that I would tell you would ... Well, here we are. You see? Here we *are*. But ... I don't know ... could I have planned all this? No ... no, I couldn't have. But I think I did. And now I've told you what you wanted to know, haven't I? And now you know all about what happened at the zoo. And now you know what you'll see in your TV, and the face I told you about ... you remember ... the face I told you about ... my

face, the face you see right now. Peter ... Peter? ... Peter ...
thank you. I came unto you (*He laughs, so faintly*) and you have
comforted me. Dear Peter.

PETER (*Almost fainting*): Oh my God!

JERRY: You'd better go now. Somebody might come by, and you
don't want to be here when anyone comes.

PETER (*Does not move, but begins to weep*): Oh my God, oh my God.

JERRY (*Most faintly, now; he is very near death*): You won't be coming back here any more, Peter; you've been dispossessed.
You've lost your bench, but you've defended your honor. And
Peter, I'll tell you something now; you're not really a veg-
etable; it's all right, you're an animal. You're an animal, too.
But you'd better hurry now, Peter. Hurry, you'd better go ...
see?

(JERRY *takes a handkerchief and with great effort and pain wipes
the knife handle clean of fingerprints*)

Hurry away, Peter.

(PETER *begins to stagger away*)

Wait ... wait, Peter. Take your book ... book. Right here ...
beside me ... on your bench ... my bench, rather. Come ... take
your book.

(PETER *starts for the book, but retreats*)

Hurry ... Peter.

(PETER *rushes to the bench, grabs the book, retreats*)

Very good, Peter ... very good. Now ... hurry away.

(PETER *hesitates for a moment, then flees, stage-left*)

Hurry away.... (*His eyes are closed now*) Hurry away, your para-
keets are making the dinner ... the cats ... are setting the table.

PETER (*Off stage*): (*A pitiful bowl*) OH MY GOD!

JERRY (*His eyes still closed, he shakes his head and speaks; a combination
of scornful mimicry and supplication*): Oh ... my ...God.

(*He is dead*)

   CURTAIN

Screaming with the fury of a fatally wounded animal, Jerry begins his
final moments, attempting to tell Peter and the audience just what happened at the zoo, yet failing to do so, because he himself does not quite
know what happened to him there. Though he speaks the language of
annunciation, reversed ("I came unto you and you have comforted me"),
his only revelation to Peter, and to us, is that: "it's all right, you're an animal. You're an animal, too." The battle for the park bench, a territorial

imperative, has exposed to Peter, our Horatio and surrogate, that we are all animals also. Jerry's mission ends with that message, and so he is happy to die. What is superb and dreadful about Albee's great short drama is that its apocalyptic burden is both Freudian and Christian. Through Peter, we are taught again that we are all bisexual, though many if not most of us repress that psychic component. Yet we are taught also that, without the transcendental and extraordinary, we are animals indeed. The zoo story is that, without grace or a selfless love, we impale or are impaled.

Who's Afraid of Virginia Woolf?

The fame of *Who's Afraid of Virginia Woof?*, primarily because of the popular if flawed Mike Nichols film, with Elizabeth Taylor and Richard Burton, tends to obscure its close resemblance to *The Zoo Story*, since again we have a drama of impaling, of love gone rancid because of a metaphysical lack. That is Albee's characteristic and obsessive concern, marked always by its heritage, which is a similar sense of the irreconcilability of love and the means of love that dominates the plays of Tennessee Williams. Unfortunately, *Who's Afraid of Virginia Woolf?* is a kind of blowup of *The Zoo Story* and aesthetically is inferior to it, whether in the study or on the stage. Martha and George paradoxically are a less memorable couple than Jerry and Peter, perhaps because both of them, like Peter, are surrogates for the audience. Neither of them has Jerry's Hamlet-like quality of being ourselves, yet considerably beyond us. Instead, both Martha and George are Horatios, who survive only to endure the endless repetition of drawing their breaths, in this harsh world, in order to go on telling our story.

The undenied power as representation of Albee's *Virginia Woolf* is that it has become as much our contemporary version of middle-class marriage as O'Neill's *Long Day's Journey into Night* has established itself as our modern version of the American family. Yet that raises the issue of social mythology rather than of the mimesis of human reality. Albee, like O'Neill and like his own precursor, Williams, is open to the accusation that he has become more a caricaturist than a dramatist. George and Martha are cartoon figures; they cannot surprise us any more than they can surprise one another. They are shrewd imitations of a conventional foreshortening of reality, psychic and societal, a foreshortening that, alas, many of us live. But they do not compel aspects of reality, that we could not see without them, to appear, and they are incapable of change. In some sense, they cannot even listen to themselves, let alone one another. If you cannot hear yourself speak, then you cannot change by pondering what you yourself have said, which is one of the great implicit Shakespearean lessons. *The Zoo*

Story had learned that lesson, but *Who's Afraid of Virginia Woolf?* has forgotten it.

One way of observing Albee's decline in power of representation between *The Zoo Story* and *Virginia Woolf* is to contrast our first and last visions of George and Martha, and then juxtapose that contrast to the shocking difference between our first and last visions of Jerry and Peter, the protagonists of *The Zoo Story*. Jerry ends as a pragmatic suicide, and Peter as an involuntary murderer, or manslaughterer, yet their more profound change is from being total strangers to being something like fatal lovers. But, because they are caricatures, can George and Martha change at all?

GEORGE: I'm tired, dear ... it's late ... and besides....

MARTHA: I don't know what you're so tired about ... you haven't *done* anything all day; you didn't have any classes, or anything.

GEORGE: Well, I'm tired.... If your father didn't set up these goddamn Saturday night orgies all the time....

MARTHA: Well, that's too bad about you, George.

GEORGE (*grumbling*): Well, that's how it is, anyway.

MARTHA: You didn't *do* anything; you never *do* anything; you never mix. You just sit around and *talk*.

GEORGE: What do you want me to do? Do you want me to act like you? Do you want me to go around all night *braying* at everybody, the way you do?

MARTHA (*Braying*): I DON'T BRAY!

GEORGE (*Softly*): All right ... you don't bray.

MARTHA (*Hurt*): I do not *bray*.

GEORGE: All right. I said you didn't bray.

MARTHA (*Pause*): I'm cold.

GEORGE: It's late.

MARTHA: Yes

GEORGE (*Long silence*): It will be better.

MARTHA (*Long silence*): I don't ... know.

GEORGE: It will be ... maybe.

MARTHA: I'm ... not ... sure.

GEORGE: No.

MARTHA: Just ... Us?

GEORGE: Yes.

MARTHA: I don't suppose, maybe, we could....

GEORGE: No, Martha.

MARTHA: Yes. No.

GEORGE: Are you all right?

MARTHA: Yes. No.

GEORGE (*Puts his hand gently on her shoulder; she puts her head back and he sings to her, very softly*): Who's afraid of

Virginia Woolf

Virginia Woolf

Virginia Woolf,

MARTHA: I ... am ... George.

GEORGE: Who's afraid of Virginia Woolf.

MARTHA: I ... am ... George.... I ... am.

(GEORGE *nods, slowly*)

(*Silence; tableau*)

     CURTAIN

George talks, ineffectually; Martha brays, ineffectually; that is their initial reality, when we come upon them. Martha barely talks, or is silent; George is almost equally monosyllabic, when we leave them. A silent or monosyllabic ineffectuality has replaced chattering and braying, both ineffectual. Nothing has happened, because nothing has changed, and so this couple will be rubbed down to rubbish in the end. Is that enough to constitute a dramatic image? Albee, who began, in *The Zoo Story*, with the rhetorical strength and exacerbated vision of a strong dramatist, seems to have slain his own powers of representation almost before he himself can have understood them. *Who's Afraid of Virginia Woolf?*, whatever its impact upon contemporary audiences, clearly is of an age, and hardly for all time.

Harold Pinter

(1930-)

Pinter is the legitimate son of Samuel Beckett, and so has a position in contemporary drama that is both assured and, perhaps more ultimately, rather difficult to sustain. *The Birthday Party*, *The Caretaker*, *The Homecoming*, and *Old Times* form an impressive panoply, but diminish, both in the study and in the theater, when brought too close to *Waiting for Godot*, *Endgame*, *Krapp's Last Tape*, plays which are after all quite certainly as enduring as *The Way of the World*, *The Country Wife*, *The School for Scandal*, and *The Importance of Being Earnest*. This is not to suggest that Pinter, at an active fifty-five, has touched his final limits, but only to admit that this most admirable of working British dramatists is shadowed by Beckett, at once his poetic father, and certainly the strongest living writer in any Western language. Aesthetically considered, the shadow of the object that falls upon Pinter's authorial ego is Beckett, who is for Pinter very much the ego ideal. A comparison of Pinter's relation to Beckett with that of Tom Stoppard to Beckett is one way of seeing how much more persuasive a literary dramatist Pinter is than Stoppard. *Rosencrantz and Guildenstern Are Dead* is a weak misreading, though a charming one, of *Waiting for Godot*, but *The Caretaker* is a strong misreading or creative interpretation of *Endgame*.

Pinter writes of the open wound, and through him, we know it open and know it closed. We tell when it ceases to beat, and tell it at its highest peak of fever. I have plagiarized those last two sentences from Pinter, substituting "Pinter" for "Shakespeare." As an insight into Shakespeare, it hardly exists, and would be almost as inadequate if I had substituted "Beckett." But it does very well for Pinter, except that he cannot close any wound whatsoever. His art has some undefined but palpable relation to the Holocaust, inevitable for a sensitive dramatist, a third of whose people were murdered before he was fifteen. A horror of violence, with an obsessive sense of the open wound, is Pinter's unspoken first principle. Whether such an implicit principle of being can sustain the most eminent drama is open to considerable question, because the stance of a conscientious objector is, in itself, by no means dramatic. Barely repressed violence, internal or external, is necessarily the Pinteresque mode, but repression, a powerful aid to the poetic Sublime, is not a defense that enhances drama.

Pinter began as a poet, rather a bad one, Eliotic and uncertain: "... and here am I, / Straddled, exile always in one Whitbread Ale town, / Or such. / Where we went to the yellow pub, cramped in an alley bin, / a shout from the market." That is "Gerontion" ironically transformed into an East End of London Jewish vision, and reminds one of how much more effectively Beckett ironically transforms "Gerontion" in his superb Cartesian poem, *Whoroscope*. Pinter's rhetorical art in his best plays has the same close relation to Beckett's language that the early poems have to Eliot's diction, except that Pinter does far better in the plays at assimilating the precursor's style to an idiom recognizably the latecomer's own.

A clear aid to Pinter in his accommodation of Beckett is the hidden reliance upon a very different tradition than Beckett's Anglo-Irish literary ancestry. Beckett is a kind of Gnostic, religiously speaking, though a Gnostic with a Protestant sensibility. In contrast, Pinter has definite if veiled connections to the West's oldest normative tradition, which is not exactly Gnostic, despite Gershom Scholem's sly efforts to make it so. I am suggesting that, in American Jewish literary terms, Pinter has more authentic affinities with such novelists as Philip Roth and Harold Brodkey than with the greater, menacing and quite Gnostic Nathanael West. The cosmos of Beckett's plays is what the Gnostics called the *kenoma*, the emptiness into which we have been thrown by a catastrophe-creation. Implicit in the world of Pinter's dramas, however remote, however hopelessly inaccessible, are the normative values of the Jewish tradition: rational, humane, trusting in justice and the Covenant, naturalistic without being idolatrous, and at the last hopeful, above all hopeful.

The Caretaker

The Caretaker, Pinter's first success, remains a disturbing play after a quarter-century, but rereading it is a distinctly mixed aesthetic experience. A great set-piece for three virtuoso actors, its rewards for a reader deep in Kafka and Beckett necessarily are equivocal. Davies, who loses his chance to be caretaker, and goes back to his exile in the urban wilderness, is clearly a wanderer in the Kafkan and Beckettian *kenoma*, the cosmic emptiness ruled by the Archons of lies, racial hatreds, false prides, selfishnesses. That is the only universe in which Davies could be naturalized, and yet that is not the world of *The Caretaker*. Pinter's originality in the play consists in taking two nihilists—Davies and the enigmatic Mick—and one normative if damaged consciousness—Aston—and placing them together in a room that suggests a catastrophic world, smashed by a Creation-Fall, but that actually represents things as they are, our given existence, in which there can be hope even for us. In Kafka's vision there is hope, but not for us. Beckett sees no hope, apart from us, but then sees also that we have no hope. Pinter's Aston has hope, invests it in the wretched Davies, type of the natural man, and finds that the hope is betrayed. But even a betrayed hope remains a hope.

Pinter evidently first intended to end *The Caretaker* with the ambivalent brothers, Mick and Aston, combining to murder Davies in what might almost have been a parody of the Primal History Scene in Freud's *Totem and Taboo*. Martin Esslin usefully finds in Davies a kind of father archetype for Aston, and rather more precariously, for Mick as well. Aston's last words in the play, rejecting Davies, have the ironic familial reverberation of the son returning his father's complaints upon him: "You make too much noise." On Aston's part, the rest is silence, while Davies stumbles through a Pinteresque lyric of evanescence:

> ASTON *moves to the window and stands with his back to* DAVIES. You mean you're throwing me out? You can't do that. Listen man, listen man, I don't mind, you see, I don't mind, I'll stay, I don't mind, I'll tell you what, if you don't want to change beds, we'll keep it as it is, I'll stay in the same bed, maybe if I can get a stronger piece of sacking, like, to go over the window, keep out the draught, that'll do it, what do you say, we'll keep it as it is?
>
> *Pause.*
> ASTON: No.
> DAVIES: Why ... not?
>   ASTON *turns to look at him.*
> ASTON: You make too much noise.
> DAVIES: But ... but ... look ... listen ... listen here ... I mean ...
>   ASTON *turns back to the window.* What am I going to do?
>   *Pause.*
>   What shall I do?
>   *Pause.*
>   Where am I going to go?
>   *Pause.*

If you want me to go ... I'll go. You just say the word.
Pause.
I'll tell you what though ... them shoes ... them shoes you give
me ... they're working out all right ... they're all right. Maybe
I could ... get down....
ASTON *remains still, his back to him, at the window.* Listen ... if I
... got down ... if I was to ... get my papers ... would you ...
would you let ... would you ... if I got down ... and got my ...
Long silence.
Curtain.

The poignant, silent, normative level in Pinter's lyricism implies that
Davies is lost because he can only get his references by indeed getting
down and getting some truth, compassionate love, legitimate pride, self-
lessness. That is humanly moving, but not aesthetically cogent, since the
stigmata of Beckett's *Endgame* never abandon Davies. There are no original virtues available for Davies; what makes him a persuasive representation also excludes any possibility of his redemption. Pinter's longing for the
wholesomeness he cannot represent is, in itself, not an aesthetic longing.
Davies, though the most memorable figure in the *The Caretaker*, is also the
flaw in the drama.

Pinter writes tragicomedy, and Davies, properly played, is very funny,
but this is the humor more of Kafka and his circle than it is of the relatively
genial Beckett. Aston is not funny, and Mick's comedy is deliberately
cruel,. as in a first harangue at Davies:

MICK: Jen ... kins.
A drip sounds in the bucket. DAVIES *looks up.*
    You remind me of my uncle's brother. He was always on the
    move, that man. Never without his passport. Had an eye for
    the girls. Very much your build. Bit of an athlete. Longjump
    specialist. He had a habit of demonstrating different run-ups
    in the drawing-room round about Christmas time. Had a
    penchant for nuts. That's what it was. Nothing else but a pen-
    chant. Couldn't eat enough of them. Peanuts, walnuts, brazil
    nuts, monkey nuts, wouldn't touch a piece of fruit cake. Had
    a marvellous stop-watch. Picked it up in Hong Kong. The day
    after they chucked him out of the Salvation Army. Used to go
    in number four for Beckenham Reserves. That was before he
    got his Gold Medal. Had a funny habit of carrying his fiddle
    on his back. Like a papoose. I think there was a bit of the Red

Indian in him. To be honest, I've never made out how he
came to be my uncle's brother. I've often thought that maybe
it was the other way round. I mean that my uncle was his
brother and he was my uncle. But I never called him uncle. As
a matter of fact I called him Sid. My mother called him Sid
too. It was a funny business. Your spitting image he was.
Married a Chinaman and went to Jamaica.

This marvelous fellow—who may have been Mick's and Aston's otherwise forgotten real father—has considerably more gusto than the three
characters in the play, taken together. The nut-eating Sid, long-jump spe-
cialist with a fiddle upon his back, is a kind of Chagallian wandering Jew.
Mick ambiguously finds in Davies the exact image of Sid, towards whom
an authentic ambivalence is expressed in this fine outburst, at once admir-
ing and profoundly resentful. All that we can say with some assurance
about Mick is that he is playing the part of himself, without in any way
being that part, or being himself. We can surmise Mick's dialectical attitudes toward Davies, but they are minor compared to what Pinter will not
let us surmise: What is the quality of Mick's acceptance and rejection of
Aston, his brother?

Aston, rather than Davies or even Mick, seems to me the figure who
is the play's strongest representation, and in some sense can be called
Pinter's own image of voice. Damaged by the hideous shamans of our society, the psychiatrists who are the authentic incompetents and irresponsi-
bles among us, Aston remains for Pinter the barely articulate hope of kindness, of a quest for the only Western image that does not partake either of
origins or ends, the image of the father. That Aston is self-deceived into
finding the image in the unworthy Davies is hardly a fault, when we recall
Mick's association of Davies with the familial Sid. Whatever poetry Pinter
feels privileged to bring onto the stage he invests in Aston. The sadness of
that investment is humanly clear enough, but so is the aesthetic dignity
that Pinter nearly achieves, and in so unlikely a context.

Tom Stoppard

(1937-)

A character in a play, when removed from his setting, ceases to exist; everything he said in his original context, at least when related to that context, would be meaningless in a different context. Hence the part would have to be rewritten afresh. The dramatist would have to write the new words himself. This is not borrowing, but original composition.

—WILLIAM BEARE, The Roman Stage

THE ANCIENT ROMAN STAGE TROPE, *CONTAMINATIO*, WHICH COULD BE called a kind of interlacing between an old play and a new one, has found many distinguished uses in modern drama, particularly by Shaw, Pirandello, and a host of French revisers of the ancients. Tom Stoppard can be called an almost obsessive contaminator, since perhaps no other dramatist relies so crucially upon the trope of interlacing. *Rosencrantz and Guildenstern Are Dead* (1967) was the first of Stoppard's successes, contaminating *Hamlet, Prince of Denmark* with *Waiting for Godot*. The best of Stoppard, *Jumpers* (1972) and *Travesties* (1974), contaminate with more agility, *Jumpers* interlacing Shaw and Robert Dhery (among others), *Travesties* courageously mixing Shakespeare with Wilde's *The Importance of Being Earnest*, with Tristan Tzara, Joyce and Lenin appearing in their proper persons.

Interlacing, depending upon the reader's or playgoer's critical perspective, can be regarded either as a dramatist's defense against precursors (and contemporary rivals) or as the same dramatist's joyous disregard of the literary force of the past. Contamination is another term for influence (which after all began as *influenza*, a supposedly astral disease) except that true literary influence is an involuntary process. A willed influence, or contamination, does seem to me essentially apotropaic, and intends to ward off involuntary influx. Stoppard, a superb theatrical craftsman, sometimes subtly masks his true anxiety of influence (always Samuel Beckett) by seeming to accept the influence, as *Rosencrantz and Guildenstern Are Dead* seems to hold itself open to *Waiting for Godot*. But usually he evades *Endgame* and Beckett's giant shadow by travestying W.S. Gilbert, Shaw, Wilde, contemporary drama, and (endlessly) Shakespeare.

Thomas Whitaker, Stoppard's best critic, has offered the most generous overview of Stoppard's achievement, in a judgment that almost persuades me:

> At mid-career, Tom Stoppard has amply demonstrated what can be done by a self-styled entertainer who has assimilated the recent tradition of British comedy and learned much from the formal discoveries of the avant-garde. Like W.S. Gilbert, he can parody with ease the absurdities of his tune. Like Noel Coward, he keeps his eye on the popular stage as he attends to "those weary, Twentieth Century Blues." Like Bernard Shaw, he knows that the stage at its best does not set before us photographs of "real people" but invites us to participate in stylised explorations of our intellectual and emotional life. And like Oscar Wilde, who was himself far more than an aesthete, Stoppard knows what it means to write "a trivial play for serious people." His wit is often touched by an intellectual chill, a mordant fantasy, or an inarticulate pang that suggests the presence of Samuel Beckett. But his plays also complicate their artifice with various strategies that invite our intimate approach. Eliciting from actors and witnesses a more various participation than either Wilde or Beckett would have endorsed, they begin to turn the theatre itself into the model of a playful community. They ask us to accept as a finality neither Wide's delightfully brittle world of masks nor Beckett's exhilaratingly austere world of fragmentation and deprivation. Alert to the possibility of dwelling in those worlds among others, they invite us to rediscover the humane balance and freedom that constitute the open secret of play.

Myself a disciple of Wilde and Walter Pater, I do not know what it is to be "far more than an aesthete." Pater and Wilde teach us that an aesthete is "one who perceives," and so the aesthetic critic is necessarily the true critic of her or his time, as the aesthetic poet is the authentic poet of that time. Whether Stoppard merits Whitaker's implicit evaluation as the peer of Wilde and Beckett seems to me very problematic, but Whitaker is certainly accurate in portraying Stoppard's ambitions. When Whitaker names the Player in *Rosencrantz and Guildenstern Are Dead*, Sir Archibald Jumper in *Jumpers*, and Tristan Tzara in *Travesties* as Stoppard's "anxious stylists" who "dazzle us with their panache," he avoids the overt statement that they truly are Stoppard's own surrogates. Stoppard himself, in my view, is an anxious stylist who dazzles us with his panache. Such an achievement is already considerable, but whether it is likely to prove permanent is a puzzling matter, which is to say that Harold Pinter, rather than Stoppard, might prove to be Beckett's true son.

II

The study is hardly the proper context even for reading the intensely theatrical Stoppard, since the nature of Stoppard's text always is deliberately somewhat provisional. My own experience is that I benefit more by seeing a new Stoppard play before I read it, though even that procedure did not rescue *The Real Thing* for me, despite the lingering aura of the performances of Glenn Close and Jeremy Irons. In an "author's note" to *Jumpers*, Stoppard asserts that he can give only a "basic version" rather than a "definitive text." Presumably this is related to the antithetical style of discourse that moves him in Beckett. He once spoke of

> ... a Beckett joke which is the funniest joke in the world to me. It appears in various forms but it consists of confident statement followed by immediate refutation by the same voice.... That sort of Beckettian influence is much more important to me than a mere verbal echo of a line of a parallelism at the end of *Jumpers* ...

Surely the most important influence is the very idea of the Stoppardian play, which is a Beckettian idea. If there could be a Gnostic drama (and there cannot), then Beckett would write it, as only Kafka could write a Gnostic story (but there is no Gnostic story). The essential tenet of Gnosticism is that the Creation of the world and of mankind, and the Fall of the world and of mankind, were one and the same event. Stoppard, who writes well only in the shadow of Beckett, gives us Gnostic farce (which also barely can be). Whatever my doubts about Stoppard's ultimate eminence, he compels wonder and respect because he too, like Beckett and Kafka, courageously and obsessively attempts what cannot be done.

There is another Stoppard, celebrated by Whitaker as an affirmer of "freedom and moral sensitivity," and by the more positivistic Richard

Corballis as a celebrator of "the flux of reality" over "an abstract, artificial view of the world." This Stoppard exists, but he is rather mediocre when compared to the parodist, comedian, and disciple who inherits Beckett's sense of what the Gnostics called the *kenoma*, the cosmic emptiness into which we have been thrown. Here is the last of Rosencrantz and Guildenstern, fading out into that emptiness:

> ROS.: That's it, then, is it?
> *No answer. He looks out front.*
>> The sun's going down. Or the earth's coming up, as the fashionable theory has it.
> *Small pause.*
>> Not that it makes any difference.
> *Pause.*
>> What was it all about? When did it begin?
> *Pause. No answer.*
>> Couldn't we just stay put? I mean no one is going to come on and drag us off ... They'll just have to wait. We're still young ... fit ... we've got years ...
> *Pause. No answer*
>> (*A cry.*) We've done nothing wrong! We didn't harm anyone. Did we?
> GUIL.: I can't remember.
> ROS. *pulls himself together.*
> ROS.: All right, then. I don't care. I've had enough. To tell you the truth, I'm relieved.
> *And he disappears from view,* GUIL. *does not notice.*
> GUIL.: Our names shouted in a certain dawn... a message ... a summons ... There must have been a moment, at the beginning, where we could have said—no. But somehow we missed it. (*He looks around and sees he is alone.*)
>> Rosen—?
>> Guil—?
> *He gathers himself.*
>> Well, we'll know better next time. Now you see me, now you— (*and disappears*).

It is admirable, but not contaminated enough, since all too clearly we are in the abyss of Beckett's *Endgame*. And it is not so much Shakespeare's timeserving courtiers who are thrown into that abyss as it is Vladimir and Estragon, so that the true title might as well be *Rosencrantz and*

Guildenstern Are Waiting for Godot. But the true title of *Jumpers* is *Jumpers*, perhaps because the theaters of W.S. Gilbert and of Ionesco so pungently contaminate the theater of Beckett. Absurdist farce proves to be Stoppard's best mode, as in the first encounter of Sir Archibald Jumper and Inspector Bones:

> ARCHIE: Ah! Good morning!
>
> (ARCHIE *moves to come out from the bed. Meanwhile* DOTTY *looks over the top*)
>
> DOTTY: Lunch! And Bonesy!
>
> (ARCHIE *picks his coat up and hands it to* BONES, *and then readies himself to put his arms in the sleeves, as though* BONES *were a manservant.*)
>
> ARCHIE (*slipping on his coat*): Thank you so much. Rather warm in there. The lights, you know.
>
> DOTTY: Isn't he sweet?
>
> ARCHIE: Charming. What happened to Mrs. Whatsername?
>
> DOTTY: No, no, it's Bonesy!
>
> BONES: Inspector Bones, C.I.D.
>
> DOTTY (*disappearing*): Excuse me!
>
> ARCHIE: Bones ...? I had a patient named Bones. I wonder if he was any relation?—an osteopath.
>
> BONES: My brother!
>
> ARCHIE: Remember the case well. Cognomen Syndrome. My advice to him was to take his wife's maiden name of Foot and carry on from there.
>
> BONES: He took your advice but unfortunately he got interested in chiropody. He is now in an asylum near Uxbridge.
>
> ARCHIE: Isn't that interesting? I must write him up. The Cognomen Syndrome is my baby, you know.
>
> BONES: You discovered it?
>
> ARCHIE: I've got it. Jumper's the name—my card.
>
> BONES (*reading off card*): "Sir Archibald Jumper, M.D., D.Phil., D.Litt., L.D., D.P.M., D.P.T. (*Gym*)" ... What's all that?
>
> ARCHIE: I'm a doctor of medicine, philosophy, literature and law, with diplomas in psychological medicine and P.T. including gym.
>
> BONES (*handing back the card*): I see that you are the Vice-Chancellor of Professor Moore's university.
>
> ARCHIE: Not a bad record, is it? And I can still jump over seven feet.

BONES: High jump?

ARCHIE: Long jump. My main interest, however, is the trampoline.

BONES: Mine is show business generally.

ARCHIE: Really? Well, nowadays, of course, I do more theory than practice, but if trampoline acts appeal to you at all, a vacancy has lately occurred in a little team I run, mainly for our own amusement with a few social engagements thrown in—

The Cognomen Syndrome is worthy of Ionesco, and Archie's voiced qualifications are from the world of W.S. Gilbert. Perhaps only the trampoline is Stoppard's own, but in farce at so sublimely exuberant a level all indebtedness can be discounted. Alas, *Jumpers* is unmatched elsewhere in Stoppard. *Travesties* comes closest, particularly in the agon of James Joyce and Tristan Tzara, where most critics have given the victory to Tzara, who speaks with the exuberance of Shaw's surrogates, as he denounces Joyce's aestheticism:

Your art has failed. You've turned literature into a religion and it's as dead as all the rest, it's an overripe corpse and you're cutting fancy figures at the wake. It's too late for geniuses! Now we need vandals and desecrators, simple-minded demolition men to smash centuries of baroque subtlety, to bring down the temple, and thus finally, to reconcile the shame and the necessity of being an artist!

In contrast, Stoppard's Joyce is a failure, and his credo lacks a countervailing eloquence:

An artist is the magician put among men to gratify—capriciously—their urge for immortality. The temples are built and brought down around him, continuously and contiguously from Troy to the fields of Flanders. If there is any meaning in any of it, it is in what survives as art ...

Though we are told that Stoppard regards this as the most important moment in his play, it is clearly a failure in contamination, an interlacing that does not work. *Travesties* is a splendid notion not properly worked through, though its triple agon of Modernism against Dada against Lenin's ardor has given it an inevitable panache. Stoppard remains one of the most audacious legatees of Modernism, and at forty-eight is hardly to be judged as being beyond the centerpoint of his theatrical quest.

The Invention of Love

The Invention of Love seems to me Tom Stoppard's masterpiece to date. He long ago transcended the influence of Samuel Beckett, which still clouds (for me) *Rosencrantz and Guildenstern Are Dead*. His true precursor has become the divine Oscar Wilde, and one feels that if another *Importance of Being Earnest* ever is going to be composed, it will be by Stoppard.

Unless I misread Stoppard (always possible with so great an ironist) the closing contrast between A.E. Housman and Oscar Wilde is not much to Housman's credit. Wilde lived and loved; Housman stayed home and avoided scandal. For Stoppard, these are questions of success or failure. But are they?

What has happened to the Aesthetic in a play about the Aesthetic Movement, whose high priest, the sublime Walter Pater, is badly travestied in Stoppard's play? Would you know from Stoppard that Oscar rarely had an idea that was not vulgarized from Pater?

Housman however is the point, because he was a great poet, as you could not know from reading *The Invention of Love*. Try the effect of reading just four or five lyrics by Housman, in the midst of your reading *The Invention of Love*. They might include some of my favorites: "Into my heart an air that kills," "Eight O'Clock," "The Night is Freezing Fast," and the lovely "Tell me not here, it needs not saying." Or try a more radical experiment. Read against Stoppard's play, as counterpoint, Housman's magnificent and perpetually relevant "Epitaph On an Army of Mercenaries."

> These, in the day when heaven was falling,
> The hour when earth's foundations fled,
> Followed their mercenary calling
> And took their wages and are dead.
>
> Their shoulders held the sky suspended;
> They stood, and earth's foundations stay;
> What God abandoned, these defended,
> And saved the sum of things for pay.

Housman, a great classical scholar, has written an epitaph worthy of Simonides. But my interest is elsewhere. Did Stoppard's Housman write this strong and uncompromising poem? Heaven always is falling, and earth's foundations perpetually flee away. All callings are mercenary, whether Oxford dons or dramatists or what you will. We are all God's mercenaries, Housman suggests, and must defend what He abandoned. *The Invention of Love* is an admirable play, but hardly just to the poet Housman, whose difficult, evasive poetry also saved the sum of things for pay.

Sam Shepard

(1943–)

Fool for Love

INCEST, ACCORDING TO SHELLEY, IS THE MOST POETICAL OF CIRCUMSTANCES. This brief prelude to Sam Shepard centers upon *Fool for Love*, which I like best of his several dozen plays. Walt Whitman, an authentic forerunner of Shepard, denied being influenced by anyone, though without Ralph Waldo Emerson one can doubt Whitman would have happened. Shepard similarly denies all literary and dramatic indebtedness, insisting he emanates from Jackson Pollack and the Who. Plays however are written with words, and Shepard, if your perspective is long enough, is another Expressionist dramatist, a very good one, with a definite relation to "Brecht"! The quotation marks are there because we know that most of "Brecht" was written by two very talented women whom the rascal exploited.

Shepard also shows some touches of Pinter, and even of Pinter's precursor, Beckett. There seems no clear American lineage in dramatic tradition for the very American Shepard. I find a touch of Tennessee Williams in Martin, May's date in *Fool for Love*, and dimly in the background are the Strindbergian asperities of Eugene O'Neill's destructive family romances. Yet no one can dispute that Sam Shepard is an American Original. Emerson, everyone's American grandfather, told us: "The originals are not original." Rock and roll performers, whom Shepard so envies, all have their formative phases, in which their ancestry is quite clear, the Who included. Shepard, who battles so fiercely against categorization, resembles a tradition in American literature that R.W.B. Lewis has called Adamic. Like Walt Whitman, Sam Shepard seeks to be Adam early in the morning, but a Western American Adam.

Fool for Love has four characters, all American archetypes. The incestuous lovers are half-siblings, May and Eddie, who is a dead-end cowboy. May, a drifter, is caught up with Eddie in a hopelessly ambivalent relationship, always about to end but unable to do so. Their common father, the Old Man, is dead, but highly visible, at least to us in the audience. He too is a cowboy, rocking away and consuming whiskey beyond the grave. That leaves only Martin, May's would-be date, who appears to be a surrogate for the audience.

Everything about *Fool for Love* suggests a controlled hallucination. Nothing is certain, least of all incest; since the Old Man insists he sees nothing of himself in either of the lovers. Nor can we believe anything that May and Eddie say about one another. We can be certain that they inspire obsessiveness, each in himself or herself and in the (more-or-less) beloved.

The paradox in Shepard is why any of his people matter, to us or to him. The answer, which confers aesthetic dignity, is altogether Whitmanian. *Song of Myself* anticipates Shepard: his burned-out Americans were Whitman's before they were Shepard's. Walt Whitman, the true American shaman, would have been at home in *Fool for Love*, *Buried Child*, and *True West*.

Shepard's people are lyrical selves, desperately seeking a stable identity. They are not going to find it. Their dramatist remains our major living visionary, stationed at the edge of our common abyss.

August Wilson

(1945-)

I RECALL ATTENDING A PERFORMANCE OF *JOE TURNER'S COME AND GONE* AT Yale in 1986, and came away more moved than I had been by *Ma Rainey's Black Bottom* and *Fences*. *Two Trains Running* I have never seen, and have just read for the first time, after rereading three earlier plays in the University of Pittsburgh Press's very useful *Three Plays* (1991), which has a stern Preface by the dramatist, and a useful Afterword by Paul Cater Harrison. Returning to the text of *Joe Turner's Come and Gone* after a decade is a remarkable experience in reading, since few plays by American dramatists hold up well away from the stage. As a literary work, *Joe Turner's Come and Gone* is authentically impressive, particularly in its spiritual insights. August Wilson's political stance as a black nationalist is present in *Joe Turner's* (to give it a short title), but his art as a dramatist surmounts the tendentiousness that elsewhere distracts me. Whether or not his other celebrated plays may prove to be period pieces (like those of Bullins and Baraka), I am uncertain, but there is a likely permanence in *Joe Turner's*, perhaps because of its profound depiction of the African American roots of what I have learned to call the American Religion, the actual faith of white Protestants in the United States.

The summer of 2001 is hardly a good time anyway to argue nationalist stances among African Americans, now that the full extent of black disenfranchisement in Jeb Bush's Florida is being revealed. It is clear that if there had been an unimpeded African American vote in Florida, the Supreme Court would not have been able to appoint George W. Bush as President. Since August Wilson's project is to compose a play for every decade of the black experience in twentieth century America, one wryly awaits what he might choose to do with the Florida Outrage of November 2000.

Wilson, in his Preface to *Three Plays*, offers a powerful reading of his masterwork:

> There is a moment in *Joe Turner's Come and Gone* at the end of the first act when the residents of the household, in an act of tribal solidarity and recognition of communal history, dance a Juba. Herald Loomis interrupts it to release a terrifying vision of bones walking on the water. From the outset he has been a man who has suffered a spiritual dislocation and is searching for a world that contains his image. The years of bondage to Joe Turner have disrupted his lie and severed his connection with his past. His vision is of bones walking on water that sink and wash up on the shore as fully fleshed humans. It is not the bones walking on the water that is the terrifying part of the vision—it is when they take on flesh and reveal themselves to be like him. "They black. Just like you and me. Ain't no difference." It is the shock of recognition that his birth has origins in the manifest act of the creator, that he is in fact akin to the gods. Somewhere in the Atlantic Ocean lie the bones of millions of Africans who died before reaching the New World. The flesh of their flesh populates the Americas from Mississippi to Montevideo. Loomis is made witness to the resurrection and restoration of these bones. He has only to reconcile this vision with his learned experiences and recognize he is one of the "bones people." At the end of the play he repudiates the idea that salvation comes from outside of himself and claims his moral personality by slashing his chest in a bloodletting rite that severs his bonds and demonstrates his willingness to bleed as an act of redemption.

Spiritually, this is both greatly suggestive and not unconfusing. Why does Loomis slash himself? There is a deep pattern of African gnosticism in the colonial black Baptists, who carried on from their heritage in affirming "the little me within the big me," the spark of the Alien God that was the best and oldest part of them, free of the Creation-Fall. Michal Sobel has shown how this pattern recurs in African American religion, and I suspect it was transmitted by the African Baptists to the original Southern Baptists. If Loomis slashes himself as a parody of and against Christian blood atonement, I could understand it more readily, but Wilson violates African tradition by the chest-slashing that is a bloodletting, bond-severing act of redemption. Perhaps Wilson felt he needed this self-violence as a dramatic gesture, and yet it may detract from the rebirth of Loomis. If this is a flaw, it is a small one in so strong a play.

David Mamet

(1947–)

VERY FEW CONTEMPORARY DRAMAS OF AUTHENTIC EMINENCE DEPRESS ME quite so much as does *Sexual Perversity in Chicago*, whether I see it at a theater, or reread it in my study. Doubtless, Mamet wants that affect in auditor or reader. I have encountered only one photograph of Mamet, the Brigitte Lacombe shot of the playwright as Groucho Marx that adorns the paperback of *SPC* (a short version of the title). One could argue that Groucho is more of an influence upon Mamet than are Beckett, Pinter, and Albee, since *SPC* seems (to me) best acted as parodistic farce. T.S. Eliot, still the major poet who makes me most uneasy, had a great regard both for Groucho and for Marlowe's Jew of Malta, Barabbas. I cannot read *The Jew of Malta* without casting Groucho in the role, and sometimes I wish I could direct *SPC* with Groucho playing Bernie and Chico as Danny.

The epigraph to *SPC* might be Marlowe's Mephistophiles cheerfully answering: "Why this is Hell, nor am I out of it." Though Douglas Bruster usefully compares Mamet to Ben Jonson of the City Comedies, I suspect that Mamet actually resembles Marlowe more than Jonson. The savagery of Mamet's stance towards his protagonists, particularly in *SPC*, is Marlovian, as is Mamet's fierce obsession with hyperbolical rhetoric. Here is Bernie, wildly prevaricating, and approaching the vaunting terms of Sir Epicure Mammon in *The Alchemist*:

> BERNIE: So wait. So I don't know what the shot is. So all of a sudden I hear coming out of the phone: "Rat Tat Tat Tat Tat. Ka POW! AK AK AK AK AK AK AK *Ka Pow!*" So fine. I'm pumping away, the chick on the other end is making airplane noises, every once in a while I go BOOM, and the broad on the bed starts going crazy. She's moaning and groaning and about to

go the whole long route. Humping and bumping, and she's screaming "Red dog One to Red dog Squadron" ... all of a sudden she screams "Wait." She wriggles out, leans under the bed, and she pulls out this five-gallon jerrycan.

DANNY: Right.

BERNIE: Opens it up ... it's full of gasoline. So she splashes the mother all over the walls, whips a fuckin' Zippo out of the Flak suit, and WHOOSH, the whole room is in flames. So the whole fuckin' joint is going up in smoke, the telephone is going "Rat Tat Tat," the broad jumps back on the bed and yells "Now, give it to me *now* for the love of Christ." (*Pause.*) So I look at the broad ... and I figure ... fuck this nonsense. I grab my clothes, I peel a sawbuck off my wad, as I make the door I fling it at her. "For cab fare," I yell. She doesn't hear nothing. One, two, six, I'm in the hall. Struggling into my shorts and hustling for the elevator. Whole fucking hall is full of smoke, above the flames I just make out my broad, she's singing "Off we go into the Wild Blue Yonder," and the elevator arrives, and the whole fucking hall is full of *firemen.* (*Pause.*) Those fucking firemen make out like bandits. (*Pause.*)

Bernie is confidence man rather than gull, so that we dislike him, whereas the outrageous Sir Epicure Mammon is weirdly endearing. And yet Bernie's obsessive rhetoric has an hallucinatory quality that is more than Jonsonian enough. No audience easily tolerates Bernie, whose final tirade manifests what could be called a negative pathos, which involuntarily expresses a desperate sense of damnation:

BERNIE: Makes all the fucking difference in the world. (*Pause.*) Coming out here on the beach. Lying all over the beach, flaunting their bodies ... I mean who the fuck do they think they are all of a sudden, coming out here and just flaunting their bodies all over? (*Pause.*) I mean, what are you supposed to think? I come to the beach with a friend to get some sun and watch the action and ... I mean a fellow comes to the beach to sit out in the fucking sun, am I wrong? ... I mean we're talking about recreational fucking space, huh? ... huh? (*Pause.*) What the fuck am I talking about?

The fear of female sexuality hardly could be more palpable, and a new kind of Inferno beckons in: "What the fuck am I talking about?" Hell, according to Jean-Paul Sartre's *No Exit*, is Other People. Like Rimbaud's Hell, Bernie's Inferno is not less than the existence of women as such.

Tony Kushner

(1956-)

AS AN AMERICAN DRAMATIST, TONY KUSHNER REPRESENTS (AMIDST MUCH else) the confluence of several literary traditions that, to me, seem antithetical to one another: Bertolt Brecht's Marxist stage epics; the lyrical phantasmagorias of Tennessee Williams; Yiddish theater in its long history from the earliest *purimshpil* (Leipzig, 1697) to the exuberant flourishing that was still prevalent in my own youth. A fierce admirer of Kushner's work, I confess an increasing aesthetic aversion to Brecht as I age. Politically I have no differences with Kushner, but for more than a decade now, I have experienced a purely literary anxiety that this dramatist's genius might be so deformed by public concerns that he could dwindle into another Clifford Odets, rather than fulfill his extraordinary gifts by transcending even Tennessee Williams and Thornton Wilder among his American precursors.

Kushner passionately insists that he is a political dramatist, but reading his plays and attending their performance persuade me otherwise. His largest American ancestors are Walt Whitman and Herman Melville, and while *Song of Myself* and *Moby-Dick* are the epics of democracy, their spiritual and metaphysical elements are far more vital than their politics. Brecht's dramas (if they *are* his, rather than Elizabeth Hauptmann's, Margarete Steffin's, and Ruth Berlau's) increasingly threaten to become Period Pieces, just as Clifford Odets's *Waiting for Lefty* is now nothing but a Period Piece. Kushner's *A Bright Room Called Day* (1985) is a Ronald Reagan Period Piece which depresses me, two decades later, because Reagan now appears virtually harmless in comparison to our astonishing current President, who defies any ironic representation whatsoever. Shakespeare himself could not render George W. Bush dramatically plausible. Nathanael West's Shagpoke Whipple, in *A Cool Million*, cannot match

Bush II in blatancy, patriotic religiosity, and bland righteousness. Reality in America has beggared fantasy and one wants to implore Kushner to turn inward, rather than dramatically confront a continuous outrageousness that no stage representation can hope to rival. I need only turn on Fox TV to witness parodistic excess accepted as reality by a majority of my fellow citizens who cared enough to vote. Oscar Wilde, wisely urging art to be perfectly useless, would at this moment be the best of mentors for Tony Kushner.

II

Roy Cohn, to date, is Kushner's best creation, an all but Shakespearean hero-villain. The three versions I have seen of the Kushnerian Cohn were performed by Ron Leibman, F. Murray Abraham, and Al Pacino. All were effective, but Leibman was the best, because he played it with a Yiddish aura of outrageousness and of having been outraged. The only time I recall being moved by Arthur Miller's *Death of a Salesman* was when I saw it in Yiddish translation in 1952, with Joseph Buloff as Loman. I wish that Joseph Wiseman had been young enough to play Roy Cohn. Wiseman was a magnificent Edmund in a terrible *King Lear* I recall seeing in 1950, and later he performed an unforgettable mad Duke in John Webster's *The Duchess of Malfi*. Watching and listening to Leibman flooded me with memories of Wiseman, presumably because both actors played with excess and *sprezzatura*, in a mode I had worshipped in Maurice Schwartz, who perhaps had learned it from Jacob Adler. Kushner, whose superb *A Dybbuk* is undervalued, is a natural throwback to the hyperbolical Yiddish theater where I first saw Shylock, played by Schwartz as hero, not as hero-villain or the farcical bogyman that Shakespeare designed to go Marlowe's Barabas, Jew of Malta, one better.

Kushner is a whirligig of change, unpredictable and unprecedented, except for Tennessee Williams at his strongest. The one time I met Williams (was it in the late Seventies?) he proudly handed me his treasured copy of *The Collected Poems of Hart Crane*, so that I could see he had liberated it from the Washington University of St. Louis Library. We talked about Crane, our mutually favorite poet. I have met Kushner at length primarily in front of a large audience, and so have not been able to ascertain his favorite poet, but surely it must be Walt Whitman, still (in my judgment) the greatest writer brought forth by our Evening Land, the Americas. I delight that *Perestroika* boldly plagiarizes Whitman, just as it is audacious enough to send up Blance DuBois's: "I have always depended upon the kindness of strangers." But that is High Camp, whereas the employment of the sublime Walt seems to me crucial; since he *is* the Angel Principality of America, despite her inconvenient gender, and her negativity:

> Hiding from Me one place you will find me in another.
> I I I I stop down the road, waiting for you.

That is an Angelic variation upon the very close of *Song of Myself*, substituting "hiding" for "seeking." Just before, this negative version of Whitman has proclaimed: "Forsake the Open Road." What Hart Crane was to Tennessee Williams, a fusion of Whitman and Melville is for Kushner, except that the overwhelmingly personal investment of Williams in Crane is not present in Kushner's veneration of his American fathers, Melville and Whitman. Williams's other prime precursor was D.H. Lawrence, like Melville an evader of homoeroticism.

III

Angels in America, indisputably Kushner's masterwork to date, is accurately described by him as "fantasia." A careful rereading of it demonstrates that Kushner's mastery of controlled phantasmagoria is his highest dramatic gift. Except for Roy Cohn, the double-play has no characters wholly memorable as personalities, fully endowed with individuated voices. The black, gay male nurse Belize has been much praised, but I fear that is mere political correctness. Louie Ironson seems a self-parody on Kushner's part, and the prophet Prior Walter is poignant but scarcely persuasive. The Mormon closet gay and right-wing lawyer, Joe Pitt, is a caricature. Except for Cohn, Kushner's women are stronger, Harper in particular, but then she is at home in fantasy. What carries *Angels in America*, the daemonic Cohn aside, is its extraordinary inventiveness in regard to what might as well be termed the spirit world.

Having been defeated by a stubborn Kushner in a public debate on theatre and religion (March 22, 2004), in New York City, I am only too aware he will continue to insist he is a political dramatist, rather than a theological one, long after I have departed for whatever spirit-world there may be. Not being exactly a devoted Brechtian, I am unable to see how "a relationship of complaint and struggle and pursuit between the human and divine"—Kushner's eloquent characterization of his own Judaism—involves politics. When Kushner declares that "drama without politics is inconceivable," I wonder just how he reads Shakespeare. Those who endeavor to interpret *Hamlet* or *King Lear* or *Macbeth* as political theater lose my interest rather quickly. Is Reagan or Bush II really Kushner's motive for metaphor? No. Kushner has more in common with Kafka than with Brecht, though he does not want to see this. Like his angels, Kushner has filed a suit against God for desertion. God shrewdly has taken on Roy Cohn as his defense attorney and so the angels (and Kushner) are going to lose their case.

IV

I have read *Caroline, or Change* in manuscript, but have not seen it performed, and doubtless by now Kushner has revised it anyway. I do not know how much intrinsic relevance it will retain a decade hence, an apprehension I experience also in regard to *Homebody/Kabul*. Kushner hardly is going to agree with me on this, but I think *A Dybbuk* will outlast them both. Social ironies, like political concerns, drive Kushner into the composition of Period Pieces. The dramatic impulse towards phantasmagoria always will be his aesthetic redemption.

Roy Cohn is a hero-villain and a strong individuality. To Kushner, that individuality is one with Cohn's evil. Yet that seems to me Kushner's incessant error. To invoke what ultimately is an Hegelian distinction, singularity *cares* about itself *and others*, while individuality is indifferent, whether to the self or to otherness. Rosalind, in *As You Like It*, is a singularity, as is Falstaff in his plays. Hamlet is an individuality, who loves neither himself nor others, but I can locate nothing political in Hamlet, or in Iago.

Kushner's Roy Cohn is a fascinating blend of singularity and individuality, neither of them a source of his murderous malice. Coleridge mistakenly spoke of Iago's "motiveless malignancy", but Iago, like his disciple, Satan in Milton's *Paradise Lost*, suffers from a Sense of Injured Merit. So, as I read him, does Tony Kushner's Roy Cohn. He wants to have been a major demon like Joe McCarthy, but God has passed him over for promotion. Iago, passed over for Cassio, determines to bring his war-god Othello down to the abyss, to uncreate Othello. Cohn, outraged and outrageous, finds his proper employment only in the afterlife, in the superb (and invariably unperformed) Scene 7 of Act V of *Perestroika*:

> *As Prior journeys to earth he sees Roy, at a great distance, in Heaven, or*
> *Hell or Purgatory—standing waist-deep in a smoldering pit, facing*
> *a volcanic, pulsating red light. Underneath, a basso-profundo roar,*
> *like a thousand Bessemer furnaces going at once, deep underground.*
> ROY: Paternity suit? Abandonment? Family court is my particular
> metier, I'm an absolute fucking demon with Family Law. Just

tell me who the judge is, and what kind of jewelry does he like? If it's a jury, it's harder, juries take more talk but sometimes it's worth it, going jury, for what it saves you in bribes. Yes I will represent you, King of the Universe, yes I will sing and eviscerate, I will bully and seduce, I will win for you and make the plaintiffs, those traitors, wish they had never heard the name of ...

(*Huge thunderclap.*)

ROY: Is it a done deal, are we on? Good, then I gotta start by telling you you ain't got a case here, you're guilty as hell, no question, you have nothing to plead but not to worry, darling, I will make something up.

Is it possible to read this without delighting in Roy Cohn? He *will* win God's case, thus vindicating his entire career, and severely putting into question all Kushnerian dramatic politics. The Messenger, who is the Angel of *A Dybbuk*, at the play's close receives Rabbi Azriel's eloquent charge:

(*Softly*) It doesn't matter. Tell Him that. The more cause He gives to doubt Him. Tell Him that. The deeper delves faith. Though His love becomes only abrasion, derision, excoriation, tell Him, I cling. We cling. He made us, He can never shake us off. We will always find Him out. Promise Him that. We will always find Him, no matter how few there are, tell Him we will find Him. To deliver our complaint.

Kushner, like Azriel, always will deliver his complaint. Pathos, eloquence, fantasia: these never will forsake him. If, as I firmly believe, he yet will surpass Tennessee Williams, it will not be because of his Brechtian faith in the political possibilities of theater.

Further Reading

Barranger, Milly S. *Understanding Plays*, 3rd ed. Boston: Allyn & Bacon, 2003.

Beacham, Richard C. *The Roman Theatre and Its Audience*. Cambridge, M.A.: Harvard University Press, 1996.

Beadle, Richard, ed. *The Cambridge Companion to Medieval English Theatre*. Cambridge: Cambridge University Press, 1994.

Bentley, Eric. *The Life of the Drama*. New York: Applause Books, 2000.

———. *Thinking About the Playwright: Comments from Four Decades*. Evanston: Northwestern University Press, 1987.

Bigsby, C.W.E. *A Critical Introduction to Twentieth-Century American Drama: Volume 1, 1900–1940*. Cambridge: Cambridge University Press, 1982.

———. *A Critical Introduction to Twentieth-Century American Drama: Volume 3, Beyond Broadway*. Cambridge: Cambridge University Press, 1985.

Bloom, Harold. *The Western Canon: The Books and School of the Ages*. New York: Harcourt Brace & Company, 1994.

Bordman, Gerald and Thomas S. Hischak. *The Oxford Companion to American Theatre*, 3rd ed. New York: Oxford University Press, 2004.

Bradby, David. *Modern French Drama 1940–1980*. Cambridge: Cambridge University Press, 1984.

Brecht, Bertolt. *Brecht on Theatre: The Development of an Aesthetic*. John Willett, trans. New York: Hill and Wang, 1964.

Brockett, Oscar G. and Franklin J. Hildy. *History of the Theatre*, 9th ed. Boston: Allyn & Bacon, 2002.

Brown, John Russell, ed. *The Oxford Illustrated History of Theatre (Oxford Illustrated Histories)*. New York: Oxford University Press, 2001.

Carlson, Marvin. *Theories of the Theatre: A Historical and Critical Survey, from the Greeks to the Present*. Ithaca.: Cornell University Press, 1993.

Fischer-Lichte, Erika and Jo Riley, trans. *History of European Drama and Theatre*. London: Routledge, 2002.

Fortier, Mark. *Theatre/Theory: An Introduction*. London: Routledge, 2002.

Freedley, George and John a. Reeves. *A History of the Theatre*. New York: Crown Publishers, 1968.

Gassner, John. *Masters of the Drama*. New York: Dover Publications, 1954.

Hemmings, Frederic William John. *The Theatre Industry in Nineteenth-Century France*. Cambridge: Cambridge University Press, 1993.

Kewes, Paulina. *Authorship and Appropriation: Writing for the Stage in England, 1660–1710 (Oxford English Monographs)*. New York: Oxford University Press, 1998.

Kolin, Philip C. and Colby H. Kullman, ed. *Speaking on Stage: Interviews with Contemporary American Playwrights*. Tuscaloosa: University of Alabama Press, 1996.

Lev, Graham. *A Short Introduction to the Ancient Greek Theater*. Chicago.: University of Chicago Press, 1991.

Londre, Felicia Hardison. *The History of World Theater: From the English Restoration to the Present*. New York: Continuum International Publishing Group, 1991.

Longman, Stanley Vincent. *Page and Stage*. Boston: Allyn & Bacon, 2003.

Nagler, A.M. *A Source Book in Theatrical History*. Mineola: Dover Publications, 1959.

Nicoll, Allardyce. *World Drama from Aeschylus to Anouilh*. London: Harrap, 1976.

Styan, J.L. *Modern Drama in Theory and Practice*. New York: Cambridge University Press, 1981.

Trussler, Simon. *The Cambridge Illustrated History of British Theatre*. Cambridge: Cambridge University Press, 1994.

Watt, Stephen Myers. *Postmodern/Drama: Reading the Contemporary Stage (Theater: Theory/Text/Performance)*. Ann Arbor: University of Michigan Press, 1998.

Weber, Samuel. *Theatricality as Medium*. New York: Fordham University Press, 2005.

Wickham, Glynne. *A History of Theater*. New York: Phaidon Press, 1994.

Index

About the Author

HAROLD BLOOM is Sterling Professor of the Humanities at Yale University. He is the author of over 20 books, including *Shelley's Mythmaking* (1959), *The Visionary Company* (1961), *Blake's Apocalypse* (1963), *Yeats* (1970), *A Map of Misreading* (1975), *Kabbalah and Criticism* (1975), *Agon: Toward a Theory of Revisionism* (1982), *The American Religion* (1992), *The Western Canon* (1994), and *Omens of Millennium: The Gnosis of Angels, Dreams, and Resurrection* (1996). *The Anxiety of Influence* (1973) sets forth Professor Bloom's provocative theory of the literary relationships between the great writers and their predecessors. His most recent books include *Shakespeare: The Invention of the Human* (1998), a 1998 National Book Award finalist, *How to Read and Why* (2000), *Genius: A Mosaic of One Hundred Exemplary Creative Minds* (2002), *Hamlet: Poem Unlimited* (2003), and *Where Shall Wisdom be Found* (2004). In 1999, Professor Bloom received the prestigious American Academy of Arts and Letters Gold Medal for Criticism, and in 2002 he received the Catalonia International Prize.